# TEACHING RELIGIOUS EDUCATION CREATIVELY

*Teaching Religious Education Creatively* offers a brand-new approach for the primary classroom and is crammed full of innovative ideas for bringing the teaching of religious education (RE) to life. It helps teachers understand what constitutes a healthy curriculum that will encourage children to appreciate and understand different belief systems. Perhaps most importantly, it also challenges teachers to understand RE as a transformatory subject that offers children the tools to be discerning, to work out their own beliefs and to answer puzzling questions.

Underpinned by the latest research and theory and with contemporary, cutting-edge practice at the forefront, expert authors emphasise creative thinking strategies and teaching creatively. Key topics explored include:

- What is creative teaching and learning?
- Why is it important to teach creatively and teach for creativity?
- What is religious education?
- Why is it important for children to learn 'about' and 'from' religion?
- How can you teach non-biased RE creatively as a discrete subject and integrate it with other curriculum areas?

*Teaching Religious Education Creatively* is for all teachers who want to learn more about innovative teaching and learning in RE in order to improve understanding and enjoyment and transform their own as well as their pupils' lives.

**Sally Elton-Chalcraft** is Reader in Education at the University of Cumbria, UK.

D0219226

# THE LEARNING TO TEACH IN THE PRIMARY SCHOOL SERIES

**Series Editor:** Teresa Cremin, The Open University, UK

Teaching is an art form. It demands not only knowledge and understanding of the core areas of learning, but also the ability to teach these creatively and foster learner creativity in the process. *The Learning to Teach in the Primary School Series* draws upon recent research which indicates the rich potential of creative teaching and learning, and explores what it means to teach creatively in the primary phase. It also responds to the evolving nature of subject teaching in a wider, more imaginatively framed 21st century primary curriculum.

Designed to complement the textbook, *Learning to Teach in the Primary School Series*, the well informed, lively texts offer support for student and practising teachers who want to develop more creative approaches to teaching and learning. The books highlight the importance of the teachers' own creative engagement and share a wealth of innovative ideas to enrich pedagogy and practice.

Titles in the series:

**Teaching English Creatively**
*Teresa Cremin*

**Teaching Science Creatively**
*Dan Davies*

**Teaching Mathematics Creatively**
*Trisha Pound and Linda Lee*

**Teaching Geography Creatively**
*Edited by Stephen Scoffham*

**Teaching History Creatively**
*Edited by Hilary Cooper*

**Teaching Music Creatively**
*Pam Burnard and Regina Murphy*

**Teaching Physical Education Creatively**
*Angela Pickard and Patricia Maude*

**Teaching Religious Education Creatively**
*Edited by Sally Elton-Chalcraft*

# TEACHING RELIGIOUS EDUCATION CREATIVELY

## Edited by Sally Elton-Chalcraft

Routledge
Taylor & Francis Group

LONDON AND NEW YORK

First published 2015
by Routledge
2 Park Square, Milton Park, Abingdon, Oxon OX14 4RN

and by Routledge
711 Third Avenue, New York, NY 10017

*Routledge is an imprint of the Taylor & Francis Group, an informa business*

*British Library Cataloguing in Publication Data*
A catalogue record for this book is available from the British Library

*Library of Congress Cataloging-in-Publication Data*
Teaching religious education creatively / edited by Sally Elton-Chalcraft.
      pages cm. — (Learning to teach in the primary school series)
  1. Religious education.   I. Elton-Chalcraft, Sally.
  BV1471.3.T38 2014
  372.84—dc23
  2014025138

ISBN: 978-0-415-74257-3 (hbk)
ISBN: 978-0-415-74258-0 (pbk)
ISBN: 978-1-315-81453-7 (ebk)


Typeset in Times New Roman and Helvetica Neue
by Apex Covantage, LLC


Printed and bound in the United States of America by Publishers Graphics,
LLC on sustainably sourced paper.

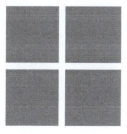

# CONTENTS

# CONTENTS ▨ ▨ ▨ ◼

# LIST OF CONTRIBUTORS

**Lat Blaylock** is the editor of *RE Today* magazine and a national RE adviser in the UK. He has written many RE syllabuses and schemes of work and trains about 3,000 teachers a year. He has published a number of RE resources and made six series of broadcasts with the BBC. He has written four packages of visual learning materials, called 'Picturing Jesus', which use the global art of the contemporary Christian communities for RE. He was the specialist writer of the RE Council's new National Curriculum Framework for RE 2013.

**Siobhán Dowling Long** is a lecturer in the School of Education, University College Cork. She holds a PhD from the University of Wales, Trinity-St-David, Lampeter. As a former secondary school teacher of religious education and music, she served as head of Religious Education and Liturgical Music. She is a specialist in the area of the reception of the Bible in music. Her monograph, *The Sacrifice of Isaac: The Reception of a Biblical Story in Music* (2013), is published by Sheffield Phoenix Press.

**Sally Elton-Chalcraft** is reader in education at the University of Cumbria. She has worked in several primary and middle schools and three higher education institutions. She leads the dissertation part of the master's programme and also works with student teachers on religious education, equality and diversity issues. She has researched and published in the areas of creative teaching and learning, religious education, spirituality and the debate concerning British values and education. She is currently engaged in a research project investigating perceptions of disability in India and the UK.

**John Hammond** taught RE in schools in London and Preston and lectured in religious studies and religious education at St Martin's College, Lancaster, now the University of Cumbria. Working with David Hay of the Religious Experience Research Unit he co-authored *New Methods in Religious Education* and, for Multiverse, the TDA online resource for trainees, contributed a series of articles on the religious dimension of multi-ethnicity including multiculturalism, faith schools and Islamism. Retired, he continues to work on the interface between religion, culture and RE.

**Penny Hollander** has been a teacher with experience in primary and secondary schools and higher education at the University of Cumbria. Her major teaching interests are effective RE provision in schools and particularly children's spiritual development. She is currently working as a freelance consultant, mainly with Carlisle diocese, in an advisory capacity and delivering training in RE and collective worship. She has recently written some materials for the National Society's Christianity Project. She is also a trained SIAMS inspector.

**Julia Ipgrave** is senior research fellow in Warwick Religion and Education Research Unit, University of Warwick. She has researched and published widely in the field of religion in schools, religious education, children's religious understanding, young people's attitudes to religious diversity and inter-religious dialogue. Her work involves comparative studies of inter-religious engagement in school and society with colleagues in other European countries. Before moving into higher education she worked for 16 years in Leicester schools in teaching and management roles.

**Carrie Mercier** has worked in a number of schools in England, Scotland and the US. She has taught in both primary and secondary classrooms and has published many school textbooks for religious education. Moving into teacher education she became involved in leading the Postgraduate Certificate in Education (PGCE) in secondary RE at York St John before moving to St Martin's College, where she was to become head of the Department of Philosophy and Religion. More recently she has been running the MTL while continuing to teach on various ITE programmes as well as religious studies and religious education.

**Fiona Moss** is an RE adviser for *RE Today* and edits their Primary Curriculum books. She speaks at conferences, training events and schools across the country on all aspects of RE but particularly enjoys working on creativity. She was a member of National Association of Teachers of Religious Education and is now their executive officer. For 15 years she was a teacher in a large inner-city primary school in Leicester.

**Georgia Prescott** is a senior lecturer in primary religious education at the University of Cumbria. She is currently a member of Cumbria Standing Advisory Council for Religious Education (SACRE). Her research interests include religious education, philosophy for children (P4C), and spiritual, moral, social and cultural development (SMSC). She has published articles in these areas in *RE Today* and *REsource*.

**Lynn Revell** is a reader in religion in education at Canterbury Christ Church University where she is the programme director for the doctorate of education. She is interested in the ways teachers understand and respond to inequality in education especially in relation to religion, beliefs and ethnicity. In 2011 she published *Islam* *and Education – The Manipulation and Misrepresentation of a Religion*, published by Trentham Press, and she is involved in research projects examining Islamophobia and teaching and the legitimacy of faith in education.

**Geoff Teece** is currently part-time lecturer in RE at the University of Exeter. Geoff trained as a junior/secondary teacher, studying theology and English, and subsequently taught for 16 years in primary and middle schools. After studying for a master's in education Geoff joined the staff at the Westhill RE Centre in Birmingham, eventually becoming its director. Geoff then moved to Birmingham University as lecturer in RE to work with Michael Grimmitt on the secondary PGCE course.

# SERIES EDITOR'S FOREWORD

Over the last two decades, teachers in England, working in a culture of accountability and target setting, have experienced a high level of specification both of curriculum content and of pedagogy. Positioned as recipients of the prescribed agenda, practitioners – it could be argued – have had their hands tied, their voices quietened and their professional autonomy constrained. Research reveals that during this time some professionals have short-changed their understanding of pedagogy and practice (English *et al.* 2002; Burns and Myhill 2004) in order to deliver the required curriculum. The relentless quest for higher standards and 'coverage' may well have obscured the personal and affective dimensions of teaching and learning, fostering a mindset characterised more by compliance and conformity than curiosity and creativity.

However, alongside the standards agenda, creativity and creative policies and practices also became prominent and a focus on creative teaching and learning developed. Heralded by the publication *All Our Futures: Creativity, Culture and Education* (NACCCE 1999), this shift was exemplified in the Creative Partnerships initiative, in the Qualifications and Curriculum Authority's creativity framework (QCA 2005) and in a plethora of reports (e.g. OfSTED 2003; DfES 2003; CapeUK 2006; Roberts 2006). It was also evident in the development of the Curriculum for Excellence in Scotland. The definition of creativity frequently employed was 'imaginative activity fashioned so as to produce outcomes that are both original and of value' (NACCCE 1999: 30). Many schools sought to develop more innovative curricula, and many teachers found renewed energy through teaching creatively and teaching for creativity.

Yet tensions persist, not only because the dual policies of performativity and creativity appear contradictory, but also because the new National Curriculum draft programmes of study in England at least afford a high degree of specificity and profile the knowledge needed to be taught and tested. We need to be concerned if teachers are positioned more as technically competent curriculum deliverers rather than artistically engaged, research-informed curriculum developers. I believe, alongside Eisner (2003) and others, that teaching is an art form and that teachers benefit from viewing themselves as versatile artists in the classroom, drawing on their personal passions and creativity as they research and develop practice. As Joubert observes,

> Creative teaching is an art. One cannot teach teachers didactically how to be creative; there is no fail safe recipe or routines. Some strategies may help to promote creative thinking, but teachers need to develop a full repertoire of skills which they can adapt to different situations.
>
> (Joubert 2001: 21)

However, creative teaching is only part of the picture, since teaching for creativity also needs to be acknowledged and their mutual dependency recognised. The former focuses more on teachers using imaginative approaches in the classroom in order to make learning more interesting and effective; the latter, more on the development of children's creativity (NACCCE 1999). Both rely upon an understanding of the notion of creativity and demand that professionals confront the myths and mantras which surround the word. These include the commonly held misconceptions that creativity is connected only to participation in the arts and that it is confined to particular individuals, a competence of a few specially gifted children.

Nonetheless, creativity is an elusive concept; it has been multiply defined by educationalists, psychologists and neurologists, as well as by policy makers in different countries and cultural contexts. Debates resound about its individual or collaborative nature, the degree to which it is generic or domain-specific, and the difference between the 'Big C' creativity of genius and the 'little c' creativity of the everyday. Notwithstanding these issues, most scholars in the field perceive it involves the capacity to generate, reason and critically evaluate novel ideas and imaginary scenarios. As such, I perceive it encompasses thinking through and solving problems, making connections, inventing and reinventing and flexing one's imaginative muscles in all aspects of learning and life.

In the primary classroom, creative teaching and learning have been associated with innovation, originality, ownership and control (Jeffrey and Woods 2009), and creative teachers have been seen, in their planning and teaching and in the ethos which they create, to afford high value to curiosity and risk taking, to ownership, autonomy and making connections (Cremin 2009; Cremin et al. 2009). Such teachers, it has been posited, often work in partnership with others: with children, other teachers and experts from beyond the school gates (Cochrane and Cockett 2007). Additionally, in research exploring possibility thinking, which it is argued is at the heart of creativity in education (Craft 2000), an intriguing interplay between teachers and children has been observed; both are involved in possibility thinking their ways forwards and in immersing themselves in playful contexts, posing questions, being imaginative, showing self-determination, taking risks and innovating (Craft et al. 2012; Burnard et al. 2006; Cremin et al. 2006). A new pedagogy of possibility beckons.

This series, Learning to Teach in the Primary School, which accompanies and complements the edited textbook Learning to Teach in the Primary School (Arthur and Cremin 2010), seeks to support teachers in developing as creative practitioners, assisting them in exploring the synergies and potential of teaching creatively and teaching for creativity. The series does not merely offer practical strategies for use in the classroom, though these abound, but more importantly seeks to widen teachers' and student teachers' knowledge and understanding of the principles underpinning a creative approach to teaching, principles based on research. It seeks to mediate the wealth of research evidence and make accessible and engaging the diverse theoretical perspectives and scholarly arguments available, demonstrating their practical relevance and value to the profession. Those who aspire to develop further as creative and curious educators will, I trust, find much of value to support their own professional learning journeys and enrich their pedagogy and practice and children's creative learning right across the curriculum.

## ABOUT THE SERIES EDITOR

**Teresa Cremin** (Grainger) is a professor of education (literacy) at the Open University and a past president of UKRA (2001–2) and UKLA (2007–9). She is currently co-convenor of the BERA Creativity SIG and a trustee of Booktrust, the Poetry Archive and UKLA. She is also a fellow of the English Association and an academician of the Academy of Social Sciences. Her work involves research, publication and consultancy in literacy and creativity. Her current projects seek to explore children's make-believe play in the context of storytelling and storyacting, their everyday lives and literacy practices, and the nature of literary discussions in extracurricular reading groups. Additionally, Teresa is interested in teachers' identities as readers and writers and the characteristics and associated pedagogy that fosters possibility thinking within creative learning in the primary years. Teresa has published widely, writing and co-editing a variety of books including *Writing Voices: Creating Communities of Writers* (Routledge, 2012); *Teaching English Creatively* (Routledge, 2009); *Learning to Teach in the Primary School* (Routledge, 2010); *Jumpstart! Drama* (David Fulton, 2009); *Documenting Creative Learning 5–11* (Trentham, 2007); *Creativity and Writing: Developing Voice and Verve* (Routledge, 2005); *Teaching English in Higher Education* (NATE and UKLA, 2007); *Creative Activities for Character, Setting and Plot, 5–7, 7–9, 9–11* (Scholastic, 2004); and *Language and Literacy: A Routledge Reader* (Routledge, 2001).

## REFERENCES

Arthur, J. and Cremin, T. (eds) (2010) *Learning to Teach in the Primary School* (2nd edition). London: Routledge.

Burnard, P., Craft, A. and Cremin, T. (2006) 'Possibility thinking', *International Journal of Early Years Education*, 14(3): 243–62.

Burns, C. and Myhill, D. (2004) 'Interactive or inactive? A consideration of the nature of interaction in whole class teaching', *Cambridge Journal of Education*, 34: 35–49.

CapeUK (2006) *Building Creative Futures: The Story of Creative Action Research Awards, 2004–2005*. London: Arts Council.

Cohrane, P. and Cockett, M. (2007) *Building a Creative School: A Dynamic Approach to School Development*. London: Trentham.

Craft, A. (2000). *Creativity Across the Primary Curriculum*. London: Routledge.

Craft, A., McConnon, L. and Mathews, A. (2012). 'Creativity and child-initiated play'. *Thinking Skills and Creativity*, 7(1): 48–61.

Cremin, T. (2009) 'Creative teaching and creative teachers', in A. Wilson (ed.) *Creativity in Primary Education*. Exeter: Learning Matters, pp. 36–46.

Cremin, T., Barnes, J. and Scoffham, S. (2009) *Creative Teaching for Tomorrow: Fostering a Creative State of Mind*. Deal: Future Creative.

Cremin, T., Burnard, P. and Craft, A. (2006). 'Pedagogy and possibility thinking in the early years', *International Journal of Thinking Skills and Creativity*, 1(2): 108–19.

Department for Education and Skills (DfES) (2003) *Excellence and Enjoyment: A Strategy for Primary Schools*. Nottingham: DfES.

Eisner, E. (2003) 'Artistry in education', *Scandinavian Journal of Educational Research*, 47(3): 373–84.

English, E., Hargreaves, L. and Hislam, J. (2002) 'Pedagogical dilemmas in the National Literacy Strategy: primary teachers' perceptions, reflections and classroom behaviour', *Cambridge Journal of Education*, 32(1): 9–26.

Jeffrey, B. and Woods, P. (2009) *Creative Learning in the Primary School*. London: Routledge.

Joubert, M.M. (2001) 'The art of creative teaching: NACCCE and beyond', in A. Craft, B. Jeffrey and M. Liebling (eds) *Creativity in Education*. London: Continuum.

National Advisory Committee on Creative and Cultural Education (NACCCE) (1999) *All Our Futures: Creativity, Culture and Education*. London: Department for Education and Employment.

OfSTED (2003) *Expecting the Unexpected: Developing Creativity in Primary and Secondary Schools*, HMI 1612. E-publication. Available at www.ofsted.gov.uk. (Accessed 9 November 2007)

Qualifications and Curriculum Authority (QCA) (2005) *Creativity: Find It, Promote It! – Promoting Pupils' Creative Thinking and Behaviour across the Curriculum at Key Stages 1, 2 and 3 – Practical Materials for Schools*. London: QCA.

Roberts, P. (2006) *Nurturing Creativity in Young People: A Report to Government to Inform Future Policy*. London: DCMS.

# SECTION 1

# TEACHING RELIGIOUS EDUCATION CREATIVELY

## Aims and principles

# INTRODUCTION

## CREATIVE RELIGIOUS EDUCATION

### *Sally Elton-Chalcraft*

This chapter sets the scene for the whole volume by outlining what is meant by creative teaching and learning and how this can be put into practice in religious education. The book, and this chapter in particular, attempts to answer the following five questions.

1.  What is creative teaching and learning?
2.  Why is it important to teach creatively and teach for creativity?
3.  What is religious education?
4.  Why is it important for children to learn 'about' and 'from' religion?
5.  How do I teach non-biased RE creatively as a discrete subject and integrated with other curriculum areas?

This first chapter introduces all five elements. Subsequent chapters expand on these topics, drawing on each author's wealth of experience and knowledge.

## WHAT IS CREATIVE TEACHING AND LEARNING?

Creativity has been notoriously difficult to define – in some literature it is defined as an abstract noun with particular characteristics as described in the NACCCE 1999 policy document (Table 1.1). In contrast, some authors define creative strategies actively as a verb – creative thinking (Buzan's 2014 mind mapping, de Bono's 2014 thinking hats, Cremin *et al.*'s 2012 possibility thinking). Some authors approach creativity in education in terms of strands – creative thinking, creative teaching and teaching for creativity, and creative integration of subjects (Copping and Howlett 2008).

Creativity also has been discussed from different cultural perspectives (Craft *et al.* 2007), which is pertinent to the debate because at the heart of religious education is a desire to learn about a variety of cultures.

## School CCAF (challenging, creative and fun) and school HEBS (hard/easy, boring, scary)

To gain an understanding of creative teaching and learning in practice we could transport ourselves to two hypothetical schools in the UK where the children are engaged in learning.

---

▨ **Table 1.1** Definition of creativity from National Advisory Committee on Creative and Cultural Education (NACCCE 1999:29)

---

The policy document for creativity, *All Our Futures* (NACCCE 1999:29), defines the four features of creativity as:

1. Using imagination – generating something original, providing an alternative to the expected.
2. Pursuing purposes – applying imagination to produce something (an idea, a performance, a product).
3. Creativity involves originality.
   - ▨ Individual, in relation to their own previous work
   - ▨ Relative, in relation to their peer group
   - ▨ Historic, uniquely original
4. Judging value – evaluating the imaginative activity as effective, useful, enjoyable, satisfying, valid, tenable.

---

▨ **Table 1.2** Characteristics of caricatured CCAF and HEBS schools

---

| *CCAF (challenging, creative and fun) school* | *HEBS (too hard/easy, boring, scary) school* |
|---|---|
| Children and teachers are challenged, have fun and are creative at school. | Teachers and learners find school too hard or too easy, boring or scary. |
| Children possess the magnificent eight qualities of a powerful learner (Claxton 2007; see Table 1.3) – curious, imaginative, disciplined, reflective etc. | Children are unmotivated to learn, get upset when they make mistakes or fail, are bullies or victims of bullying. |
| Teachers enjoy the challenge of planning, teaching and assessing. They have positive relationships with their pupils and find their jobs tiring but rewarding. | Teachers put minimum effort into planning, teaching and assessing. They dominate or are scared by their pupils. They are miserable, feel powerless and only work to pay their bills. |

---

From the very first moment the children enter the classroom, in school CCAF (challenging, creative and fun), the enthusiastic teacher engages them in creative learning, see Table 1.2. Children experience a vibrant classroom environment with interactive displays and activities which encourage them to generate novel ideas or ways of working. Both the teacher and the children are having fun but are also challenged. If you have read *Hooray for Diffendoofer Day* (Prelutsky and Smith 1998 but inspired by Dr Seuss) you may have some idea of what this exciting classroom looks like and what its mirror image in Dreary town is like too (which I call HEBS – hard/easy, boring, scary). Both the teacher and children will look forward to coming to CCAF school most of the time. Things do not always run smoothly in our hypothetical classroom – which is, after all, in the 'real' world, but there is usually an excited 'buzz' and any visitor will instantly know that learning is taking place.

The learners at CCAF (challenging, creative and fun) school would possess characteristics which Claxton has defined as the 'magnificent eight' (Claxton 2007:123), listed in Table 1.3.

So the teachers in CCAF school build their children's 'learning muscles' and 'learning stamina' (Claxton 2007) to achieve the magnificent eight characteristics of a powerful

---

■ **Table 1.3** Guy Claxton's 'magnificent 8 qualities of a powerful learner' (Claxton 2007:123–6)

1. First a powerful learner is *curious*: they wonder about things, are open-minded and ask pertinent and productive questions.
2. Confident learners have *courage* to deal with uncertainty and complexity and admitting 'I don't know'. Mistakes are for learning from, not getting upset about.
3. Powerful learners are good at *exploration* and *investigation* – they are good at finding, making and capitalising on resources that will help them pursue their projects (tools, places, other people).
4. Powerful learning requires *experimentation* – they draft/make something, then evaluate, and redraft/revise. They try different approaches, mess things up, make mistakes (if they are not too costly).
5. Powerful learners have *imagination* and draw on their own inner creativity. They make 'mental simulations' of tricky situations to smooth their own performances in their mind's eye. They know when and how to put themselves in another's shoes.
6. Creativity needs to be yoked to *reason* and *discipline* – powerful learners think carefully, rigorously, methodically. They analyse and evaluate as well as being imaginative. They spot holes in their own argument as well as other people's. Disciplined thinking enables knowledge and skill to guide learning.
7. Powerful learners have the virtue of *sociability*, making good use of collaboration. They are good at balancing sociability with solitariness – they are not afraid to go off by themselves when they need to think and digest.
8. Powerful learners are *reflective*. They step back and evaluate how the learning is going but avoid being too self-critical.

---

learner. But Claxton (2007) warns the teacher against being overly stringent in 'building learning power' – the children are not to be seen as mini athletes who must be challenged almost to the breaking point. Elton-Chalcraft and Mills (2013) state that learning should be challenging and yet also it must be fun. But it is a tall order for the primary teacher to plan and facilitate lessons which will allow children to be creative, use their imagination, be challenged and also have fun. However, these are not mutually exclusive. If children have a positive mindset towards learning then they will be intrinsically motivated to learn – the fun will spring from the satisfaction of struggling with a task but eventually making some progress. Creative teaching and learning can be fun if both the teacher and the children gain satisfaction from the challenge, if they know what it is like to feel exhilaration after a struggle. The children at CCAF (creative, challenging and fun) school enjoy the challenge of learning compared with their counterparts in HEBS (hard/easy, boring, scary) school, who are bored. While this is an exaggerated caricature, nevertheless these two schools illustrate two opposing approaches to learning. Similarly children may display opposing characteristics as learners. Two characters in the film version of the Dr Seuss (1997) book *The Cat in the Hat* demonstrate this point – a sister's over-cautious disposition and fear of fun are contrasted with her brother's reckless risk taking and fun-loving disposition. By the end of the film both children have moved from their polarised positions, realising that fun and risk taking (the characteristics of creativity) are necessary but in moderation. Their opposing characteristics were measured on a 'phunometre' (fun measurement) scale. Elton-Chalcraft and Mills (2013:2) adopt this fictitious 'phunometre' scale to evaluate teaching and learning contexts – the learning environment (for example interactive displays, working wall, mind mapping, use of stimulating resources) and planned activities (problem solving, open-ended investigation, creative thinking strategies). See Table 1.4.

■ **Table 1.4** The 'phunometre scale' used by Elton-Chalcraft and Mills (2013) for measuring fun and challenge for both the learning environment and planned activities

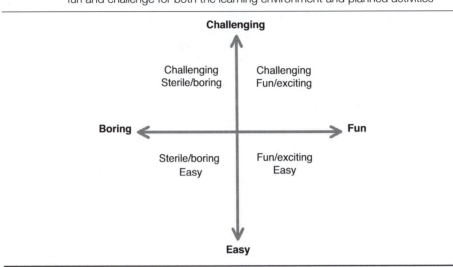

# WHY IS IT IMPORTANT TO TEACH CREATIVELY AND TEACH FOR CREATIVITY?

First I argue that it is more fulfilling to work and learn in a school which exhibits creative and challenging learning and teaching. Second I argue that teachers who teach creatively, and teach for creativity, move beyond a transmission model to a powerful and transformative model of teaching, thus the curriculum is more meaningful. In the third part of my argument I suggest that a creative and transformative model of teaching and learning provides the children with resilience and learning power to prepare them for their future lives.

## 1. Better to work and learn in a creative school

Our two schools, CCAF (creative, challenging and fun) and HEBS (hard/easy, boring, scary), may be caricatures; however, they show the extremes of two opposing philosophies. At school CCAF there are enthused, curious, resilient life-long learners working with motivated, hard-working and happy teachers dedicated to building the children's 'learning muscles' and 'learning stamina', thus avoiding 'learned helplessness' (Claxton 2007, 2008). In contrast school HEBS is populated with bored and disaffected children frightened of failure with scared, demotivated and unhappy teachers. In reality most schools have elements of both these characteristics, but the aim would be to strive to be school CCAF. Thus it is important to teach creatively and teach for creativity so that both the teachers and the children feel fulfilled, enjoy the learning and experience a sense of achievement. Cullingford (2007) has argued that children need extrinsic rewards if the curriculum is sterile and boring, and behaviour management strategies are needed to keep children on task, whereas if children are given more ownership of their learning in an engaging and creative curriculum they are more likely to be motivated to learn.

## 2. A meaningful curriculum

Educationalists such as Bruner (1996) and neuroscientists such as Heilmann (2005) and Claxton (1997) have all argued that children are more motivated by a creative curriculum which makes sense to them, includes problem solving and child-led investigation and develops their thinking skills. Neuroscience teaches us that knowledge makes more sense when it is contextualised (Heilmann 2005). Teachers who are skill and concept builders play a crucial role in making the curriculum meaningful as opposed to task managers and curriculum deliverers who merely transmit knowledge or keep children busy with tasks (Twiselton 2004). Task managers are described by Twiselton (2004) as teachers who view their role in terms of task completion, order and business with little reference to children making sense of their learning. Teachers who are curriculum deliverers also lack an understanding of a meaningful curriculum, seeing their role merely as delivering an externally decided set of skills and knowledge (Twiselton 2004). Skill and concept builders on the other hand see the 'bigger picture' and endeavour to design a meaningful curriculum which makes sense in terms of principles and concepts (Twiselton and Elton-Chalcraft 2014). Thus a creative and effective teacher is also a skill and concept builder (Twiselton 2004) who thinks carefully about what the children need to learn and why this knowledge and these skills are relevant. Such a teacher ensures the learning fits into the wider curriculum and she/he scaffolds the learner's experience. Teachers at CCAF school would be skill and concept builders designing and implementing a creative and challenging curriculum which is more meaningful for the learners.

## 3. Resilient learners prepared for an uncertain future

A third reason for teaching creatively and teaching for creativity is that such an approach prepares children more effectively for an uncertain future. Children attending CCAF school (see Table 1.2) would be better prepared to engage with what life throws at them in their future lives. Humanity is evolving at a fast pace with new technologies and new ways of thinking, working and living. To keep abreast of, and not be daunted by, such unprecedented change, the children from school CCAF might be better prepared to deal with the demands of an uncertain future than children from HEBS school, who may exhibit fear or anger towards situations where they feel unprepared or 'out of their depth'.

Creative teaching and learning encourages children to learn from mistakes to pick themselves up and move forwards. Hymer and Gershon (2014) talk about the power of failure and making mistakes in order to progress; they cite a poster seen in one school they visited, see Table 1.5.

---

■ **Table 1.5** Poster in a school cited by Hymer and Gershon (2014:27)

---

**F**irst
**A**ttempt
**I**n
**L**earning

---

In CCAF school the children are encouraged to try out ideas, and their 'bounceback-ability' allows them to have another go if their first attempt fails.

In the next sections I apply some of the principles of creativity discussed previously to show what characterises effective and creative RE.

# WHAT IS RELIGIOUS EDUCATION AND WHY IS IT IMPORTANT FOR CHILDREN TO LEARN CREATIVELY 'ABOUT' AND 'FROM' RELIGIOUS EDUCATION?

Before outlining the aims, principles and values underpinning RE, I begin this section by asking you to evaluate your own starting point.

## 1. Your baggage

Before going any further it is important for the teacher to consider their own attitudes towards religion and RE. Religion and beliefs are notoriously contentious topics. So, reader, please consider the questions in Table 1.6.

Your values and attitudes (your baggage) can have a positive or negative influence on your capacity to engage children in creative and effective RE. Before commencement of planning the teacher of RE must ask themselves what 'baggage' they bring? Returning to our two schools described in Table 1.2, CCAF and HEBS, examples of good and bad RE planning are identified in Table 1.7.

▪ **Table 1.6** Questions to ask oneself before planning any RE

| | |
|---|---|
| YOUR BAGGAGE | What do you think about religion? <br> What influence did your upbringing have on the values you hold? <br> What do you think the aims of RE ought to be? |

▪ **Table 1.7** Examples of how to plan good (or bad) RE

| To plan creative and effective RE (akin to CCAF school – Table 1.2): | To plan dangerous or uninspiring RE (akin to HEBS school – Table 1.2): |
|---|---|
| Acknowledge your 'baggage'. | Let your 'baggage' influence you. |
| Understand aims and principles of RE (see next section). | Misunderstand/ignore aims and principles of RE. |
| Encourage children to *investigate* and *evaluate* a variety of belief systems. Support children in their realisation that sometimes belief systems contradict each other. | *Indoctrinate* children into your belief system (e.g. Catholicism, atheism, Islam etc.), or pretend that all belief systems are actually the same in essence. |
| Plan RE which explores a range of belief systems through role play, re-enactments, artwork, lively discussion, visits, visitors, problem solving etc. | Ask children to 'research' belief systems by copying from websites or printing out colourful pictures. Never discuss work with the children. |

*(Continued)*

▨ **Table 1.7** *Continued*

| | |
|---|---|
| Encourage a safe, open-minded environment for children to voice their opinions and challenge others respectfully. Try your best to manage controversial discussions, helping children critically evaluate the validity of different views. | Avoid controversial discussions. Or make sure you are always in control so children know there is a 'right' or 'wrong' viewpoint, i.e. the teacher's view is always 'right'. |
| Provide opportunities for children to solve problems (e.g. how would you ensure a year 1 boy's leaving party would provide suitable food and party games for a Jewish girl, several vegetarian children, a diabetic child, a Muslim etc.?). | Ask children to colour in and label a photocopied resource sheet showing halal and Kosher food laws. |

## 2. Aims and principles of RE

Once a teacher has acknowledged his/her baggage – see Table 1.6 – the aims and principles of RE can be introduced. RE holds a unique position as part of the 'basic' but not the national curriculum. In state schools the RE syllabus is determined by the local authority, Standing Advisory Council for Religious Education (SACRE). Many SACREs draw on the Non-Statutory National Framework for RE (QCA 2004) to write their Agreed Syllabus for RE. In faith schools a faith-based curriculum for RE is often drawn on – for example Church of England schools use a diocesan syllabus.

There are some overlaps of aims and principles of RE in both state and faith schools, and in this volume we draw on the aims for RE as articulated in the Non-Statutory National Framework for RE (REC 2013) summarised below. RE should ensure that all pupils:

A. Know about and understand a range of religions and worldviews.
B. Express ideas and insights about the nature, significance and impact of religions and worldviews.
C. Gain and deploy the skills needed to engage seriously with religions and worldviews.

(REC 2013:11–12)

In chapter 2 of this volume Teece eloquently shows how these aims can best be implemented in practice by adopting two pedagogical principles:

▨  Learning about religion/belief systems/worldview
▨  Learning from religion/belief systems/worldview

The Non-Statutory National Framework for RE identifies four attitudes requisite for RE – self-awareness, respect for all, open-mindedness, and appreciation and wonder (QCA 2004:13) (this QCA document has been superseded by the National Curriculum Framework for religious education – REC 2013). Such attitudes and indeed the aims and principles of RE are underpinned by values as discussed in the following section.

## 3.  Values, beliefs and RE

In this section I investigate educational values and beliefs and show how RE can contribute to the debate. My argument is based on the following premises:

- ▨ Teaching and learning in school is not value free.
- ▨ Values and beliefs are communicated through school ethos.
- ▨ RE provides an opportunity to evaluate, nurture, re-enforce or challenge values and beliefs.

Alexander and his team, in the acclaimed and influential Cambridge Review, asked the question 'what is primary education for?' and deduced that it is 'fundamentally a moral pursuit' (Alexander 2010:174).

Values and beliefs are communicated through the school ethos – the displays, curriculum content, body language and interactions and so on. In faith-based and community schools RE is an ideal place for teachers and children to explore different belief systems and values. For example in many schools there are 'codes of conduct' or 'school rules' and sometimes these are developed together by both children and adults working in the school, thus everyone shares ownership of the 'rules' or 'ethos'. Examples might include 'overarching values' such as 'Respecting everyone's right to education' and also specific rules such as 'don't run in the corridor'.

During a topic on 'Rules' children could examine the reasons why rules are important; they might investigate the Ten Commandments of Judaism and Christianity and compare this with the Eightfold Path of Buddhism, looking at similarities and differences. This investigation can then encompass their own school rules, ethos and values with the children learning 'about' different traditional belief systems and then learning 'from' these belief systems to reflect on how moral values relate to their own behaviour.

While RE in a community school should not be religious instruction or faith nurture, even in a faith school RE should enable children to critically examine their own belief system in RE lessons. Acts of collective worship provide opportunities for faith nurture in faith schools, but we would argue that in both faith-based and community schools RE should be *education* not *indoctrination*. In faith-based and community schools beliefs and values may be communicated through the school ethos. RE provides a forum for open discussion about a range of values and different views of morality.

Within teaching itself there are values which are communicated via governmental directives. At the time of writing the government has been keen to implement PREVENT (part of the government's anti-terrorism strategy called Contest) which came into force in 2011. In this document 'extremism' is defined as 'vocal or active opposition to fundamental British values' (Elton-Chalcraft, Lander and Revell 2014). On the face of it such a strategy would seem legitimate but, as Revell (2012) argues, such a policy has fuelled Islamophobia; in chapter 11 she discusses how Islam can be approached creatively and in an unbiased manner in the classroom. Chapter 10 (Elton-Chalcraft) and chapter 12 (Hammond) both argue that RE has an important role to play in challenging racism, homophobia and scapegoating. OfSTED (2013) stated,

Religious education (RE) should make a major contribution to the education of children and young people. At its best, it is intellectually challenging and personally enriching. It helps young people develop beliefs and values, and promotes the virtues of respect and empathy, which are important in our diverse society. It fosters civilised debate and reasoned argument, and helps pupils to understand the place of religion and belief in the modern world.

Values permeate our lives, and when we have the space to do so, children and adults alike contemplate 'our place in the world', for example which friends to talk to, which hobbies to engage in, which food to eat etc. We act, sometimes unconsciously, according to a set of beliefs/social conventions, or values, which are often determined by our upbringing. Children, like adults, are usually very aware of injustices; but also children, like adults, delight when something inspires them. Primary school education can play a crucial role in how a child develops – how they begin to understand the world in which they live. RE, because of its nature to question and explore in a safe environment, can play a significant role in supporting a child's understanding of the varied nature of belief systems. RE can encourage children to respect but also critically evaluate their own and other belief systems in a non-biased fashion. So RE, in both faith-based and community schools, seeks to investigate and evaluate a range of beliefs and values, but RE sometimes should also allow children to nurture, re-enforce or challenge particular values and beliefs. While many teachers may desire to present non-biased RE, in practice they lack the confidence to achieve this. In some previous research I found that while the majority of the student teachers in my sample were keen to teach for diversity they also acknowledged lack of confidence and competence to do so (Twiselton and Elton-Chalcraft 2014). *Teaching Religious Education Creatively* aims to provide the teacher with examples of effective and creative non-biased RE rooted in evidence from research.

## HOW DO I TEACH NON-BIASED RE CREATIVELY, AS A DISCRETE SUBJECT AND INTEGRATING WITH OTHER CURRICULUM AREAS?

The previous sections outlined the aims and principles of effective RE – what should be learnt and why. In this section I aim to explain how to make teaching and learning in RE creative, effective, non-biased and engaging for the learners and the teacher alike.

The chapters in this volume provide insight into the characteristics of creative and effective RE. OfSTED's report highlights characteristics of effective enquiry which have been adapted in Table 1.8 into a series of dos and don'ts.

Putting these dos and don'ts from Table 1.8 into practice entails emulating the CCAF (challenging, creative and fun) school rather than the HEBS (hard/easy, boring, scary) school approach and ethos (see Table 1.2). In RE children use their imagination; they know when and how to put themselves in another's shoes. This can be quite challenging for the RE teacher so an example is provided in Table 1.9 to illustrate how this might be managed.

### Creatively learning about food in RE and other subjects

Teaching non-biased RE means encouraging children to see the familiar in an unfamiliar light and to make the unfamiliar more familiar. Using the topic of food as a way of achieving this in RE is suggested in Table 1.9.

■ **Table 1.8** Characteristics of effective and creative enquiry in RE (adapted from OfSTED 2013)

| Do | Don't |
|---|---|
| **Involve the children, giving them ownership of learning.** Teacher and pupils discuss what the lesson will be about and where it will lead, making sure they can see the relevance and importance of the enquiry and how it relates to their own concerns. Children set up their own enquiry. | **Communicate learning objectives mechanistically.** Pupils copy the objectives for the lesson into their books, taking up most of the lesson. |
| **Allow pupils to use their creativity and imagination** – ensuring that experiential learning and opportunities to foster spiritual and creative development are built into the process of enquiry. | **Avoid risks.** Teachers were unwilling to open up enquiry in case pupils asked challenging or controversial questions with which they felt ill equipped to deal. |
| **Extend the enquiry** – into more challenging areas of evaluation and reflection. | **Focus too much on the product of the enquiry rather than the process.** Teachers drew attention to the way in which the pupils presented what they had found out. |

## Creative integration of RE and other subjects

Taking the lesson ideas in Table 1.9 it is possible to link RE with other subjects using a webbed integration approach (see Table 1.10). Copping (2011:30) discusses Robin Fogarty's models of curriculum design, which include shared, threaded, integrated and webbed. The shared model is like viewing the curriculum through binoculars where two distinct subject areas are brought together into a single focus (Fogarty 1991:62), for example integrating two subjects emphasising their common skills and concepts. The threaded approach views the curriculum through a magnifying glass where the 'big ideas' are enlarged and given more prominence than the content (Fogarty 1991:63). Fogarty (1991:63) likens the integrated approach to a kaleidoscope where subjects overlap and are not distinct. The webbed approach, adopted in Table 1.10, identifies a single theme; subject content, skills and concepts overlap in a relevant and meaningful way (Fogarty 1991:63, Copping 2011:33).

In the lesson ideas in Table 1.9 the children are invited to investigate the idea behind 'we are what we eat' both from an RE perspective and linking with other curriculum subjects in a meaningful way using a webbed approach to integration.

Throughout the cross-curricular topic children are engaging in planning and designing investigations themselves, so they have ownership of their learning. They study new, interesting, contentious ideas – making the familiar unfamiliar and the unfamiliar familiar. Before the commencement of this cross-curricular topic the children may have not questioned what they ate or why, but by the end of the topic children should have learnt a great deal about the food we eat and the values and reasons underpinning choice. Throughout the topic they will be reflecting deeply, increasing

■ **Table 1.9** We are what we eat: making the familiar unfamiliar and the unfamiliar familiar

Working on their own, then in pairs or trios, and finally in small groups children investigate what they eat and why.

- List your favourite 3 meals
- List 3 food you don't eat
- Discuss in 2s or 3s why you chose the foods in the first and second lists
- In groups of 4 or 5 compare what you and others eat and reasons why
- In your group of 4 or 5 list reasons why people eat or don't eat certain foods

Working as a class with the teacher as a scribe on the whiteboard

- List all the reasons why people eat or don't eat particular foods
- Discuss reasons: medical (allergies), preferences (appearance, texture, taste), religious, cultural, bad/good experiences or memories, availability, cost, political etc.
- Encourage the children to evaluate their own biases and preferences in a different light (for example would they eat snake, octopus, seaweed, human?)
- Encourage children to put themselves into the shoes of another. Why would other people not eat what they eat? (For example why do some people not eat meat or fish, or not eat dairy and meat dishes at the same meal?)

Working in groups utilising thinking skills to investigate food laws

- As tenacious researchers children investigate religious food laws – in Islam (halal and haram), in Judaism (kosher separation of dairy and meat) etc.
- As skilled researchers children plan, design and implement an enquiry asking friends and family what they eat and why. Investigate religious/cultural/moral reasons behind choices. Decide the mode of presentation: a play, a poster, a PowerPoint presentation, a quiz, an information leaflet, artwork, a podcast

■ **Table 1.10** Webbed integration (Fogarty 1991, Copping 2011) links RE with some curriculum areas

**History:** *How status defines what is eaten.* Investigate meals eaten in the period of history being studied, e.g. Tudor England, looking at the differences between the diets of rich and poor people.

**Food technology:** *Making meals that we eat.* Design, prepare and cook a meal which is halal or kosher or suitable for a vegetarian.

**We are what we eat**

**Maths:** *Gathering data about what we eat.* Design and produce a tally chart in maths showing which are the most popular foods eaten by children's family and friends. This enquiry can be designed by the children in groups – a problem-solving exercise.

**Geography:** *How place defines what is eaten.* Investigate global and political trends – cost, availability and country of origin of food.

their subject knowledge and skills in both RE and other subject areas. Creative teaching and learning must be both challenge and fun (see Table 1.4) and some children may find some of the tasks challenging. For example when designing a questionnaire to collect data about family and friends' meals choices some children may make mistakes in their tally sheets, or they may be unhappy about their cooking or their PowerPoint presentations, see Table 1.10. So the teacher's role is to encourage 'bouncebackability' (Hymer and Gershon 2014). Creative teaching and learning requires children to be tenacious researchers, having the motivation to keep looking for that piece of information about kosher food, having the determination to get the texture of their halal burger right, re-doing their tally chart, working on their ICT skills to improve their podcast (Barber and Cooper 2012, Moss 2010) etc. Creative teaching and learning also requires providing 'incubation time' where children have time to ponder overnight their failed questionnaire design, cooking or podcast and return to school the next day with a better plan (FAIL = first attempt at learning; Table 1.5).

## CREATIVE RE – HOW THE CHAPTERS IN THIS VOLUME CAN HELP

There are many RE books which focus on what to teach and appropriate approaches (e.g. McCreery, Palmer and Voiels 2008, Webster 2010 and Teece 2012). Some books focus on pedagogy and underlying principles of religious education suitable for master's-level enquiry, for example Stern (2006), Jackson (1997), Erricker, Lowndes and Bellchambers (2011), Gates (2007) and Grimmitt (2000). There are many books and resources about creative RE with practical examples of good classroom practice, e.g. Webster (2010), Teece (2001) and *RE Today* publications.

This book draws on all these approaches and brings together the theory and practice in one volume aimed at the discerning student teacher and in-service teacher, as well as those studying at the master's level, wanting to learn more about innovative teaching and learning in RE which will transform their own as well as their pupils' lives. This book treads the fine balance between, on the one hand, educating the conscientious teacher about the 'accepted' canon of what constitutes a healthy RE curriculum and supporting children to become religiate (Gates 2007), appreciating and understanding the motivations behind belief systems and so on. On the other hand, this volume challenges the reader to understand religious education as both a transformatory and liberatory subject, thus ensuring children have the tools to be discerning of belief systems, to be challenged by and enjoy working out their own responses to puzzling questions.

### Section 1
### Aims and principles of RE are articulated.

Chapter 1 has set the scene by discussing the characteristics of creative teaching and learning and the implications for RE.

In **chapter 2** Geoff Teece argues that learning 'about' religion and learning 'from' religion were never originally conceived as attainment targets but were thought of as a pedagogical strategy to improve teaching and learning.

**Section 2**
**The seven chapters in this section present a variety of approaches for creative teaching and learning in religious education.**

> **Chapter 3**, by Georgia Prescott, discusses how P4C (philosophy for children) and the community of enquiry can be powerful approaches to engage the learner in RE. She draws on classroom examples and practical activity ideas to illustrate good RE practice.
>
> In **chapter 4** Penny Hollander explains the TASC (thinking actively in a social context) model with examples of how the model has been used successfully in schools during RE lessons.
>
> Fiona Moss in **chapter 5** provides some key pointers for effective planning for RE. She discusses six learning methods which are cross-referenced in other chapters in this volume.
>
> **Chapter 6** by Sally Elton-Chalcraft, Penny Hollander and Georgia Prescott discusses what is meant by spirituality, and creative lesson ideas are suggested which support children's spiritual development in the classroom context.
>
> In **chapter 7** Carrie Mercier and Siobhán Dowling Long explore ideas for enriching RE through music, art and creativity and through engaging pupils in the aesthetic dimension of religion.
>
> **Chapter 8** by John Hammond provides a rationale and practical examples for the experiential approach in RE.
>
> Drawing on her own research Julia Ipgrave in **chapter 9** argues for the inclusion of inter-faith dialogue in RE and she shows how this can be achieved creatively in the classroom.

**Section 3**
**The three chapters in section 3 encourage the teacher of religious education to widen his/her understanding about the relevance of the subject and its role in education.**

> **Chapter 10**, by Sally Elton-Chalcraft, considers widening the scope of RE to include a range of contrasting belief systems such as minority denominations of Christianity and atheist belief systems such as Humanism. Creative lesson activities and examples of good and bad practice are provided.
>
> In **chapter 11** Lynn Revell examines how teachers can approach Islam and Islamophobia with their children. She suggests strategies for developing skills and attitudes that challenge the way we think.
>
> John Hammond in **chapter 12** argues for a new dimension in RE's approach to community cohesion. Practical activities and resources are suggested for challenging scapegoating.

I hope the chapters in this book will help to convince you (whatever your starting point) that RE, if engaged with creatively, can be an enlightening, transformative and liberating subject.

# REFERENCES

Alexander, R. (2010) *Children, Their World Their Education: Final Report and Recommendations of the Cambridge Primary Review*. Abingdon: Routledge.

Barber, D. and Cooper, L. (2012) *Using New Web Tools in the Primary Classroom: A Practical Guide for Enhancing Teaching and Learning*. Abingdon: Routledge.

de Bono, E. (2014) 'Six thinking hats'. Available at www.debonogroup.com/six_thinking_hats.php (accessed 18 April 2014).

Bruner, J. (1996) *The Culture of Education*. Cambridge, MA: Harvard University Press.

Buzan, T. (2014) 'Mind mapping'. Available at www.tonybuzan.com/about/mind-mapping (accessed 18 April 2014).

Claxton, G. (1997) *Hare Brain Tortoise Mind: Why Intelligence Increases When You Think Less*. London: Fourth Estate Ltd.

Claxton, G. (2007) 'Expanding young people's capacity to learn'. *British Journal of Educational Studies*, 55 (2): 115–34.

Claxton, G. (2008) *What's the Point of School*. Oxford: Oneworld Publications.

Copping, A. (2011) 'Curriculum approaches'. In Hansen, A. (ed.), *Primary Professional Studies*. Exeter: Learning Matters, pp. 23–43.

Copping, A. and Howlett, D. (2008) 'Intervention, innovation and creativity in the classroom: using findings to improve practice'. In Elton-Chalcraft, S., Hansen, A. and Twiselton, S. (eds), *Doing Classroom Research: A Step-by-Step Guide for Student Teachers*. Maidenhead: Open University Press, ch. 8.

Craft, A., Cremin, T. and Burnard, P. (2007) *Creative Learning 3–11 and How We Document It*. Stoke-on-Trent: Trentham Books Ltd.

Cremin, T., Chapell, K. and Craft, A. (2012) 'Reciprocity between narrative, questioning and imagination in the early and primary years: examining the role of narrative in possibility thinking'. *Thinking Skills and Creativity* 9: 135–51. Available at http:dx.doi.org/10.1016/j.tsc.2012.11.003 (accessed 20 March 2014).

Cullingford, C. (2007) 'Creativity and pupil experience of school'. *Education 3–13*, 35(2): 133–42.

Elton-Chalcraft, S., Lander, V. and Revell, L. (2014) 'Fundamental British values in education: an investigation into teachers' and student teachers' perceptions of values.' Paper presented at the European Conference of Educational Research, Porto, Portugal, September 2014.

Elton-Chalcraft, S. and Mills, K. (2013) 'Measuring challenge, fun and sterility on a "Phunometre" scale: evaluating creative teaching and learning with children and their student teachers in the primary school'. *Education 3–13*, DOI:10.1080/03004279.2013.822904. Available at www.tandfonline.com/doi/abs/10.1080/03004279.2013.822904 (accessed 20 March 2014).

Erriker, C., Lownded, J. and Bellchambers, E. (2011) *Primary Religious Education – A New Approach: Conceptual Enquiry in Primary RE*. Abingdon: Routledge.

Fogarty, R. (1991) 'Ten ways to integrate curriculum'. *Educational Leadership*, 49(2): 61–5.

Gates, B. (2007) *Transforming Religious Education: Beliefs and Values under Scrutiny*. London: Continuum.

Grimmitt, M. (ed.) (2000) *Pedagogies of RE*. Great Wakering: McCrimmon.

Heilman, K. (2005) *Creativity and the Brain*. Psychology Press.

Hymer, B. and Gershon, M. (2014) *Growth Mindset Pocketbook*. Teachers' Pocketbooks.

Jackson, R. (1997) *Religious Education: An Interpretive Approach*. London: Hodder and Stoughton.

McCreery, E., Palmer, S. and Voiels, V. (2008) *Teaching RE: Primary and Early Years, Achieving QTS*. Exeter: Learning Matters.

Moss, F. (ed.) (2010) *Opening up Creativity RE*. Derby: RE Today Publications.

NACCCE (National Advisory Group for Creative and Cultural Education) (1999) *All Our Futures: Creativity, Culture and Education*. Available at www.cypni.org.uk/downloads/alloutfutures.pdf (accessed 20 February 2014).

OfSTED (2013) *Realising the Potential* (130068). Available at www.ofsted.gov.uk/resources/130068

Prelutsky, J. and Smith, L. (1998) *Hooray for Diffendoofer Day*. London: Collins.

REC (Religious Education Council) (2013) National Curriculum Framework for RE available at www.natre.org.uk/uploads/Free%20Resources/RE_Review_Summary%20&%20Curriculum%20Framework.pdf (accessed 10 September 2014)

Revell, L. (2012) *Islam and Education*. Stoke-on-Trent: Trentham Books Ltd.

QCA (2004) *Religious Education: The Non-Statutory National Framework for RE*. London: Qualifications and Curriculum Authority.

Seuss, Dr (1997) *The Cat in the Hat*. London: Collins.

Stern, J. (2006) *Teaching Religious Education*. London: Continuum.

Teece, G. (2001) *A Primary Teacher's Handbook to RE and Collective Worship*. Oxford: Nash Pollock.

Teece, G. (2012) *Primary Teacher's Guide to Religious Education*. Witney: Scholastic.

Twiselton, S. (2004) 'The role of teacher identities in learning to teach primary literacy'. *Education Review: Special Edition: Activity Theory*, 56(2): 88–96.

Twiselton, S. and Elton-Chalcraft, S. (2014) 'Developing your teaching skills'. In Arthur, J. and Cremin, T. *Learning to Teach in the Primary School*, 3rd edition. London: Routledge, unit 2.4.

Webster, M (2010) *Creative Approaches to Teaching Primary RE*. Harlow: Pearson.

# CHAPTER 2

# CREATIVE LEARNING ABOUT AND FROM RELIGION

## PRINCIPLES UNDERPINNING EFFECTIVE RE PLANNING AND RELIGIOUS UNDERSTANDING

*Geoff Teece*

## INTRODUCTION

For the last twenty years learning about religion and learning from religion have become recognised as attainment targets in RE. They appeared initially as learning about religions and learning from religion in the 1994 SCAA Model Syllabuses, designed to inform the local planning of agreed syllabuses. They then became embedded in the Qualifications and Curriculum Authority (QCA) Non-Statutory National Framework for RE in 2004. However, despite their almost universal use, OfSTED (2007, 2010 and 2013) have reported that many teachers have been unsure how to understand and implement them. Furthermore in 'A Review of Religious Education in England' (REC 2013), learning about and from religion have been replaced as attainment targets by a single target that follows the same wording found in the programmes of study of the national curriculum subjects. The target states, 'By the end of each key stage, students are expected to know, apply and understand the matters, skills and processes specified in the relevant programme of study' (REC 2013, 15).

So what does this mean for learning about and from religion? This chapter recognises that one of the problems teachers may have had with these terms is that they were never originally conceived as attainment targets; instead they were meant as a pedagogical strategy to improve teaching and learning. Their disappearance as attainment targets throws open the possibility that teachers can be helped to understand them as useful ways to inform their thinking about creative planning and teaching of religions in the classroom.

**Learning 'about' religion and learning 'from' religion were intended to be seen as pedagogical strategies NOT attainment targets.**

In the next section we will explore from where these terms came and what they were originally intended to mean. We will then trace briefly the history of their development in curriculum documents and consider some of the confusions and misunderstandings before moving to a section on putting the theory into practice, where we will consider what it is we might expect our students to understand in RE with examples of how to use 'learning about' and 'learning from' to think creatively about planning and teaching RE.

# WHERE DID IT ALL BEGIN AND WHAT DID IT MEAN?

The terms 'learning about religion' and 'learning from religion' were first introduced by Michael Grimmitt and Garth Read in 1975. They were working on a curriculum model that identified RE's field of enquiry initially as traditional belief systems (nowadays we would refer to religions and worldviews; see REC 2013, 14) and shared human experience (those common human experiences that give rise to the 'big' questions of life such as 'who am I?', 'why is there suffering?', 'who is my neighbour?' and 'what happens when we die?'), represented diagrammatically by two circles. The model reflected the inter-relationship between the beliefs and concepts of the major world religions and the ultimate questions and issues raised by our shared (human) experience of the world around us. This reflected Grimmitt's and Read's longstanding conviction that education in general and RE in particular was all about human personal development.

The first curriculum outcome of this work resulted in a publication called *Teaching Christianity in RE* (Grimmitt and Read 1975). Garth Read is an Australian religious educator, and on returning to Queensland he joined the Religious Education Curriculum Project team who were responsible for an important development of the diagram. According to Read, the team recognised that each student brings a particular (though developing) belief system and set of experiences, knowledge and understandings to the classroom learning situation. The team believed that these were sources of potential content for exploration and reflection during the learning process. They could, of course, only become available to the class as and when any student chose or was able to make them so. Therefore, the teaching process needed to encourage this to happen in a natural, respectful and non-threatening way. Thus the Queensland RE Project extended RE's field of enquiry to include what is represented in the diagram by a third circle, 'individual patterns of belief'. It was this model which was to become the basis for the Westhill Project (led by Read on his return to the Regional RE Centre), as described in *How Do I Teach RE?* (Read *et al.* 1986) and in an extensive series of publications providing a comprehensive 5–16 programme of RE.

Grimmitt, meanwhile, re-visited some of these earlier ideas but set about re-working them into a comprehensive theory of the relationship of education in general, and RE in particular, to human development. His book, *Religious Education and Human Development* (Grimmitt 1987) contains a detailed rationale for the human development approach as well as a curriculum framework which sought to bring into a dialectical relationship the *life world* of the student and the *religious life world* of the various religious traditions. Consequently, the curriculum should be designed to enable pupils to develop the skills and abilities required to apply insights gained from their study of religion to an understanding of their own situations and experiences (Grimmitt 2000, 20).

Such pedagogical principles illustrate Grimmitt's conviction that the study of religion should play an *instrumental* role in RE pedagogy. What is important for the learner is

---

▨ **Table 2.1** Grimmitt's (2000) view of the study of religion

---

The pupil should understand:

▨   the way in which a religious believer perceives the world;
▨   how these insights can inform how the learner sees the world.

---

not knowledge of religion *per se*, but the way in which a religious believer perceives the world and how these insights can inform how the learner sees the world (see Table 2.1).

Grimmitt makes a distinction between 'abilities in pure religion' for the purposes of nurturing religious faith and the educational task of enabling pupils to develop 'abilities in applied religion'. Also, 'the achievement of such learning outcomes . . . hinges on devising a curriculum which does not restrict itself to description but engages pupils in evaluative interaction with religious beliefs, values and perspectives' (Grimmitt 1991, 77).

Central to this is the pedagogical *procedure* or *strategy* of learning about and from religion. This is what Grimmitt said about learning about and from religion:

> When I speak about pupils *learning about religion* I am referring to what the pupils learn about the beliefs, teachings and practices of the great religious traditions of the world. I am also referring to what pupils learn about the nature and demands of ultimate questions, about the nature of a 'faith' response to ultimate questions, about the normative views of the human condition and what it means to be human as expressed in and through Traditional Belief Systems or Stances for Living of a naturalistic kind.

(Today he would probably refer to religions and worldviews.)

> When I speak about *learning from religion* I am referring to what pupils learn from their studies in religion about themselves – about discerning ultimate questions and 'signals of transcendence' in their own experience and considering how they might respond to them. . . . The process of learning from religion involves, I suggest, engaging two, though different, types of evaluation. Impersonal Evaluation involves being able to distinguish and make critical evaluations of truth claims, beliefs and practices of different religious traditions and of religion itself. . . . Personal evalua-tion begins as an attempt to confront and evaluate religious beliefs and values [and] becomes a process of self-evaluation.
>
> (Grimmitt 1987, 225–6)

We shall see what that can mean in practice in the latter sections of this chapter.

## SUBSEQUENT DEVELOPMENTS

Despite Grimmitt's insistence that learning about and from religion were to be seen as teaching and learning strategies, when, in 1994, the Schools Curriculum and Assessment Authority (later QCA) published two Model Syllabuses for RE, they became 'adopted' as attainment targets. Furthermore they were changed to 'Learning about *religions*' and 'Learning from *religion*'. They were described thus:

Attainment Target 1: Learning about religions
This includes the ability to:

■ identify, name, describe and give accounts in order to build a coherent picture of each religion;
■ explain the meaning of religious language, story and symbolism;
■ explain similarities and differences between, and within, religions.

Attainment Target 2: Learning from religion
This includes the ability to:

■ give an informed and considered response to religious and moral issues;
■ reflect on what might be learnt from religions in the light of one's own beliefs and experience;
■ identify and respond to questions of meaning within religions.

As the new millennium dawned there was increasing debate as to the benefits or not of a national (albeit non-statutory) approach to the subject. In 2003 the QCA published a feasibility study that resulted in the publication of a national non-statutory national framework for religious education (QCA 2004). Central to the framework was the use of the two attainment targets: Learning about religion and learning from religion (reverting to Grimmitt's original titles).

Finally in 2010 QCA published some non-statutory guidance which based its understanding of RE on the 2004 framework and listed three major areas to which RE is intended to make an important contribution: spiritual, moral, social and cultural development; personal development and well-being; and community cohesion.

However, there were problems with these developments.

## CONFUSIONS AND MISUNDERSTANDINGS

There is evidence, largely from OfSTED reports (for example OfSTED 2005, 2007, 2010) that many teachers were not comfortable with this model – the major criticism being that learning *about* religion lacks depth and that consequently learning *from* religion is too 'narrowly conceived only as helping pupils to identify and reflect on aspects of their lives, with lessons used narrowly as a springboard for this reflection' (OfSTED 2005, 2).

Appropriate sections from OfSTED's report *Making Sense of Religion* (2007) contain the following criticisms.

■ In many cases, teachers perceive that AT1 (learning about religion) work is essentially descriptive and a lower order of challenge. They assume that short answers are all that is required to check basic knowledge and understanding. More extended answers are always linked to AT2 (learning from religion) alone. As a result, AT1 tasks too often demand that pupils 'report on' or 'write about' rather than asking them to analyse and process the material (10).
■ Unevenness in the progress that pupils make across the two attainment targets of 'learning about' and 'learning from' religion reflects the continuing emphasis that many schools place on 'learning about' religion. Where provision is particularly weak, pupils learn about only superficial features of the religion, rather than deepening their understanding through investigation. This tends to happen when

---

▨ **Table 2.2** Teachers' confusion about the purpose of RE (identified by OfSTED's report *Realising the Potential*, 2013)

---

Key points in the report were:

- ▨ In many schools visited, the subject was increasingly losing touch with the idea that RE should be primarily concerned with helping pupils to make sense of the world of religion and belief.
- ▨ Many primary teachers, including subject leaders, were finding it difficult to separate RE from the more general, whole-school promotion of spiritual, moral, social and cultural development.
- ▨ Many schools showed a strong tendency to detach learning in RE from the more in-depth study of religion and belief. Too often teachers thought they could bring depth to the pupils' learning by inviting them to reflect on or write introspectively about their own experience rather than rigorously investigate and evaluate religion and belief.
- ▨ In the primary schools visited, considerable weaknesses in teaching about Christianity frequently stemmed from a lack of clarity about the purpose of the subject. For example, Christian stories, particularly miracles, were often used to encourage pupils to reflect on their own experience without any opportunity to investigate the stories' significance within the religion itself.

---

teachers assume that more analytical and reflective tasks are linked predominantly to attainment target 2, 'learning from' religion; as a result, they do not include challenging tasks in work related to 'learning about' religion (38).

OfSTED (2010) in their second 'long report' on religious education, *Transforming Religious Education*, found (among other things) that whilst RE made a positive contribution to pupils' personal development in terms of appreciating the diverse nature of society, its contribution to spiritual development is limited. There is uncertainty among many teachers of RE about what they are trying to achieve in the subject.

The OfSTED survey in 2013 found further evidence of teachers' confusion about what they were trying to achieve in RE and how to translate this into effective planning, teaching and assessment (see Table 2.2).

## Research into resources to teach world religions

Recent research on materials used to teach about world religions in schools found problems with the conceptualisation of learning from religion. In a section that analyses whether current textbooks present religion in depth in terms of its 'deeper significance', there are a number of comments to support a rethink about how religion is presented to students (Jackson *et al.* 2010, 99–100). One example from this section reads,

Even where texts are encouraging a 'learning from' approach to religious education the reviewer found that students were not necessarily encouraged to delve much more deeply into the significance of the religion; '"*learning from ideas*" *tend to operate at the level of functionality – e.g. how they might show someone/something respect, the role of having a uniform etc.*' They do not explore Sikh ideas about human values and are interested in parallel practices rather than resonating with values in other traditions and students' lives.

This research and the evidence from the OfSTED reports gives weight to the argument that effective learning from religion depends on the prior clarification of what exactly pupils should learn about.

## WHAT SHOULD PUPILS BE LEARNING ABOUT IN RELIGIOUS EDUCATION?

In one sense this may appear quite straightforward. For example, the new curriculum review of religious education (REC 2013, 14) states that all pupils should 'know about and understand a range of religions and world views'. What does knowing and understanding mean in this context? We can get some way towards an answer by looking at a section from the statement of the 'purpose of study' in the curriculum review (REC 2013, 14). See Table 2.3.

This is helpful in a number of ways. First it puts the study of religions and world-views within the context of the process of teaching and learning in RE. As it suggests in point 2, religions and worldviews are a source from which pupils can learn about and form big questions in life, which includes (see point 3) enabling the pupils to develop their ideas, values and identities.

Notwithstanding this, it is true that religions and worldviews are many-faceted and complex traditions. Indeed in some ways the idea of religions is a particularly Western construction. It suggests that religions are things to be studied when in fact they are more like ways of seeing the world. It's not insignificant that in some traditions, for example Islam, Hinduism and Buddhism, the term 'religion' was never used. For Muslims it is *din*, which means the path, a complete way of life. For Buddhists it is about following the dharma, one definition of which is the teachings of Buddha. Those who have taken religious studies as a degree will probably know that terms like 'Buddhism' and 'Hinduism' are relatively recent labels applied to these traditions by Western scholars. Hinduism is more appropriately referred to as Sanatana Dharma, the eternal way.

---

■ **Table 2.3** The purpose of RE (identified by REC *Review of RE in England*, 2013)

---

1. Religious education contributes dynamically to children and young people's education in schools by provoking challenging questions about meaning and purpose in life, beliefs about God, ultimate reality, issues of right and wrong and what it means to be human.
2. In RE they learn about and from religions and worldviews in local, national and global contexts, to discover, explore and consider different answers to these questions. They learn to weigh up the value of wisdom from different sources, to develop and express their insights in response, and to agree or disagree respectfully.
3. Teaching therefore should equip pupils with systematic knowledge and understanding of a range of religions and worldviews, enabling them to develop their ideas, values and identities.

---

Why is this important? For one thing it is tempting to just see religions as a set of beliefs and practices to be studied and religious believers as those who go around believing things about the world. Whilst beliefs and doctrines are an important aspect of religions, a more helpful and possibly a more comprehensive approach is to see them as ways of seeing the world. Two words that can often confuse a teacher are *faith* and *belief*. This is because, in modern times, they are often used synonymously and interchangeably. So we talk about 'the Christian faith', 'the Sikh faith' etc., often meaning the Christian religion and the Sikh religion. To have faith is often seen as believing a set of statements about the world, for example, that Jesus is the Son of God, that believing in him will bring me salvation, that the Bible is the word of God etc. However, if we look back in Christian theology, for example, we find that 'believing' meant much more than merely assenting to a set of statements about the world. St Anslem's famous statement 'Credo ut Intelligam' (I believe in order to understand) does not refer to belief in this way. Rather it speaks of believing in terms of how we orientate ourselves. If we tell someone, 'I believe in you', we do not mean 'I believe certain statements about you, you are 5 feet tall and slightly overweight'; we mean, 'I trust you, I commit myself to you, I have faith in you.' So in this reading of things, 'belief' arises out of our efforts to interpret our experiences into concepts and propositions. The American scholar Wilfred Cantwell Smith put it like this:

> Prior to our being religious or irreligious, before we come to think of ourselves as Catholics, Protestants, Jews or Muslims, we are already engaged with issues of faith. Whether we become nonbelievers, agnostics or atheists, we are concerned with how to put our lives together and with what will make our life worth living. Moreover, we look for something to love that loves us, something to value that gives us value, something to honour and respect that has power to sustain our being.
>
> (Cantwell Smith 1978, 5)

This is important if we are to find an approach to studying religions and worldviews that makes sense to young people and makes sense within the process of RE that is suggested in the curriculum review. So a confident RE teacher is one who has a good knowledge and understanding of the beliefs and practices of religious traditions and how these beliefs and practices express the way that people in that tradition see the world. It is not enough merely to know some information about the festivals, key figures and other aspects of the religious traditions. As teachers we have to 'get inside' the tradition as far as we can. This means attempting to understand the tradition conceptually. This is important because the subject knowledge needed by a good teacher of RE includes knowledge and understanding not only of religions but also of how this knowledge and understanding contributes to the process of teaching and learning in the subject, what we call pedagogical knowledge.

In terms of the process of RE then, it is important for us, as teachers, to try and understand how a Hindu, Jew, Christian etc. 'sees' the world and its 'big' or ultimate questions. However, we must start from the idea of what it is to be human before we consider how another might see the world. This involves knowing something about how the idea of what it is to be human is understood within a particular tradition and how the tradition itself provides a spiritual 'path' for the believer to become as fully human as possible and so live a more rounded, fulfilling and holy life. Attempting to understand this is no easy task but the ideas expressed here are particularly well expressed by Wilfred Cantwell Smith in the following passage, where he calls for 'us on the outside' who wish to understand a Muslim to understand not his religion but his religiousness.

So for the Hindu, the Buddhist, the Tierra del Fuegin. If we would comprehend these we must look not at their religion but at the universe so far as possible through their eyes. It is what the Hindu is able to see, by being a Hindu that is significant. Until we can see it too, we have not come to grips with the religious quality of his life. And we can be sure that when he looks around him he does not see 'Hinduism'. Like the rest of us, he sees his wife's death, his child's minor and major aspirations, his money lender's mercilessness, the calm of a starlight evening, his own mortality. He sees things through coloured glasses, if one will, of a 'Hindu' brand.

(Cantwell Smith 1978, 138)

Therefore, we can say that religious education is a subject which deals not with religion as an object out there to be studied, but with religions and worldviews as ways of interpreting the world – some of these are Buddhist, some are Christian, some are humanist and some are atheist.

## WHAT DO WE WANT PUPILS TO UNDERSTAND?

Key to helping pupils to understand anything is to enable them to understand concepts. How do we choose these concepts? One way to look at this is to think of concepts in three categories.

### Category one: concepts from the religious traditions

First, there are the concepts and ideas which belong within a particular religious tradition and which relate to the key beliefs and values of the tradition but also provide the lens through which a follower views the world. Potentially there are an enormous number of these and we have to be selective. The ones here are chosen because they reflect what we might call the spirituality or religiousness of the tradition. Or in other words, they are concepts that are essential if one is to understand something of how a Christian, Buddhist, Hindu etc. sees the world. To improve subject knowledge the teacher can investigate these (see Table 2.4).

### Category two: concepts derived from our shared human experience

Although the following concepts are not in themselves religious, they are very helpful in enabling pupils to make links among religions, worldviews and the types of questions referred to in the purpose of study (see Table 2.5). They might be referred to as 'spiritual' as they can help us make sense of our shared human experience.

### Category three: concepts derived from the study of religion

The concepts in Table 2.6 can help pupils make sense of religion in a general way. For example it is important that pupils begin to understand something about the nature of religious language and communication. All religions communicate essential truths in non-literal ways. Therefore a concept like myth is important in this sense. It's also important because, like a number of concepts in this category, it has been devalued and reduced in its meaning in many Western societies. See Table 2.6.

**■ Table 2.4** The concepts (lenses) through which the believer sees the world

| **Buddhist** | **Christian** | **Hindu** |
|---|---|---|
| Anatta | Church | Ahimsa |
| Anicca | Discipleship | Atman |
| Buddha | Faith | Avatara |
| Dhamma | Forgiveness | Bhakti |
| Dukkha | God the Father | Brahman |
| Kamma | Holy Spirit | Dharma |
| Metta | Jesus the Christ | Karma |
| Nibbana | Love | Maya |
| Sangha | Mother of God | Moksha |
| Tanha | Resurrection | Samsara |
| | Salvation | Shakti |
| | Sin | Smriti |
| | Trinity | Sruti |
| | | Varna |
| | | Yoga |

| **Jewish** | **Muslim** | **Sikh** |
|---|---|---|
| Brit | Akhirah | Anand |
| Halakhah | Allah | Akhand Path |
| Israel | Din | Brace |
| Kedusha | Ibadah | Gurmukh |
| Kashrut | Iman | Guru |
| Mitzvah | Islam | Haumai |
| Shabbat | Jihad | Ik Onkar |
| Shalom | Qadar | Jivan Mukhti |
| Synagogue | Qur'an | Khalsa |
| Tenakh | Rasul | Langar |
| Teshuvah | Salah | Nam Simran |
| Torah | Shari'ah | Sewa |
| Tzedekah | Shirk | Sikh |
| | Sunnah | |
| | Tawhid | |
| | Ummah | |

**■ Table 2.5** Concepts derived from our shared human experience

service, wonder, guidance, relationship, teacher, commitment, suffering, duty, purity, festival mystery, authority, unity, care, special place, growth, identity, difference, ritual, celebration, truth pattern, community, responsibility, forgiveness, belonging, wholeness, change, leadership, rule special time, custom, peace, equality

**■ Table 2.6** Concepts derived from the study of religion

fasting, initiation, pilgrimage, belief, religious tradition, worldview, worship, creation, devotion, prayer, God, god, faith, blessing, symbol, myth, scripture

# WHAT MIGHT THIS LOOK LIKE IN PRACTICE?

Let's take an example of visiting a place of worship. The first thing to remember if we are to make learning about and from religions meaningful is that there is no such place as a place of worship; there are only churches, mosques, viharas, synagogues, gurdwaras etc. That is one of the mistakes that is easy to make in thinking about setting a 'learning from' activity. For example, a teacher might assign students to write about a special place that they go on their own for quiet. That may be appropriate for some experiences but often a visit to a 'place of worship' is neither quiet nor solitary! It's best to think back to our sets of concepts and try to make links between them. Table 2.7 shows what is being suggested here.

---

■ **Table 2.7** Learning about and from religions through visiting places of worship

### *Learning about and from Sikhism and a visit to a gurdwara:*

Hospitality/sharing/respect/gifts/learning and sharing music/humility/holiness/generosity/ beauty/unity/commitment/honesty/devotion/importance of identifying that which is important/God's words are to be found in many places/listening to the praise of God is a good thing/reciting God's praise continually is a good thing

*Specific concepts from Sikhism, for example sewa, akhand path, langar, wahiguru, diwan, Guru Granth Sahib.*

### *Learning about and from Islam and a visit to a mosque:*

Unity/commitment/devotion/humility/brotherhood/respect for Allah/submission/obedience/ importance of cleanliness inside and out/importance of prayer together/gratitude/authority/ modesty/beauty in pattern, colour and shape/taking care to make something beautiful for Allah/importance of not making images/importance of memorisation of important words/ holiness/honesty/authority/importance of ritual

*Specific concepts from Islam, for example dhikr, ibadah, Qur'an, ummah, tawhid, wudu.*

### *Learning about and from Buddhism and a visit to a vihara:*

Commitment/respect/devotion/all life changes and decays/obedience/value of silence/ meditation/difficulty of silence/struggle with oneself and one's mind/honesty/gratitude/ importance of ritual

*Specific concepts from Buddhism, for example anapanasati, annica, Brahma Viharas, dukkha, samadhi, samatha, upaya, upekkha.*

### *Learning about and from Hinduism and a visit to a mandir:*

God can be understood in many different ways/God is bigger than the human mind can comprehend/the senses can be used in worship/gratitude/vibrancy and joy in worship/ devotion/holiness/generosity/importance of ritual

*Specific concepts from Hinduism, for example atman, avatara, bhakti, Brahman, dharma, trimurti.*

---

*(Continued)*

■ **Table 2.7** Continued

---

*Learning about and from Judaism and a visit to a synagogue:*

Respect/holiness/importance of the words of God/authority/obedience/importance of ritual/
community/importance of prayer together/remembering the acts of God/remembering those
who have died/importance of symbol to communicate that too holy for words/everlasting
presence of God/commitment/gratitude

*Specific concepts from Judaism, for example kedusha, ner tamid, bet tefillah.*

*Learning about and from Christianity and a visit to a church:*

Holiness/importance of symbol for communicating ideas/importance of sacrifice/
remembering the acts of God/authority/commitment/duty/confession/importance of ritual/
forgiveness/repentance/beauty/expressing ideas about God in a creative form/devotion/
gratitude/importance of prayer together

*Specific concepts from Christianity, for example communion of saints, reconciliation,
forgiveness, prayer, thanksgiving.*

---

**Source:** From Maybury and Teece (2005, 187–8)

You'll notice that there are many more concepts than included in the previous tables
but hopefully you can see that the concepts in italics are taken from category one, whilst
the other concepts are a mixture of the other two categories.

# HOW DO I THINK ABOUT PLANNING FOR LEARNING ABOUT AND FROM RELIGION? AN EXAMPLE FROM SIKHISM

If we take the first example from Table 2.7, visiting a gurdwara, we can think about it in
the following way.

## How Sikhs understand human nature and humans' place in the world

For Sikhs *avidya* (spiritual blindness) and *maya* (illusion as to what is ultimately real) cause
the condition known as *haumai* which means ego or I-centredness. A person who is subject
to *haumai* is known as *manmukh*:

> Under the compulsion of *haumai* man comes and goes, is born and dies, gives and takes,
> earns and loses, speaks truths and lies, smears himself with evil and washes himself of it.
> (Adi Granth 466)

According to Guru Nanak it is *haumai* which controls unregenerate man to such an extent
that it 'binds him more firmly to the wheel of transmigration' (McLeod 1968, 182).

For Sikhs, following a path of *nam simran* (keeping God constantly in mind) and
*sewa* (selfless service) and hence developing *gurmukh* (God-centredness) leads to a state
of *mukhti* (spiritual liberation).

> Salvation is achieved through self-realisation by the process of meditation on the
> Nam (name), which is a subjective or mystical experience, assisted by the Guru. This

process destroys *Haumai* [egotism]. . . . The grace of the personal Guru, as well as the invisible God-Guru, is the prerequisite for achieving salvation, on the basis of service rendered to the Guru [*Guru Sewa*].

(Rahi 1999, 83)

## A visit to the gurdwara

How might a visit to the gurdwara enable students to understand something of this view of the world and to learn something from it?

During such a visit pupils would probably have the experience of sitting in the prayer hall listening to the *Guru Granth Sahib* being read, after which they would sit together and be served *langar*. In addition, they may be taken on a 'tour' of the gurdwara and listen to Sikhs talking about their beliefs and how serving in the gurdwara influences the way they live their lives. In response to these experiences we might want the students to reflect on their thoughts and feelings during the visit. It is not unusual for a teacher to ask the pupils to talk about special places they like to visit, to consider the importance of worship to religious people and to consider the things that influence the way they live their own lives. The question that begs to be asked about such activities is how do we intend these reflections to enable the pupils to learn about and from Sikhism? We can only answer this if we know what we intend the pupils to understand about Sikhism, which means focussing on certain key Sikh concepts (see category one). Without such specific concentration on Sikh beliefs and practices these activities are merely about the students' experiences and are not necessarily related to what they might learn from Sikhism. For example, in order really to learn from Sikhism, they will have experienced Sikhs doing *sewa* so pupils can reflect on ideas such as generosity, service, sharing and humility. From the experience of *langar* they might reflect on ideas of equality, willingness to give and receive, or caring for others. The experience of listening to the continuous reading of the *Guru Granth Sahib* (*akhand path*) might lead to pupils reflecting on the importance or not of God's word being continuously heard, on what in their view are the most important sounds in the world, or perhaps on the very idea that God's word can be heard in the world and what that might mean in their own lives. Thinking of the importance of the *Guru Granth Sahib* for Sikhs, they might consider ideas such as respect, guidance, authority and what a teacher means.

So the Sikh concepts and values involved in this example are indicative of what we might call the spirituality of Sikhism. Of course, students often learn about phenomena of Sikhism such as the Five Ks, which can go some way to developing students' understanding of an aspect of Sikh identity, but the material which has the richest potential for students to understand Sikhism and, as importantly, learn from Sikhism, is more likely to be found in an exploration of *sewa* because, as indicated, it is an important aspect of *gurmukh* (God-centeredness), which leads to spiritual liberation, is transformative and is central to how Sikhs see other people, how they see what being God-centred means and how they see the world in general (Table 2.8).

---

■ **Table 2.8** Studying religion should enrich (not be reduced to) the experience of the learner

Learning 'about' the religion through the lens of the believer, e.g. the concept of sewa in Sikhism
Learn from the religion – what sense this makes to their own understandings of generosity

## SUMMARY AND CONCLUSION

In this chapter we have seen how many teachers have been confused about how to apply learning from and about religion in their planning and teaching. This was largely because 'learning about' and 'learning from' religion were taken up as attainment targets when they were never intended to be so. Despite their disappearance as attainment targets in the curriculum review, it is still expected that pupils learn about and from religion. What we have explored in this chapter is a coherent way of thinking about this. We have highlighted that the secret to good practice is identifying key concepts that should underpin our thinking and planning. One of the most important things to remember is that learning from religion should be based on what is learnt *about* a religion, not just on the pupil's experience. Another way of putting it is that studying religion should enrich the experience of the learner rather than religion being reduced to the experience of the learner. In the latter case nobody ends up learning very much at all.

## ADDITIONAL RESOURCES

Baumfield, V., *et al.* (1995) 'Model syllabuses: the debate continues' in *Resource* 18 (1), pp. 3–6.

Cush, D. & Francis, D. (2001) '"Positive pluralism" to *Awareness, Mystery and Value*: a case study in religious education curriculum development' in *British Journal of Religious Education* 24 (1), pp. 52–67.

Everington, J. (2000) 'Mission impossible? Religious education in the 1990s' in Leicester, M., Mogdil, C. & Mogdil, S. (eds), *Spiritual and Religious Education*. London, Falmer Press.

Hella, E. & Wright, A. (2009) 'Learning "about" and "from" religion: phenomenography, the variation theory of learning and religious education in Finland and the UK' in *British Journal of Religious Education* 31 (1), pp. 53–64.

Hull, J. (2002) 'Spiritual development: interpretations and applications' in *British Journal of Religious Education* 24 (3), pp. 171–82.

Teece, G. (2012) 'Learning about and from religion'. Unpublished monograph prepared for the canton of Zurich.

Teece, G. (2010) 'Is it learning about and from religions, religion or religious education and is it any wonder some teachers don't get it?' in *British Journal of Religious Education* 30 (3), pp. 89–103.

Teece, G. (2009) 'Religion as human transformation' in *Resource* 31 (3), pp. 4–7.

Teece, G. (2008) 'Learning from religions as skilful means: a contribution to the debate about the identity of religious education' in *British Journal of Religious Education* 3 (3), pp. 187–98.

Teece, G. (2001) *A Primary Teacher's Handbook to RE and Collective Worship*. Oxford, Nash Pollock.

Teece, G. (1997) 'Why John Hick's theory of religions is important for RE' in *Resource* 20 (1), pp. 3–6.

Teece, G. (1993) *In Defence of Theme Teaching in RE*. Birmingham, Westhill RE Centre.

Walshe, K. & Teece, G. (2013) 'Understanding religious understanding in religious education' in *British Journal of Education* 35 (3), pp. 313–325.

Wintersgill, B. (1995) 'The case of the missing models: exploding the myths' in *Resource* 18 (1), pp. 6–11.

# REFERENCES

Cantwell Smith, C. (1978) *The Meaning and End of Religion: A New Approach to the Religious Traditions of Mankind*. London: SPCK.

Grimmitt, M. (2000) *Pedagogies of Religious Education*. Great Wakering: McCrimmons.

Grimmitt, M. (1991) 'The Use of Religious Phenomena in Schools' in *British Journal of Religious Education* 13 (2), pp. 77–88.

Grimmitt, M. (1987) *Religious Education and Human Development*. Great Wakering: McCrimmons.

Grimmitt, M. & Read, G. (1975) *Teaching Christianity in RE*. Great Wakering: Mayhew.

Jackson, R., et al. (2010) *Materials Used to Teach about World Religions in Schools in England*. London: Department for Children, Schools and Families.

Maybury, J. & Teece, G. (2005) 'Learning from what? a question of subject focus in religious education in England and Wales' in *Journal of Beliefs and Values* 26 (2), pp. 179–90.

McLeod, W.H. (1968) *Guru Nanak and the Sikh Religion*. Delhi: Oxford University Press.

OfSTED (2013) *Religious Education: Realising the Potential*. London: HMSO.

OfSTED (2010) *Transforming Religious Education*. London: HMSO.

OfSTED (2007) *Making Sense of Religion: A Report on Religious Education in Schools and the Impact of Locally Agreed Syllabuses*. London: HMSO.

OfSTED (2005) *Religious Education in the Primary School*. Document reference number: HMI 2346 (out of print).

QCA (2004) *Religious Education: The Non-Statutory National Framework*. London: QCA & DfES.

Rahi, H. Sing (1999) *Sri Guru Granth Sahib: A Reference Book of Quotations*. Delhi: Motilal Banarsidass.

REC (2013) *A Review of Religious Education in England*. London: Religious Education Council of England & Wales.

SCAA (1994) *Model Syllabuses for RE*. London: Schools Curriculum and Assessment Authority.

# SECTION 2

# CREATIVE APPROACHES IN RELIGIOUS EDUCATION

# CHAPTER 3

# CREATIVE THINKING AND DIALOGUE

## P4C AND THE COMMUNITY OF ENQUIRY

### *Georgia Prescott*

. . . the thought of a child may be a priceless gift to a parent or teacher with ears to hear.

Gareth Matthews (1994 p15)

## INTRODUCTION

Religious education (RE) creates a perfect opportunity for children to think and talk creatively and philosophically because it is concerned with exploring differing views of the world and our place as humans within it. Religions and other worldviews concern themselves with philosophical and contestable questions and issues and have their own interpretations of the world. Religious texts, stories and teachings introduce, question and explore these ideas and concepts. RE therefore can engage children in investigating and evaluating different views and in exploring their own ideas and beliefs, whatever their standpoint.

This chapter will explore reasons to include opportunities for creative thinking and dialogue in your RE lessons, as well as some practical strategies for doing so.

## CREATIVE THINKING AND DIALOGUE IN RE

Creative RE has to involve more than just imparting the 'facts' about religion to children and hoping that the students might engage with them. In inspecting RE lessons, OfSTED (2013) commented, 'While pupils had a range of basic factual information about religions, their deeper understanding of the world of religion and belief was weak' (p8).

Low-level tasks such as filling in worksheets after being given some information, writing/retelling stories in their own words and cutting and pasting activities really only require skills such as remembering or sequencing, and they do not engage children with the concepts and ideas behind the information or texts.

> Pupils rarely developed their skills of enquiry into religion: to ask more pertinent and challenging questions; to gather, interpret and analyse information; and to draw conclusions and evaluate issues using good reasoning.
>
> (ibid. p9)

Real learning has to come from getting children to engage at a deeper level with the *concepts* within the subject matter (Erriker, Lowndes & Bellchambers 2011) and apply it to their own experiences and beliefs. This should involve opportunities and space for children to think, both collectively and individually (Fisher 2013; Hymer & Sutcliffe 2012; Nottingham 2013).

One of the key ways for children to develop their thinking is through dialogue, in a setting where they feel safe enough to express themselves openly through the mutual exchange of ideas. Despite the downplaying of speaking and listening by the coalition government, its importance is still acknowledged within the National Curriculum (DfE 2013); and few educators would deny the central importance and benefits of dialogue in the classroom as a key to real learning (Littleton & Mercer 2013; Fisher 2009, 2013; Alexander 2009).

One of the key statutory requirements of the 'Spoken Language' strand in the 2013 National Curriculum includes this: 'use spoken language to develop understanding through speculating, hypothesising, imagining and exploring ideas' (DfE 2013 p17). It is this type of spoken language that has particular relevance to the use of dialogue in RE.

So what does creative thinking and dialogue look like, and how does it differ from other types of classroom talk? Ken Robinson (2011 p151) talks about creativity as 'the process of having original ideas that have value' and says 'creativity involves putting your imagination to work' (ibid. p143). Creative thinking in RE involves giving children the space and chance to think about beliefs and ideas about the world and our place in it. They can do this as individuals, but it is much more effective as a group engaged in dialogue. Through collaborative dialogue, children can be introduced to a range of ideas and can build on these together. This helps them to struggle collectively with complex concepts and possibly to create new ideas as a result. Butler and Edwards (in Nottingham 2010 p185) called this struggle the 'pit', which they see as an essential part of the process of learning. This concept is developed further by Nottingham (2010 p188, 2013 p86). Fisher (2009 p8) sees the value in 'playful and divergent ideas' and 'challenging them [children] to be creative and to think in new ways'.

For creative thinking and dialogue to be really effective, it needs time, and teachers should not be afraid of giving value to this type of learning. RE should not require written responses for everything that we do. We need to recognise, plan for and value the quality learning and engagement that can take place through dialogue. 'Creative dialogue cannot be left to chance, it must be valued, encouraged and expected – and seen as essential to good teaching and learning (Fisher 2013 p41).

There are many methods through which children can become engaged in creative dialogue in the classroom. This chapter will explore some of these in terms of how they might be applied to RE.

## P4C AND THE COMMUNITY OF ENQUIRY

Creative thinking and dialogue in RE can take place through the development of a community of enquiry. This is where the community enquires together as a group, as discussed earlier. Philosophy for Children (P4C) is now a well-established approach to learning in the classroom which involves children working in a community of enquiry. Much has already been written about P4C (Cam 1995, 2006; Fisher 2009, 2013; Haynes 2002; Hymer & Sutcliffe 2012; Nottingham 2013; Stanley 2004). P4C was originally developed by

Matthew Lipman (1993) and later Ann Margaret Sharp (Splitter & Sharp 1995) in the 1960s and continues to be developed in the UK under the direction of the Society for the Advancement of Philosophical Enquiry and Reflection in Education (SAPERE; www.sapere.org.uk/).

P4C involves children in reflecting on and enquiring into philosophical ideas, and because the philosophy of religion is a major school of philosophy, RE is a natural context in which to use P4C. P4C follows a set process, which can be used as outlined in this chapter, but also some of the techniques and approaches within P4C can be usefully applied as shorter activities to use within a RE lesson. Furthermore, P4C needs to be distinguished from circle time. The two can often be confused because both require children to sit in a circle. The distinction is that P4C requires children to talk and think *together as a group*, a process facilitated by sitting in a circle.

The full process goes as follows:

■ **Starter activity** – a community-builder type of activity which helps the group come together and work as a community
■ **Thought-provoking stimulus** – e.g. a story/photo/picture/object/music/poem
■ **Initial thoughts and question raising** – children identify concepts/ideas and raise (hopefully open-ended, philosophical) questions
■ **Question airing** – questions are shared with the group and sorted
■ **Question choosing** – a democratic process whereby questions are voted for and the most popular is chosen by the group
■ **Enquiry** – the group have an enquiry around their chosen question which is facilitated rather than led by the teacher
■ **Final thoughts** – children have a chance to reflect and air some of their final thoughts, tracking possible changes in their thinking through the enquiry
■ **Review** – students are given a chance to review the process and their involvement in it

> (For extended details about the process see Buckley 2012a, 2012b;
> Hymer & Sutcliffe 2012; Nottingham 2013.)

This can be quite a lengthy process, and undoubtedly the more children are used to it, the better at it they get. There is value in sometimes running a full enquiry process and other times doing some elements of it or running it over two sessions.

## STIMULI FOR P4C IN RE

In RE there are many things which can be used as a stimulus for an enquiry. These could include religious stories or teachings, proverbs, photographs depicting religions, religious artworks, music and religious artefacts. It is useful if the stimulus is in some way interesting, challenging or even controversial, to encourage the raising of questions. By using the P4C approach you are ensuring that the children engage with the material in their own way, and you are not setting the agenda. Sometimes a teacher will say about RE, 'I'll tell them the story and then tell them what it means.' By doing this, they are imposing their own interpretation of what the story means, rather than enabling children to work out what it might mean to them or to question the puzzling or interesting aspects of it to them. This involves a change in perception of the teacher, not always as fact/information giver, but as learning facilitator and sometimes co-enquirer.

We might also be encouraged to use a full range of stories and writings, particularly from Christianity, rather than going back to the same stories time and time again. How many times during their primary years do children hear the story of the Good Samaritan or Noah's ark from the Bible? Is there is any progression in the way they engage with the story and its messages? Using proverbs from the book of Proverbs from the Bible, for example, makes for interesting discussion. There are many of these types of 'wise' sayings within different religious traditions. There are also interesting stories that are less well-used that children can and should be introduced to.

Religious and secular artworks, in both 2D and 3D, are often thought-provoking or even controversial, and give an artist's interpretation of an aspect of religion. These can be interesting stimuli for P4C enquiry. Internet search engines make access to these relatively easy, and postcards or copies can be accessed from a range of sources. For example the REJesus website (www.rejesus.co.uk) shows a number of artworks depicting Jesus from a range of cultural perspectives, and RE Today produces a number of picture packs which contain a variety of religious artworks and images from different cultures (www.retoday.org.uk).

In Table 3.1 is a list of questions classes have asked and the one they have chosen to enquire into in response to a range of stimuli. In most cases I have not included all the questions asked; instead I provide a sample of some of the more philosophical ones. This illustrates the type of thinking children can do in order to create questions from a range of stimuli in RE.

Several observations can be made about the questions. Younger children tend to ask questions that are more rooted in the stimulus. This is a natural part of their developing the ability to ask philosophical questions, which tend to be more removed from the original stimulus. A skilled facilitator can use their chosen question to encourage the group to develop their discussion so it does begin to get into the more philosophical issues within their question. The Year 5/6 group was very experienced at P4C, so their questions tended to be more philosophical in nature. Philip Cam (2006 p32–6) has used a 'question quadrant' to help distinguish between different types of questions that children may ask, which is a useful reference point for facilitators. At Key Stage Two, it can also be used with children to help them sort the questions themselves that they have asked. In doing this, they begin to develop an understanding of the types of questions that they need to be asking.

Another observation is that many of the questions may not be specifically religious in nature. Again, this is not a problem, as the children are really engaging in issues and concepts rooted in the stimulus. Through this, their engagement with the stories or other stimuli is far greater than listening to a teacher read a story and rewriting it in their own words. Hopefully, therefore, their learning will be more inclusive of all children regardless of their faith or non-faith background, and their engagement will be far deeper.

## DEVELOPING THINKING THROUGH EXPLORATION OF CONCEPTS

In effect, through different approaches, RE can encourage children to explore and develop their thinking around various key concepts. These concepts can fall into different categories as outlined by Erriker, Lowndes & Bellchambers (2011 ch. 4) and are used as a basis for conceptual enquiry at the centre of the Hampshire Locally Agreed Syllabus for RE.

■ **Table 3.1** Examples of questions raised and chosen by children in RE

| Year Group | Stimulus | Questions Asked | Chosen Question |
|---|---|---|---|
| Y5/6 | *The Short and Incredibly Happy Life of Riley* – Colin Thompson and Amy Lissiat (Secular story – links well to Buddhist teachings) | ■ Why do humans always want more? <br> ■ Is a rat's life better than a human's? <br> ■ Was Riley happy all his life or was he sad sometimes? | Why do humans always want more? |
| Y5/6 | Images of Jesus from different cultural perspectives | ■ Why can't we have one image of Jesus in the world? <br> ■ Why do people have different opinions of Jesus? <br> ■ Does Jesus like everyone? <br> ■ How do we know what Jesus looks like if we haven't seen him? | How do we know what Jesus looks like if we haven't seen him? |
| Y5/6 | The Bowl of Milk and the Jasmine Flower – story from Sikhism | ■ Why do people have hatred in them? <br> ■ What is rudeness? <br> ■ Why are people rude? <br> ■ Why are people jealous about other people? <br> ■ Why are people selfish? | Why are people rude? |
| Y5/6 | Music – John Zorn – 'Ghetto Life' (music depicting Kristallnacht in the Holocaust) | ■ Can music tell a story? <br> ■ What is this music trying to tell us? (The children didn't know the context of the music before they heard it.) | Can music tell a story? |
| Y5/6 | Music – Queen – 'Heaven for Everyone' | ■ Could the earth be heaven for everyone? <br> ■ Do people want heaven if they don't believe in God? <br> ■ What is heaven? | What is heaven? |
| Y2 | The Man and His Goat (story from Hinduism from the Panchatantra) | ■ Why did a plan that sounded so silly work? <br> ■ How did the man end up believing the thieves? <br> ■ How did the thieves get away with it? | Why did a plan that sounded so silly work? |

They identify such concepts as *universal concepts* common to all such as 'love' or 'forgiveness' ('category A'), *universal religious concepts* common to all or many faiths such as 'prayer' or 'god' ('category B'), and finally *specific religious concepts* which are exclusive to one faith such as 'Sewa' in Sikhism or 'Incarnation' in Christianity ('category C'). Enquiry into these can be encouraged through careful selection of a stimulus for P4C that might yield questions about a concept or that might lead into discussion around one. The

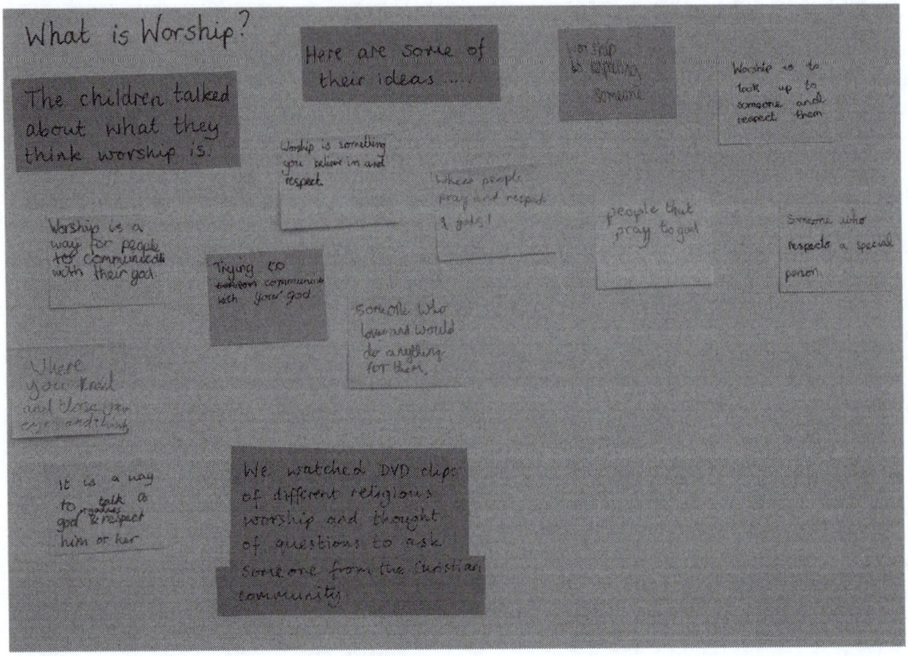

**Figure 3.1** Enquiring into the concept of worship (Photo – David Angell)

photo in Figure 3.1 shows children's work from St Mary's CE Primary School, Kirkby Lonsdale, in Cumbria after they had begun to enquire into the universal religious concept of worship and before looking at worship in Christianity specifically.

## Shorter thinking exercises

We can also do shorter P4C-style activities that help children enquire into concepts in RE. Vivianne Baumfield (2002) and Philip Cam (2006) have each introduced different thinking tools to help children develop their skills in enquiry and dialogue. Philip Cam (2006) introduced the skill of making distinctions and connections. Some examples for RE might include the following:

*What is the distinction between:*

■　*Prayer and worship?*
■　*Love and devotion?*
■　*A church and a cathedral?*

*What is the connection between:*

■　*A mosque and a synagogue?*
■　*Sewa and Zakat?*
■　*Baptism and Bar Mitzvah?*

■ **Figure 3.2** Odd one out

Doing these kinds of exercises helps children to use higher order thinking skills to explore religious concepts, practices and features more deeply.

Vivianne Baumfield (2002) also introduced the 'Odd One Out' exercises (Figure 3.2), again designed to help children think about religious objects or features in more depth.

Which is the odd one out?

The answer could be:

■ The cross because it is a symbol.
■ The mosque because it is not linked to Christianity.
■ The cross because you can hold it in your hand.

Can you think of one?

The great thing about this is it can encourage divergent thinking if you keep asking for different answers or reasons. It is also very difficult to be 'wrong'. All ideas are acceptable as long as the argument or reason given is sound.

All of these activities involve children in developing their thinking skills and involve them in RE in different ways, which is preferable to them just regurgitating information. Many of these can be developed to be interactive by creating sets of laminated cards that can be re-used for different exercises. Internet search engines can give you access to a wealth of such images.

## Thinking by sorting

Children can be asked to sort a larger group of images into sub-groups and think of a heading for the groups. This way they are thinking in order to make connections and distinctions. They could be asked to choose ten images from the group that represent Christianity for example. If we select our images carefully we can use this type of activity to challenge children's stereotypes of a faith by including images from different cultures. This is explored in more depth in chapter 10.

Another good activity is created by sorting statements, some of which are more controversial or difficult to sort than others. If you create the statements carefully to ensure they are at an appropriate level, this can even be done with children as young as four or five years old. For an example of this, see Table 3.2.

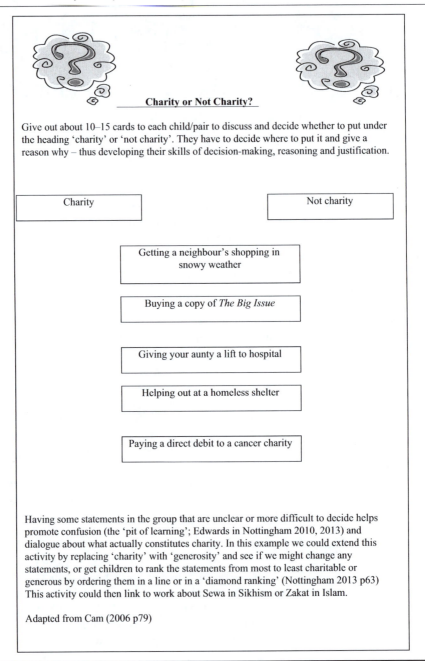

**Charity or Not Charity?**

Give out about 10–15 cards to each child/pair to discuss and decide whether to put under the heading 'charity' or 'not charity'. They have to decide where to put it and give a reason why – thus developing their skills of decision-making, reasoning and justification.

| Charity | Not charity |
| --- | --- |

Getting a neighbour's shopping in snowy weather

Buying a copy of *The Big Issue*

Giving your aunty a lift to hospital

Helping out at a homeless shelter

Paying a direct debit to a cancer charity

Having some statements in the group that are unclear or more difficult to decide helps promote confusion (the 'pit of learning'; Edwards in Nottingham 2010, 2013) and dialogue about what actually constitutes charity. In this example we could extend this activity by replacing 'charity' with 'generosity' and see if we might change any statements, or get children to rank the statements from most to least charitable or generous by ordering them in a line or in a 'diamond ranking' (Nottingham 2013 p63) This activity could then link to work about Sewa in Sikhism or Zakat in Islam.

Adapted from Cam (2006 p79)

# TYPES OF THINKING – THE FOUR CS OF P4C

Four types of thinking are identified by SAPERE as being developed through P4C when it is used to its best effect in the classroom. They could also be developed through some of the activities described earlier. These four types of thinking are caring, collaborative, creative and critical. The most effective way to explore these types of thinking is by illustrating them through a class enquiry. Development in these areas is much more likely to occur with sustained and regular use of P4C and thinking skills activities in a class and throughout a school. Table 3.3 shows edited extracts from a P4C enquiry with a class of Year 5/6 children, which was conducted as part of a research project. This class had done P4C throughout their primary years and were an experienced group. The quality of their thinking and interactions reflects their level of experience. The enquiry stimulus, as shown in Table 3.1, was the song track, 'Heaven for Everyone' by Queen. Pseudonyms have been used for the children's names. The question chosen by the group was 'What is heaven?'

**Caring thinking** demonstrates care about the subject and each other and involves showing respect for people and views. All the children in this enquiry showed caring thinking. They were all very involved in the discussion; even those who did not contribute were listening and following with interest. The children respected one another's ideas and built upon them. They show examples of 'disagreeing respectfully' (Blaylock 2007 p4) throughout because no one puts down another contribution. For example, Gloria shows that she respects but disagrees with Kate's first point, and puts forward her own ideas instead.

**Collaborative thinking** involves listening to and building on each other's ideas, but not necessarily agreeing with each other. Peter, Gloria, George and Kate all show they are building on previous contributions and develop ideas introduced earlier in the discussion. George can be seen developing his thinking in response to other ideas through his three contributions. As a group they develop their collective thinking and challenge each other to consider different ideas about heaven.

**Creative thinking** is introducing new ideas/new ways of thinking about things. George (1), Leo (1) and Kate (1) all introduce new ideas, and it is the thinking introduced by Kate (1), considering whether there is anything unpleasant in heaven, that challenges the other children and forms the basis of most of the subsequent discussion. She considers whether you can be unhappy in heaven, because sometimes she actually enjoys being grumpy. Others either reject or accept this idea and use it to develop their thinking.

**Critical thinking** involves clarifying, challenging and evaluating ideas. We can see in George's second and third contributions that he is really thinking about the ideas introduced by Kate and evaluating them. Many of the children are trying to make sense of these ideas and assimilate them into their own previous perceptions. Peter and Gloria are also evaluating and challenging Kate's ideas. Peter and George consider Kate's idea and seem to agree with it in some form, whereas Gloria rejects it.

'A vital feature of philosophy is its interest in rearranging, shifting, displacing and reframing ideas and beliefs' (Haynes 2002 p42). Through P4C, as illustrated in the previous enquiry extract, we can see children doing just this. Wittgenstein (2009) observed that all categories and concepts can be broken down under interrogation because words are tools not essences. P4C is seeking to do just this by pulling apart what we mean when we

**■ Table 3.3** Extract from discussion with children – 'what is heaven?'

| | |
|---|---|
| Teacher: | So you're thinking of heaven as being like a place? |
| George 1: | Well, yes, I think of it as a new world; a world which is basically the same but there's no death, disease sadness or anything of that – it's just endless happiness. I think that for some people who aren't Christians, they don't believe in God. Well, I think you don't have to believe in God to have a heaven. |
| Leo 1: | I think there's two types of heaven: people think that when they die they go up to heaven and then people can say that heaven is like . . . people can say they're in heaven because they've got something they really enjoy doing or they have something that they really, really like. |
| Teacher: | There's two ways of using that word isn't there? People talk about being in heaven here in this life, and they also think about heaven as an afterlife thing. That's a useful distinction isn't it? |
| Kate 1: | Well, not all people's heavens are like happiness. They are but it's sort of heaven just the way you like it really to someone. It's whatever someone likes, it probably will be there. And, and it doesn't always have to be good because you if you feel like in a bad mood, sometimes you just want everything else to be in a bad mood – it's just not everything has to be happy there – but everything's just the way you like it. |
| Teacher: | What you're saying is people would have an individual idea of what heaven looks or feels like. . . . That's an interesting new idea isn't it – related to feelings. |
| Peter 1: | Well, when I first heard the word heaven it seemed to remind me it was something happy for you. So you can make it how you want it to be and others can make it how they want it for them. |
| Gloria 1: | If you, say if you don't feel happy in a place you wouldn't really call that place heaven in a way. Heaven is for people somewhere where they can feel good and not so worried or anything. It doesn't make them feel bad. |
| George 2: | When Kate said that you could be in a bad mood and that place would be unhappy. What I think of heaven is once you're in heaven there is nothing that can make you in a bad mood. But then when I've just stopped and thinking it over there is kind of theory where you might be looking down on one of your descendants – and they might be in jail quite a lot or something and that might be you looking down on them and thinking wow that's really sad. |
| Teacher: | You mean looking down on someone who is still alive? |
| George 3: | Yep. So it's kind of hard to say whether you can be sad in heaven. After thinking that, I think perhaps you could be sad in heaven if something like that happened. But literally in the place heaven I don't think there is anything that can upset you, but if you look down on earth, not literally, but you know what I mean. |
| Teacher: | Yes – so what you're saying is that you don't think there are things in heaven that will make you sad, but there may be things – connections on earth that might make you sad. |
| Kate 2: | I know in heaven if you were sad and if you wanted everyone else to be sad that would happen. Sometimes when I'm a bit moody and someone comes along and she's really cheerful, I get really annoyed. So sometimes you wanted people to be annoyed because that would make you feel happy. Everything would go the way that you wanted it to be even if you're unhappy. Like if you were sad and everyone else was sad that's the way that you want it and that's the way it would happen. |

use words to label concepts. These are often words that we take for granted and don't take the time or opportunity to work out what they might mean. The four Cs of thinking are explored in more depth in many P4C sources. Consider Fisher (2009, 2013); Nottingham (2013); Cam (1995, 2006); Haynes (2002) and Hymer & Sutcliffe (2012).

## RECORDING CREATIVE THINKING AND DIALOGUE

As mentioned earlier, RE is a subject that should not always require children to write something every session, and that is one of the things children often enjoy about it. The challenge for the teacher, though, is when and how to record the children's attainment and progress through creative thinking and dialogue. After a wonderful discussion like the one in Table 3.3, it can be a real demotivating experience for children to have to go away and 'write about the discussion'.

There are a number of strategies for managing this process of keeping a record of children's enquiries and development of thinking skills. Here are a few suggestions:

- **Teacher's field notes** – the teacher keeps a reflective diary and records the enquiry and any notable features in terms of key contributors; progress made by particular individuals; someone who is unusually quiet or involved.
- **A record sheet** – which looks for particular thinking and speaking and listening skills, such as giving a reason; making decisions; agreeing or disagreeing; following on from a previous point. This can be recorded by an observer of the discussion such as a teaching assistant.
- **A class record/scrapbook** – where a class record is kept of children's thinking on Post-it notes and with sample pieces of work. Children can be free to add to this through the week if they think of extra ideas.
- **A child's reflective diary** – children can complete this in a variety of ways as and when they deem it necessary. They could record thoughts in thought bubbles, or on Post-its, or by drawing or creating thought maps.
- **Use of a digital recorder** – allows discussions to be recorded and analysed at a later time if needed.
- **A question/thinking wall display** – which allows children to add thoughts/questions through the week.

Below are some photos taken from the work of children in St Mary's CE Primary School in Kirkby Lonsdale, Cumbria, which demonstrate how a scrapbook for RE can effectively keep a class record of the children's talking, thinking and learning. (Thanks to Emily Morris, RE subject leader at St Mary's School, for allowing us to share the children's work.)

Figure 3.3 shows a record of the children's thoughts about the concept of love.

Figure 3.4 shows the children's work after thinking about things they feel strongly enough to stand up for.

The following photos (Figures 3.5 and 3.6) show the children reflecting their ideas about the concept of conflict through artwork in the style of artist Keith Haring. This work followed exploration of Keith Haring's artwork and a lot of discussion around the concept of conflict.

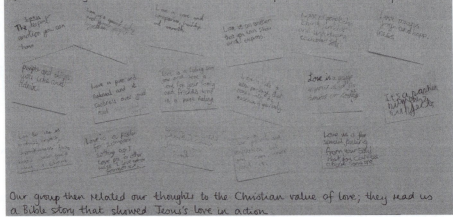

**Figure 3.3** What is love?

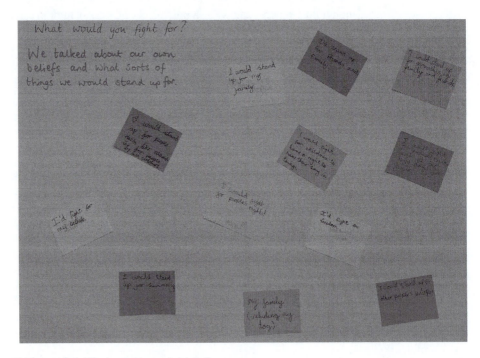

**Figure 3.4** What would you fight for?

From the "Conflict" images, we thought carefully about what conflict means to us. We portrayed our thoughts through the style of Keith Haring.

■ **Figure 3.5** 'Conflict' pictures in the style of Keith Haring (Photo – David Angell)

■ **Figure 3.6** More 'conflict' pictures in the style of Keith Haring (Photo – David Angell)

## THE POWER OF P4C

P4C and the other thinking strategies that encourage collaborative and creative thinking and dialogue in the classroom have many benefits, both visible and hidden. P4C often enables unexpected children to flourish, as it does not necessarily equate to ability in other areas, particularly literacy. It can challenge labels such as 'more able' or 'less able', which supports the arguments of Dweck (2000, 2006) against labelling children in such ways and advocates development of 'growth mindsets'. Hymer & Gershon (2014) and Nottingham (2013) explore this theory in more depth and give many more practical ideas for doing this in the classroom that could be used in RE. Because P4C is not dependent upon reading and writing skills, it allows all children to participate on an equal footing, which can be an unusual and empowering experience for many children. The value of having your voice heard or your question chosen by the group can be very transformative, particularly if this does not often happen in other areas of the curriculum. (See the section of chapter 6 entitled 'Igniting a spark'.)

Creative thinking and dialogue in RE also offers important opportunities for spiritual, moral, social and cultural development. (See chapter 6.) It allows children to develop in all these areas because it involves them in thinking for themselves in order to express their ideas. In order to operate effectively as a group, they have to develop the skills to think and listen and talk together. In RE they are often thinking about the transcendental, and so opportunities for the different dimensions of spirituality to be developed are offered. Cultural development can be offered by introducing children to music, writing and artwork from a range of cultures to show diversity within and between religions.

## CONCLUSION

In this chapter we have considered the benefits of creative thinking and dialogue in RE, as well as practical ways of making this happen in the classroom. It remains to be said that one essential requirement of the teacher in all of this is that they are willing to reflect and think for themselves about some of the questions the children will be considering. We have to model this ourselves and see ourselves as co-enquirers alongside the children. If we are obviously interested in ideas and new thoughts, we will encourage them to begin to play around with ideas and begin to develop their own arguments in support of their ideas.

In P4C enquiries we also have to let go of control somewhat in order for the process to give *them* real voice. It is important that the children choose the question they like, even if the teacher does not think it is the most interesting one. This can be difficult to do sometimes, but it is a necessary part of giving them voice, both collectively and individually.

Finally, we need to be genuinely interested in what children think and what they have to say. We need to respect their ideas and their emerging understanding of concepts. Children can surprise us with the level of their thinking, and this can happen from Early Years upwards. We need to both hear this and respect it. To return to where we started, the question to ask yourself is this: do you have the 'ears to hear'? (Matthews 1994 p15).

## REFERENCES

Alexander, R. (2009): *Children, Their World, Their Education: Final Report and Recommendations of the Cambridge Primary Review*. Abingdon: Routledge.

Baumfield, V. (2002): *Thinking Through Religious Education*. Cambridge: Chris Kington Publishing.

Buckley, J. (2012a): *Pocket P4C: Getting Started with Philosophy for Children*. Chelmsford: One Slice Books Ltd.

Blaylock, L. (2007): Inclusive RE. Birmingham: RE Today services.

Buckley, J. (2012b): *Thinkers' Games: Making Thinking Physical*. Chelmsford: One Slice Books Ltd.

Cam, P. (1995): *Thinking Together: Philosophical Inquiry for the Classroom*. Alexandria, NSW: Hale and Iremonger.

Cam, P. (2006): *20 Thinking Tools: Collaborative Inquiry for the Classroom*. Camberwell, Victoria: Australian Council for Educational Research Press.

Department for Education (DfE) (2013): *The New National Curriculum for England*. London: Department for Education.

Dweck, C. (2000): *Self-Theories: Their Role in Motivation, Personality and Development*. Hove: Psychology Press.

Dweck, C. (2006): *Mindset: How You Can Fulfil Your Potential*. London: Constable and Robinson.

Erriker, C., Lowndes, J. & Bellchambers, E. (2011): *Primary Religious Education – A New Approach: Conceptual Enquiry in Primary RE*. Abingdon: Routledge.

Fisher, R. (2009): *Creative Dialogue*. Abingdon: Routledge.

Fisher, R. (2013): *Teaching Thinking* (4th edition). London: Bloomsbury.

Haynes, J. (2002): *Children as Philosophers: Learning Through Enquiry and Dialogue in the Primary Classroom*. Abingdon: Routledge/Falmer.

Hymer, B. & Gershon, M. (2014): *Growth Mindset Pocketbook*. Alresford: Teachers' Pocketbooks.

Hymer, B. & Sutcliffe, R. (2012): *P4C Pocketbook*. Alresford: Teachers' Pocketbooks.

Lipman, M. (1993): *Thinking Children and Education*. Dubuque, IA: Kendall Hunt Publishing.

Littleton, K. & Mercer, N. (2013): *Interthinking: Putting Talk to Work*. Abingdon: Routledge.

Matthews, G. (1994): *The Philosophy of Childhood*. London: Harvard University Press.

Nottingham, J. (2010): *Challenging Learning*. Berwick upon Tweed: JN Publishing.

Nottingham, J. (2013): *Encouraging Learning: How You Can Help Children Learn*. Abingdon: Routledge.

OfSTED (2013): *Religious Education: Realising the Potential*. Manchester: OfSTED.

Robinson, K. (2011): *Out of Our Minds: Learning to Be Creative*. Chichester: Capstone Publishing Ltd.

Splitter, L. & Sharp, A. (1995): *Teaching for Better Thinking*. Camberwell, Victoria: Australian Council for Educational Research Press.

Stanley, S. (2004): *But Why? Developing Philosophical Thinking in the Classroom*. Stafford: Network Educational Press Ltd.

Wittgenstein, L. (2009): *Philosophical Investigations*. Hacker, P. & Schulte, J. (eds). Chichester: Wiley-Blackwell.

# CHAPTER 4

# CREATIVE SKILLS AND STRATEGIES

## THE TASC MODEL

*Penny Hollander*

## INTRODUCTION

Within religious education (RE) as well as other curriculum areas, the capacity for creative and critical thinking is essential for effective life-long learning. Enquiry and reflection are vital components regardless of age or ability. The recent OfSTED report *Realising the Potential* on RE provision in schools emphasises that the most effective RE placed enquiry at its heart and from the outset engaged pupils in their learning (OfSTED 2013, 5). It also corroborates findings from the earlier *Transforming Religious Education* report on RE (OfSTED 2010). There are many different ways to develop an enquiring and questioning approach to the RE curriculum but this chapter will focus on one particular model, Thinking Actively in a Social Context, commonly abbreviated to TASC. This model can be used widely across many curriculum areas, ages and contexts. It is well suited to RE in that the whole process promotes active thinking, questioning and reflection which is the bedrock of good RE in the classroom. These vital skills help children to learn both about and from religion. It is interesting that different elements of the TASC model are contained within the model recommended in the *Realising the Potential* report (OfSTED 2013, 23) for planning effective RE, including the following:

> **Asking questions**
> **Investigation**
> **Drawing conclusions**
> **Evaluation**
> **Reflection and expression**

This chapter will outline the different elements within the TASC process as a generic tool for promoting effective learning across a wide range of curriculum and also how it can be adapted for use within RE. An example of how it has been used within one primary RE classroom for the first time is also included, with both teacher and pupil evaluations of its usefulness for learning within an RE topic on Hinduism. Cross-curricular links are woven into their work. There are further suggestions for other ways of incorporating TASC into other RE topic areas.

## THE TASC MODEL

The inspiration for this approach to learning was inspired by Belle Wallace, who has written extensively about it both from a general educational perspective and also for specific subjects and for different age phases (Wallace 2001). The TASC website, www. tascwheel.com, shows how it has developed within schools of all ages and contexts, nationally and internationally, and contains many practical examples of where it has been successfully implemented. TASC is not only a practical tool but also has a strong theoretical basis drawn from the work of Vygotsky (1978) and Sternberg (1985). Wallace incorporates Vygotsky's emphasis on the importance of language in the development of higher psychological processes, using existing knowledge or 'hooks' to extend learning and create new networks of understanding (Wallace 2001, 7). For Vygotsky learning can be developed by providing educational support for the gap between what has already been mastered and further achievement. This zone of proximal development (ZPD) is an integral part of the TASC process. Sternberg's view of intelligence and effective learning processes for *all learners* by using a range of thinking skills and strategies to reflect, consolidate and transfer (i.e. key processes of metacognition) are also key to the TASC model (Wallace 2001, 8).

TASC runs alongside Bloom's taxonomy of learning (1956) which is commonly regarded as foundational within educational thinking (Figure 4.1).

More recently it has been revised by Anderson, Krathwohl *et al.* (2001) to reflect a more active form of thinking and slight re-ordering. Figure 4.2 then, perhaps, is more accurate in teachers' application in creating an effective climate for learning within their classrooms.

To understand the principles of TASC, Wallace (2009) uses the imagery of a wheel to explain the ongoing cycle of learning (see Figure 4.3).

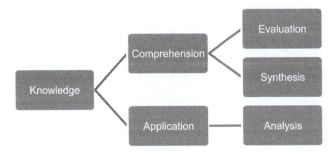

■ **Figure 4.1** Bloom's taxonomy of learning

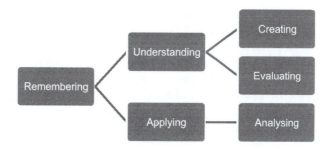

■ **Figure 4.2** Anderson, Krathwohl et al's revision of Bloom's taxonomy

■ **Figure 4.3** A wheel of learning

TASC as an acronym is explained in the following way:

**Thinking** – We are all capable of thinking and improving our thinking. Thinking makes us human, capable and caring.

**Actively** – We all need to be active and do our own thinking – no one can do our thinking *to* us. We need to be involved and interested and to do our thinking for ourselves – with appropriate guidance of course.

**Social** – We learn best when we can talk and work with others. We do a lot of learning when we share activities, testing out our ideas, listening to alternative ways of doing the task, often copying 'better' ideas.

**Context** – The context needs to be relevant to our background and stage of development. We all learn when we understand not only what we are learning but also why we are learning and where it will lead us.

The TASC wheel has different components or stages in the thinking process. Each step is essential for thinking and learning. The wheel provides visual imagery for stages in the whole process in that it can travel forwards or backwards or stop at particular points, so that children of differing abilities may move at the pace that is best suited to their learning. Some may keep moving forwards through the stages, others may need to re-trace their steps, whilst there may be those who can only go so far and then need to stop. The structure is important, and at each stage children are encouraged to reflect, question and consolidate their own learning. There is for many the temptation to skip a stage or two, e.g. from the 'generating ideas' stage to 'let's do it' without the 'best idea' segment. This needs to be resisted as too many ideas, insufficiently considered or refined in terms of whether they are possible to achieve within the constraints of the classroom, may result in both frustration and failure to complete the task. Thus, effective learning will not be achieved (except that it might be a useful lesson to bear in mind for future tasks). The last stage, 'learn from experience', is equally vital in that it crystallises learning and allows children to take what they have learnt in this context, apply it to other areas of work and reflect on what they might change on another occasion.

## THE TASC PROCESS

As a process TASC takes both time and independent thinking by the children. At each stage they are asked to reflect on the following questions to ensure that their thinking is clear, focussed and may involve risk taking which will add to their learning from experience (see Table 4.1).

Wallace (2001) points out that the TASC process can be introduced to children in a number of ways, including whole school projects, as a means of reporting back from what has been learnt from a visit and problem-solving activities. As children become accustomed to this way of working, they become increasingly effective and independent learners. However, by definition a process takes time:

> Developing children's problem-solving and thinking skills *initially* takes time, but once children are familiar with the skills and using them, they learn more efficiently and we save time.
>
> (Wallace 2001, 12)

## THE TASC MODEL AND RE

To see how the TASC model provides a good vehicle for learning in RE it is first necessary to consider the purposes and challenges of RE in the curriculum. At its best good RE makes a significant contribution to children's education by challenging them to think about the meaning and purpose of life, beliefs about God, the 'big' questions of life, what it means to be human and issues of right and wrong. They need to learn about different religious and other worldviews as well as explore their own viewpoints reflecting and expressing ideas and insights about the impact of different faith and worldviews (see Religious Education Council 2013, 10). Alongside knowledge and understanding of religion (attainment target 1, or AT1) and what they can learn from it (AT2), children's progress in RE also requires the use and application of a range of general educational skills in each key stage. These are

■ **Table 4.1** Using the TASC process (Wallace 2013)

| | |
|---|---|
| Gather and organise | What information do I have?<br>How much do I understand?<br>Have I done anything like this before?<br>What questions can I ask? |
| Identify | What are my goals? What am I trying to do?<br>What do I need to complete the task?<br>What are the obstacles to completing the task? |
| Generate | Where can I find more information?<br>Which resources will help me the most?<br>How many ways are there to complete the task?<br>What do other people think of my ideas? |
| Decide | Which idea(s) would be the most effective and why?<br>How will I plan what I am going to do?<br>(What will I need and how will I go about completing the task?)<br>How will I know if what I am doing is effective/working? |
| Implement | Is everything going to plan?<br>(Do I need to adapt or change my plan?)<br>Have I got everything I need to complete the task?<br>How well am I doing? |
| Evaluate | What have I managed to do?<br>Did everything go according to plan?<br>Did I work well on my own or as part of a group?<br>Am I ready to share my ideas/work with others? |
| Communicate | Who will I be presenting my ideas/work to?<br>How could I best present my work/ideas to others?<br>(What would I need to prepare and in what way?)<br>Have I included all of the information that I need to? |
| Learn from experience | *Looking at the whole task from start to finish:*<br>What do I feel worked particularly well and why?<br>How could I improve aspects of my work if<br>completing similar tasks in the future? |

outlined by Rivett and Blaylock (2006, 54–5) in their handbook for teachers of RE and incorporate both critical and creative thinking skills to:

- ■ Investigate – Use books or websites to select information and highlight what is relevant; collect information from churches, other places of worship, charities etc.; watch and listen to video/audio sources about different religious stories, beliefs and practices.
- ■ Interpret – Talk about meaning in artefacts, pictures, paintings, symbols and respond to questions about them (e.g. what do you think it is? What is going on?). Read prayers and talk about what they show about a person's beliefs and feelings.

- Reflect – Provide opportunities for pupils to describe how actions and atmosphere in different religious situations make them feel. Ask them to explore the thoughts and feelings associated with different religious music. Can they write a prayer or poem that a Christian, Jewish or Muslim child might use? Provide a 'wall of wisdom' for pupils to record their insights.

- Empathise – Use role play or freeze frames to capture essential religious ideas or themes. Use hot seating to see another person's perspective in relation to a religious story.

- Analyse – What are the key beliefs and religious vocabulary associated with a particular aspect of a religion? Identify similarities and differences between religious faiths and practices and practices within and between faiths studied.

- Synthesise – Notice similarities between stories and practices from religions, and talk about the prayers, texts and places of worship, drawing conclusions about similarities.

- Express – Use creative approaches (e.g. drama, role play, dance, mime, music) to illustrate a religious story or teaching. Make a collage, diagram, video or presentation (written or oral) to show your understanding of the meaning of the particular teaching or practice.

- Apply – Write a story which shows the meaning behind a faith story or religious teaching in a different or modern context. Design your own symbols which illustrate what a particular religion believes and teaches. Think about the response of a religious leader such as Jesus, Guru Nanak or Buddha to a particular dilemma.

- Evaluate – Think about the most important statements for a Christian, Jew, Muslim, Hindu or Buddhist in relation to different life issues and contribute your own response.

These skills are outlined in locally agreed syllabuses (for example, Cumbria County Council 2011, 7–8; and Manchester 2011). They also emphasise that the need for enquiry is a central element of the learning process in RE (see Cumbria County Council 2011, 9). However, although both OfSTED reports on RE (OfSTED 2010, 2013) stress the importance of enquiry-based learning in RE to raise standards and expectations, their surveys show insufficient evidence from schools visited that this has been successfully addressed. Also the 2013 report is clear that in primary schools, 'the way in which RE was provided in many of the primary schools visited had the effect of isolating the subject from the rest of the curriculum' (OfSTED 2013, 5).

The TASC model fits well with the report's recommendation for more independent learning, cross-curricular links and challenging tasks. Webster (2010, 98–9) cites an example of how one student teacher adapted the TASC wheel to inform medium-term planning for an RE unit of work on sacred spaces.

**Sacred spaces for Year 2 pupils, within a topic on 'People Who Help Us'**

*Gather:*
Who helps you?
Who helps in religion?

*Identify:*
What is your sacred space?
How do you feel?

*Generate:*
Visit a church.
How does it help people?

*Decide:*
What do you think a special space is for?

*Implement:*
Visit a gurdwara.
Create questions.

*Evaluate:*
What do we know about sacred spaces and how people help?

*Communicate:*
What is your own special place?
Create one.

*Learn from experience:*
What have you learnt about how people use a sacred space?
How does it help people? How might a special place help you?

*Examples in practice:*
The following example is taken from RE lessons within a small village church
school. The teacher involved and the Key Stage 2 children (Years 5 and 6) had
never used the approach before. The teacher was keen to use the TASC wheel
to develop children's independence in learning and also develop their reflective
and evaluative skills within RE. She also wanted to challenge the children to use
skills they had developed through literacy, drama and IT. After the experience of
using the TASC approach in RE for the first time she evaluated the process and
shared what she had learnt from experience for both herself and the children. She
was particularly pleased with how it helped her to evaluate individual children's
progression in their learning and how she could encourage them to develop their
learning further (see Table 4.2).

## WORKING THROUGH THE TASC WHEEL IN EXPLORING HINDU BELIEFS ABOUT GOD

The RE lessons for this class were on a one-hour-per-week basis. The children worked in
small groups to plan a presentation on Hindu beliefs about God. As this was their first use
of the TASC approach, the teacher decided it would be helpful to all the children to get used

▨ **Table 4.2** A teacher's view of TASC: baking a cake

At first glance, the TASC wheel looked rather complicated to use until more research provided a wealth of information, including case studies, which I found very helpful, giving me an insight in ways to use the wheel with the class.

I used the example of baking a cake in order to explain the way the wheel works, e.g. we cannot start baking (*implement*) until we know which cake we are baking and what ingredients we need (*gather/identify/generate/decide*); we cannot taste the cake to see if it has turned out right (*evaluate/ communicate/learn from experience*) until we have baked it.

The children seemed to understand this analogy and therefore found it useful when they came to use the wheel, knowing the logical steps they needed to take to complete the overall learning objective, but also realising that they could (and often needed to) refer back around the wheel; the majority of children understood that they should always look back to the success criteria in order that they didn't migrate off topic.

I will definitely use the wheel again, especially in light of the final comment above, as it can sometimes take too long to refresh learning of a topic before moving on. I found it a helpful tool for me to assess the progression of children's learning from week to week and also their own reflections of their learning.

I will definitely use the wheel again.

▨ **Table 4.3** Using the TASC wheel to explore Hindu beliefs

| *Gather and organise* | *Identify* |
| --- | --- |
| Hinduism and God – they call God Brahman<br>Hinduism is a religion<br>There are three main deities,<br>Brahma, Vishnu and Shiva<br>The lotus flower represents cleanliness<br>When a Hindu dies they go away and<br>come back as something else<br>Reincarnation | **What do Hindus believe about God?**<br><br>*What do we need to do?*<br>▨ Find out what the following tell us<br>  about Hindu beliefs in God:<br>▨ The Trimurti<br>▨ Stories about Brahma, Vishnu and Shiva<br>▨ Stories about Brahman and Creation |

to the idea of using the TASC wheel to complete the first two sections, gather and organise and identify, as whole class activities (see Table 4.3).

The outcomes from these two parts of the wheel were added to a master copy for each group to use and to give weekly reminders about what had already been done. Ideas and information were generated through a mix of teacher-led activities and independent research from books and the internet. Success criteria were also included on the wheel to ensure that the children remained focussed on what they were trying to achieve throughout the topic. Appropriate teacher invention also ensured that pupils stayed on task. The progression through each stage of the TASC wheel addressed the issue raised by OfSTED (2013, 10) about the need for pupils to process their findings through evaluation and reflection.

As part of this whole class work, children in their small groups researched Hindu beliefs about God from both the internet and materials from *RE IDEAS: GOD* (Moss 2013, 19–24). In particular they looked at stories about Brahma, Vishnu and Shiva and thought about the questions that were posed, e.g. What does this story have to say about God? and Why do you think this story is popular today? Each group then produced a freeze frame of a key moment in their chosen story, thus linking RE with work done in drama. The intention was to help them to gain a deeper understanding of the story and what it had to say about God from a Hindu perspective, as well as to make links between Hindu teachings and their own idea of God or their beliefs about the meaning of life. This fulfils level 4 requirements in RE (the expected level of attainment for the majority of children at the end of Key Stage 2).

The other segments of the wheel, including the content of the presentation and how it would be presented, were done independently by each small group. The teacher acted as a facilitator and ensured that all children kept on task.

> *Generate ideas:* Pupils used a mixture of sources to gain information and also to generate ideas for the focus of their presentation. Ideas from information sourced from books in the school library, the internet and specific resources given by the teacher were discussed by each group as well as ideas about possible ways to present the information.
>
> *Decide:* Each group decided independently which god(s) they would use as a focus for the presentation. All groups decided to focus on only one god as this followed on from their earlier freeze frame work; this seemed the safest option given that this was a new way of working.
>
> *Implement:* PowerPoint was the universal choice for the presentations, with a mixture of images and written material. Most groups divided out the different roles of research, preparing the words to say, finding images and incorporating them into the PowerPoint presentation. Adaptations were made as they went along in order to ensure the presentation had sufficient detail but was clear enough to present to others in the class.
>
> *Evaluate and communicate:* Children in each group were pleased with what they were doing but also quite self-critical; e.g. see Figure 4.4.
>
> *Learn from experience:* Children commented on their experiences of using the TASC approach from both an RE perspective and a more general thinking skills perspective. The general consensus was that it was a good way to gain a deeper understanding of the place and purposes of different gods and goddesses in Hinduism and the significance of the symbols identified with each of them. They were more confident in using the religious vocabulary associated with some aspects of Hinduism. The structured stages of TASC helped to clarify their thinking, even though some children found it confusing at first and were anxious to create the presentation at the outset. They acknowledged that this approach requires practice and on another occasion could use alternative means

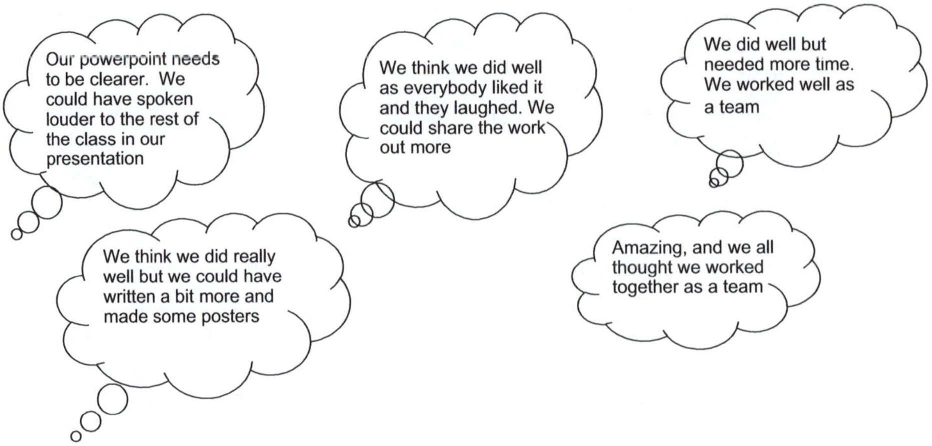

Our powerpoint needs to be clearer. We could have spoken louder to the rest of the class in our presentation
We think we did well as everybody liked it and they laughed. We could share the work out more
We did well but needed more time. We worked well as a team
We think we did really well but we could have written a bit more and made some posters
Amazing, and we all thought we worked together as a team

**Figure 4.4** Pupil reflections about the TASC process

> of presentation, e.g. the use of posters to illustrate what they were saying. Listening to the ideas of others in the group was another suggested idea of improving what they did another time.

Other comments related to general learning principles. As one pupil explained,

> If I were to use it [TASC] in future with my homework on my own I think it would help by reminding me what different aspects I need to add to my work. I think I will get more done if I use the TASC wheel.

Although she does not state this explicitly, there is perhaps the idea that more thinking through the different stages of the TASC process produces for her more effective learning.

Other thoughts expressed are pictured in Figure 4.5:

Not all comments were expressed as positively but as the teacher explained,

> The majority of children thought that although at first the TASC wheel looked complicated to use, the more they used it, the easier it became to understand how it was a helpful tool to aid their learning and progression.

AMAZING!
Helps ME A LOT!
Easy and helps you do tasks!

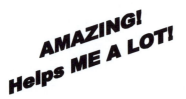

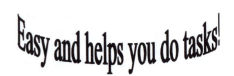

**Figure 4.5** Pupils' first reactions to learning through TASC

Other points made included:

■ The enjoyment of collaborating and working together to develop ideas made everyone feel involved in the process;

■ Visual stimulus of the TASC wheel to refer back to in order to refresh their memory and keep focussed.

# FURTHER IDEAS FOR USING TASC WITHIN THE CONTEXT OF RE

The TASC website (www.tascwheel.com) provides a hundred ideas for using the process with children of all ages and multiple abilities within different curriculum areas. Although religious education is not specifically mentioned, ideas can be easily adapted to fit in with the RE curriculum and include cross-curricular links, particularly with art, music, drama, literacy, design technology and food technology:

■ Following a visit to a place of worship, consider the most important features within a place of worship and how they are relevant for believers. Design your own place of worship, giving an explanation of what is important to include and the reasons for your choice.

■ Create a dance that describes a religious celebration and its significance for believers.

■ Create some music that can be used to tell a sacred story. Choose sounds and rhythms that match the mood of the story. Can you explain what the story teaching believers? How does this relate to your own experience?

■ Write a poem that describes a concept that is important within Christianity and what you can learn from this, e.g. creation, salvation, forgiveness, heaven.

■ Investigate what it means to belong to a community within Buddhism. How can you demonstrate that through art and drama? (Possible starting point: RE Today 2012, *Opening up Community*)

■ Design an Easter egg box which reflects the key elements of the Easter story.

■ Plan and prepare for a religious celebration meal. Get the food ready. Design the invitations and decide about music and other activities you will include (e.g. Shabbat from Judaism).

■ Create an interactive display which shows how and why a religious leader you have been studying is an inspiration to believers.

The list is not extensive or exclusive but rather provides a few suggestions as to how TASC may be flexibly applied within an RE unit of work.

# SUMMARY AND CONCLUSIONS

TASC is a tool that can be used in a wide range of effective learning experiences. It has a strong theoretical basis from two important theories about how children best learn and it underpins the practice. It is a generic model which is not confined to particular curriculum areas. Rather it helps to develop many skills that are necessary for effective learning. It can be used in a cross-curricular way, without losing sight of discrete subject learning objectives. It is essentially an interactive approach to learning, engaging pupils to share their ideas and communicate these to a wider audience. Opportunities for the students to evaluate and reflect about what they have done are integral to the process and help to consolidate learning. Pupil autonomy and independence are other key features of the approach. The wheel provides support and direction as required to ensure pupils maintain their focus on the purpose of the task. As a process it takes time to practise and refine but provides opportunity for sustained learning. It embraces both critical and creative thinking strategies. For RE teaching and learning the TASC process can address many of the weaknesses that *Realising the Potential* (OfSTED 2013) raises about clear focus and enquiry-based learning. Teachers can use TASC to develop children's skills in their questioning, knowledge and understanding of religions as well as giving opportunity to make connections and contrasts with their own experiences. Examples of how it has been and could be used within the RE classroom illustrate the potential for cross-curricular links. It is acknowledged that this is only one of many approaches that can be used to promote effective RE learning in the classrooms but certainly one that should be considered.

## Acknowledgements

Grateful thanks to the staff at Allithwaite CE primary school, particularly the RE co-ordinator Mrs Lucy Stanway, and to the Year 5 and 6 pupils who trialled the TASC approach in the RE lessons.

## ADDITIONAL RESOURCES

www.tes.co.uk/teachingresources/Thinking-Actively-in-a-Social-Context (February 2013)
www.tascwheel.com – 100 TASC ideas
www.retoday.org.uk – useful publications for many practical RE classroom activities, across different key stages
www.bbc.co.uk/learningzone/videoclips – the religious education section of clips provides many useful examples of stories, beliefs and practices from the major religions

## REFERENCES

Anderson, L. W. & Krathwohl, D. R., *et al.* (eds) (2001) *A Taxonomy for Learning, Teaching and Assessing: A Revision of Bloom's Taxonomy of Educational Objectives*, New York: Longman.

Bloom, B. S., *et al.* (1956) *Taxonomy of Educational Objectives: The Classification of Educational Goals. Handbook 1 Cognitive Domain*, New York: Longmans Green.

Cumbria County Council (2011) *Cumbria Agreed Syllabus for Religious Education 2011–16*, Cumbria: Cumbria County Council.

Manchester (2011) Revised Manchester Agreed Syllabus. Available from www.mewan.net. Manchester Education Wide Area Network

Moss, F. (ed.) (2013) *RE IDEAS: GOD*, Birmingham: Christian Education Publications.

OfSTED (2010) *Transforming Religious Education* (090215), Manchester: OfSTED; www.ofsted.gov.uk/resources/090215

OfSTED (2013) *Realising the Potential* (130068), Manchester: OfSTED; www.ofsted.gov.uk/resources/130068

Religious Education Council (2013) *A Curriculum Framework for Religious Education in England*, London: Religious Education Council for England and Wales.

RE Today (2012) *Opening up Community*, Bedfordshire: Newnorth Print Ltd.

Rivett, R. & Blaylock, L. (2006) *A Teacher's Handbook for Religious Education*, Birmingham: Christian Education Publications.

Sternberg, R. J. (1985) *Beyond IQ: A Triarchic Theory of Human Intelligence*, Cambridge: Cambridge University Press.

Vygotsky, L. S (1978) *Mind in Society: The Development of Higher Psychological Processes*, Cole M. *et al.* (eds), Cambridge, MA: Harvard University Press.

Wallace, B. (2001) *Teaching Thinking Skills across the Primary Curriculum*, London: David Fulton Publishers Ltd.

Wallace, B. (2009) *Developing Problem-Solving and Thinking Skills in the Mainstream Curriculum*; www.tascwheel.com

Webster, M. (2010) *Creative Approaches to Teaching Primary RE*, Essex: Pearson Education Ltd.

# ENGAGING CHILDREN CREATIVELY

## EFFECTIVE PLANNING FOR DEVELOPING ENQUIRY

*Fiona Moss*

Engaging and effective RE supports children to ask questions, challenge their ideas, and learn about and from the beliefs and lifestyles of different religious and belief communities. Children need to understand what the purpose of their learning is and how the knowledge, skills and understanding they are developing are relevant either to their lives or to their interests. This chapter will explore ways of supporting children to become enquirers into religion and belief. This is an area that OfSTED in their subject-focussed reports have highlighted as an effective approach to learning. Examples will be shared of strategies linking meaningful learning in RE to learning in other subject areas. The work in this chapter will draw on thinking skills strategies (Baumfield 2002), *Transforming Religious Education* (OfSTED 2010) and *Religious Education: Realising the Potential* (OfSTED 2013).

## THE CONCERNS

Poor learning in RE has several characteristic features in relation to planning, teaching and learning. OfSTED and RE advisers including the RE Today team observe, for example,

a.  Planning: Ineffective planning has led inspectors to criticise RE's coherence. A critique of the two attainment targets 'learning about religion' and 'learning from religion' by a senior inspector in a recent lecture suggested that teacher plans lead to 'a series of unrelated fact gathering exercises on the one hand, coupled with unrelated navel gazing on the other'. This is a travesty of good practice, but where teachers' grasp of the aims of the subject is insecure and no robust planning process is in place, which moves from enquiry questions through religious content to pupil engagement and allows pupils to meet challenging outcomes, this separation of the two attainment targets can occur.

b.  Teaching: Teachers with poor subject knowledge struggle to make sense of the religious materials syllabuses suggest they use (sacred text, religious practice, religious expression). Teachers respond by offering thin content and fall back on 'tame' pedagogy: learning methods such as oversimplified worksheets or even word searches are too commonly seen. 'Draw the Ten Plagues of Egypt in the right order' avoids the question 'What kind of God would so harm the ordinary people of Egypt with lice, hailstorms and rivers of blood?'

c.   Learning: Many pupils report that they find RE 'boring', but what do they mean? This blanket negative may mean it is too easy. Lacking challenge, poor learning opportunities can be repetitive. Teaching Divali each year may be justified, but if the tasks for 7- to 11-year-olds are no more difficult than those offered to 4- and 5-year-olds, then pupils will be speaking fairly when they say they are bored. If we banned the mention of the Good Samaritan from RE, then standards might rise: learning activities from other parts of Christian scripture, less repetitive and predictable, could emerge.

Now if this negative picture, which we think is not universal, merely too widespread, is inverted, then the contours of quality in planning, teaching and learning in RE emerge. This section will give three examples of how teachers can build quality into their RE work at every stage, drawing implications from them at each point. It will then go on to offer creative examples of teaching and curriculum organisation that support good-quality RE.

# SOME SOLUTIONS

## Planning

Whilst we know learning can happen in moments of inspiration, a sudden question or opportunity grabbed in the school day, teachers need to use a clear planning process to enable learning in RE. The temptation is of course to use an engaging strategy that you have seen in action, but in order to counter the critique of RE as 'providing poor and fragmented curriculum planning' (OfSTED 2013), we must consider how sequences of learning are constructed. These sequences of learning need to build on pupils' knowledge, understanding and skills whilst still being engaging, creative and memorable experiences.

A series of recent agreed syllabuses have used planning processes to support and encourage teachers in planning clear sequences of learning. Bedford Borough, Central Bedfordshire and Luton; Gloucestershire; Herefordshire; and Wiltshire are four recent examples of agreed syllabuses which have suggested a planning process. See Table 5.1. (Based on the planning process in *Identities, Meanings and Values* [Bedford Borough, Central Bedfordshire and Luton SACRE 2012].)

This process of planning enables a teacher to focus on key questions that will unlock the pupils' interest and have a clear RE focus. Following a planning structure creates an emphasis on learning outcomes and content rather than only on the engaging strategies used in teaching.

A Bedfordshire teacher stated,

The planning advice for the new syllabus [was] very helpful in guiding my planning and giving me a clear direction to take the lessons. The non-specialist RE teachers in the school have been able to plan and teach relevant and inspiring RE lessons. It can be easy to go off at a tangent, but having clear guidance ensures that my staff stay on the right track. We like the key question starting points, and can plan for the topic, instead of the topic narrowing the options.

Sarah Payne, Bedfordshire

▨ **Table 5.1** A planning process

| | |
|---|---|
| **Step 1: Key question** | Devise a key question of your own.<br>Ensure that the key question fits with the themes for your age group.<br>Ensure that the key question is sufficiently open to allow enquiry, ideally a question that will trigger further questions for investigation and enquiry from pupils.<br>Make sure that it has a clear focus on learning about and from religion and belief.<br>Explain where this unit/question fits into RE planning, e.g. how it builds on previous learning in RE; what other subject areas it links to, if appropriate. |
| **Step 2: Learning outcomes and assessment** | Select learning outcomes for the key question. Ensure there is a balance of learning about and from religion.<br>Are the learning outcomes set at the appropriate level for your children? Do they need to be further differentiated?<br>Use level descriptions; develop specific 'I can . . .' statements as appropriate to the age and ability of the pupils.<br>These 'I can' statements help you to integrate assessment for learning within the unit. There is then no necessity for an end-of-unit assessment within each unit. |
| **Step 3: Content** | Select relevant content from the programme of study to explore this key question. In general, depth is preferable to breadth. |
| **Step 4: Teaching and learning activities** | Develop active learning opportunities and investigations, using some engaging stimuli, to enable pupils to achieve the levelled outcomes. Don't forget the skills you want pupils to develop. Make sure that the activities allow pupils to practise these skills. |

# TEACHING

## Subject knowledge in RE

The quality of teaching in RE is inescapably dependent on some subject knowledge. RE betrays itself unless pupils find out about the Christians, the Muslims, the worldviews they study. Teachers are often concerned that this is an impossibility: how can I be an instant expert in six religions – and atheism? But the truth is that primary teachers do gather sufficient understanding of the curriculum in other areas, and to do so in RE is, at one level, merely professional. Additionally, they really need to know perhaps two religions, in relation to the themes of their syllabus, to teach one year group. Good-quality information is readily available but teachers need to take care how they source their knowledge. Websites such as www.reonline.org/uk provide information on religions and worldviews that has been checked, and books such as *Representing Religions* (Blaylock 2004) express how teachers of RE from different religions would like their religions to be represented. To be better equipped, readers might consider what core knowledge they expect the pupils to have in the religion and worldviews that are taught when they leave the school. Do the adults in the school also have this core knowledge, or at least know how to access it? Find the nugget of religious belief, practice or exemplary material that you can make engaging, that is relevant, and begin to enthuse your pupils about RE. However, remember an apple has a core; it's the least appetising bit but contains the possibility of growth, the pip. In RE, we don't just want the core but the whole fruit. Cores matter, but fruitiness matters too.

## Untamed pedagogy

Whilst 'bad RE' can be easily described, good learning methods in the subject are almost endlessly variable. Here are six examples to consider, each related to one of the major schools of thought in RE pedagogy. Whilst you may not use all the pedagogies in your teaching, using a variety of pedagogies will both engage learners and ensure different insights. Whichever school of thought is home territory for you, your practice will be enriched by learning from one of the others. So if your pupils' RE diet has been mostly phenomena, then get out the candle, the matches and the incense. If it's been mostly ultimate questions, then why not try a bit of ethnographic listening and interpretation for a change?

The chapters in this volume offer examples from several of these 'schools of thought'. A fuller discussion of several of them can be found in Grimmitt (2000) and Table 5.2.

## QUESTIONS

I consider that questions are the lifeblood for RE. When I taught 9- to 11-year-olds I was pleased to use a device shown to me by Anne Krissman, special needs teacher in Redbridge, called the wall of wisdom. On a large display board pupils could add any questions about religion or belief, and there was often a stimulus picture related to recent news and information about whatever we were studying in RE. Questions were displayed and over time a selection of answers were added. It was a real sign that in our class we were open to questions and finding a selection of responses to the questions. Woe to the adult who entered the classroom just after a question had been posted; they were often asked to jot down their ideas and add them to the wall. So if questions are a major key to engagement and enquiry, what type of questions might we ask?

Imagine any topic in RE where pupils are gathering facts and understanding about particular religious beliefs, practices and ways of living. Are there questions (maybe generic) that teachers can keep on asking which enable pupils to develop increasing insight and discernment? Here I propose some age-related, progressed questions that might help any teacher to push and probe children's understanding, and enable next steps through thoughtful conversation. Don't be scared of thinking time – always allow 15 seconds thinking time for pupils. Don't be scared to take risks, and always plan a few teaser, quirky questions. They can get the best stimulation flowing (see Table 5.3)

**Table 5.2** Six learning methods in RE

### Seeing things as they really are: the phenomena of religion (Smart, in Grimmitt 2000:24; chapter 1 this volume)

Sometimes pupils need to build their understanding of the phenomena of religion. They gather information, learn about religious activities, consider what symbols mean. A teacher plans to introduce a class to the Muslim religion for the first time and uses a selection of artefacts from the mosque. Children are asked to develop their understanding of what Muslims do and say, and then to think about Muslims' actions. Pupils make a selection of 10 artefacts images and texts to sum up all they have learnt about the Muslim faith so far.

**A phenomenological approach** focusses on studying Islam through stories, moral behaviour, rituals, beliefs, experiences and community life, and the art and architecture of the faith.

### Experiential religious education: educating the spirit (Hay in Grimmitt 2000:70, Wright in Grimmitt 2000:170; chapters 6 and 8 this volume)

A teacher wants to enable spiritual development through RE so she uses stilling, guided story and creative imagination to explore religious and spiritual experiences, questions and beliefs in increasing depth in the classroom. After a guided story on Pesach, students express their own spiritual ideas about concepts like love, sacrifice, submission or thankfulness in sculptures and poems.

**An experiential approach** uses the idea that children have some spiritual capacities of their own, and develops these through curricular RE.

### Interpretive RE (Jackson in Grimmitt 2000:130; chapter 1 this volume)

Starting work on Hindu dharma, a teacher begins with four rather contradictory accounts of how Divali is practised in Leicester today. With the emphasis on religion as it is lived (not merely history, texts or beliefs), pupils become enquirers themselves into the varieties of religion and belief. The key skill of making sense, or interpreting, gradually extends pupils' awareness of living communities of faith.

**Interpretive approaches** take authentic account of the ways members of religions today practise their faith. These learning methods aim to enable pupils to draw meaning from the encounter with religion for themselves.

### Concepts for learning in RE (Cooling in Grimmitt 2000:153; chapter 4 this volume)

In a unit about Christian beliefs, pupils learn three concepts: incarnation, Trinity, resurrection. They enquire into the ways these concepts make sense of the Christmas and Easter narratives and festivities. They develop understanding of beliefs and think about how beliefs can be tested by argument or experience.

**Conceptual learning, for religious literacy,** takes key concepts from the religions and from religious studies as a discipline and enables pupils to be increasingly reasonable about religion.

### Ultimate questions as a focus in RE (Grimmitt 2000:207; chapters 3 and 4 this volume)

Pupils begin a unit of work by raising all the questions they would like to ask of God/the creator/the ultimate brain. With stimulus from religious texts and practices, the class uses a philosophy for children (P4C) method. A 'community of enquiry' for pupils explores their own questions. Afterwards, the class develops pieces of personal work using religious ideas about their ultimate questions.

**A humanising approach** to RE uses 'big questions' of meaning, purpose and truth to explore the impact of religion on life and challenges the learners to deepen their own ideas.

### Pupils' worldviews in RE (Erricker in Grimmitt 2000:188; chapter 1 this volume)

After the instructor's teaching about commitment and values, pupils begin with their own commitments and generalise from these. Exploring the ways their everyday commitments can be structured into a view of what matters, a view of the world, is more important than gathering understanding of religion, as the aim of RE is to clarify the learner's vision of life.

**A worldviews approach** is about developing answers to human questions, using religious ideas and teachings as a resource for pupils' own development.

■ **Table 5.3** Questions for RE enquiry

| Age | Useful question stems typical for this age |
|---|---|
| **For 5- to 7-year-olds** | ■ Can you remember . . . ?<br>■ What did you notice about . . . ?<br>■ What did you like about . . . ?<br>■ What would you like to ask about . . . ?<br>■ Did you learn a new word? What did it mean?<br>■ What are your ideas about . . . ?<br>■ What is this a bit like? |
| **For 7- to 9-year-olds** | **Use some of the previous questions, and also try these:**<br>■ Why do these people . . . ?<br>■ Do you think this is similar to . . . ?<br>■ I wonder: (say it, and leave a pause)<br>■ Is there another (maybe deeper) meaning to this . . . ?<br>■ What matters most here?<br>■ Does this connect up to . . . ? How . . . ?<br>■ Did you learn something about ideas to do with God (or another big concept)? |
| **For 9- to 11-year-olds** | **Use some of the previous questions, and also try these:**<br>■ Can you explain what Muslims/Hindus/Christians/non-religious people believe about . . . ?<br>■ Can you explain what you think about . . . ?<br>■ What bit of this did you not understand?<br>■ What other ideas do you know about this?<br>■ Can you explain what you mean by . . . ?<br>■ Have you got a good 'hard question' to ask about this? |
| **More able learners** | **Use some of the previous questions, and also try these:**<br>■ Can you give two reasons for . . . ?<br>■ What evidence is there for . . . ?<br>■ Who thinks the opposite of this? |

## Learning

> It was difficult to get a proper answer but we managed to sort it out
>
> Alex, age 9, in response to an 'Is God real?' investigation

Alex, Iona and Sunika's teacher spent time planning an investigation where the pupils acted as detectives, collected evidence and wrote reports (see Figure 5.1) to answer an engaging question. More details of this task can be found in *RE Ideas: God* (Moss 2013). The pupils seem to have risen to the challenge of learning about a complicated

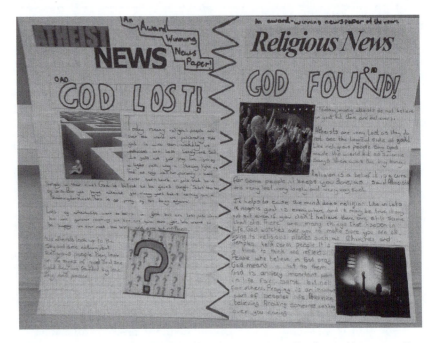

■ **Figure 5.1** Is God real? A literary and creative response, Sunika and Iona, year 5

concept, the existence of God. How else might we create this challenging, interesting learning for pupils in RE?

## INNOVATIVE AND CREATIVE LEARNING STRATEGIES IN RE

### Enquiry-based learning

Enquiry-based learning involves pupils in often rigorous discussion, formulating questions, researching, evaluating and reflecting on findings to develop their understanding. Good RE enables pupils to pursue enquiries of their own, stimulated by compelling teaching (see Table 5.4).

Recent OfSTED reports have been clear about the evidence they have found showing that 'in the most effective RE teaching, enquiry is placed at the heart of learning. However, few of the schools visited had a well-defined approach to this' (OfSTED 2013, 24).

In this section you will find a wide variety of strategies which provide pupils with opportunities to develop their ideas, understandings and questions in RE through enquiry, for example through asking good questions, interviewing visitors, solving mysteries, analysing problems, speculating and taking the role of envoy.

Enquiring RE begins with young children: their first skills as enquirers come from exercising curiosity and pursuing the will to discover. This leads to increasingly sophisticated research, in which pupils investigate for themselves, set their own agendas for learning and become researchers in simple ways.

**▨ Table 5.4** Enquiry-based planning (Blaylock and Moss 2011: 12)

| Select the content and create the enquiry | Planning some stimulating learning activities | Planning to develop reasoning | Planning to secure understanding of Christian faith | Planning to enable creative expression |
|---|---|---|---|---|
| **Why are we teaching about Jesus' parable of the lost sheep?** | **How can we make this story come alive for this group of children?** | **What questions or activities enable children to develop deeper understanding of the story?** | **How can children understand why this story matters to Christians?** | **What can children do to link or relate their own experience to the story they have been learning from?** |
| RE studies living religious traditions in terms of their sources – so Bible stories fit. | Use a creative story box approach to tell the story to the class: this communicates both the story's narrative and the value of the story to Christians. | Give the children four reasons why this story, 2,000 years old, might be still told so much and so often. | ▨ Look at some paintings or stained-glass images of the story. | Many activities facilitate this kind of linking. In this case we suggest the following: Give the children this list of words: |
| The stories Jesus told illustrate key beliefs and ideas for the Christian community – so this work is about being 'found by God', a key Christian idea. | Use Nick Butterworth and Mick Inkpen's (2008) telling of the story to explore it again. The method includes 'I wonder' questions: | Why did Jesus tell this story? Was it . . . | ▨ Think about how they were made, by whom, and why. How long did they take? | ▨ Lost<br>▨ Finder<br>▨ Searcher<br>▨ Carer<br>▨ Looker<br>▨ Brave<br>▨ Strong<br>▨ Weak<br>▨ Scared/ fearful |
| Christians believe that God seeks and rejoices in lost humanity in the same way as the shepherd. | ▨ I wonder what might be dangerous for this lost sheep?<br>▨ I wonder why the shepherd cares so much for the sheep?<br>▨ I wonder if the lost sheep matters more than the other sheep?<br>▨ I wonder what being lost feels like? Why?<br>▨ I wonder if there are things that are dangerous for us if we are lost?<br>▨ I wonder if being lost is always about not knowing where we are – are there other kinds of 'lost' too? | ▨ Because he liked sheep more than other animals?<br>▨ Because he thinks God loves people like a shepherd loves the sheep?<br>▨ Because we all get lost sometimes and need help?<br>▨ Because breaking the rules can be dangerous?<br><br>Choose the two best reasons, and think about why they are good reasons. | ▨ What does this tell you about how much the story matters to Christians?<br>▨ Many Christians call Jesus 'the good shepherd'. There are even some churches called 'The Church of the Good Shepherd'. Why? | ▨ In danger<br>▨ Like God<br>▨ Like any person<br>▨ Loving<br><br>Ask them in turn which 3 words apply to the sheep, to the shepherd, to themselves and to God. There are no right answers – this is all about helping children to be interpreters! |

How can we encourage our youngest learners to raise questions? In *Opening up Education Creativity*, Pett (2013) outlines a sequence of learning on asking and answering puzzling questions for 5- to 7-year-olds. Within this article he uses creative strategies such as identifying big and little questions, harvesting pupils questions in a class 'why' book, suggesting wondering questions from a story and posing questions for God. The proposed sequence of learning is completed with the class standing around a chalk or tape outline of a question mark and a question is posed that has been investigated within the unit; anyone with an answer or even part of an answer steps into the question mark to offer what they think or what a Hindu, Muslim, etc. might think. Using strategies like these encourages pupils to understand that RE is a place for questions and that RE is also a time to look at a series of different answers.

Tom, aged 6, wrote his four questions for God into a poem (see Figure 5.2). Consider asking an able writer to capture ideas for a whole group. A question poem could be written by a whole class.

Training children in the skills of enquiry is a focus for the whole curriculum, but in RE with 5- to 7-year-olds we can begin to model enquiry skills and construct teacher-led enquiries for children to participate in. In this planned enquiry on the lost sheep (see Table 5.4), notice that the children are given a reason to conduct the enquiry.

Why might this story, 2000 years old, be still told so much and so often?

Why did Jesus tell this story?

The creative sharing of this story using a series of artefacts and a series of 'I wonder' questions is inspired by the godly play strategy – see Berryman (2006) – and is used in

■ **Figure 5.2** Tom, 6, questions for God poem

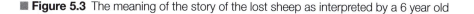

**Figure 5.3** The meaning of the story of the lost sheep as interpreted by a 6 year old

many church schools. However, if the questions are chosen with care, as in the following example, this strategy is perfectly suitable for use in community schools. The 'I wonder' questions support children to enquire into the meaning of the story for Christians. The combination of the creative sharing of the story, 'I wonder' questions and suggestions as to what the deeper meanings of the story are allows children with a range of abilities to express profound ideas about the meaning of the story. In one example, though the child, Francca, didn't find writing easy (the version in Figure 5.3 had spellings improved and was copied out clearly for display), she has been able to express a clear interpretation of the meaning of the story. Her teacher was surprised at the depth of her response and believed that this structured enquiry supported Francca to express her ideas clearly.

A semi-structured enquiry method can be used with 7- to 11-year-olds to focus enquiries in RE: raising pupil interest, focussing questions on a particular concept or piece of religious material and then supporting the subsequent enquiries. Start with a strategy to get children engaged and interested in the religious material, such as a piece of music, short film or picture. If the initial material is a picture, the thinking skills strategy 'maps from memory' (Baumfield 2002) is a creative and entertaining way of interesting children in the material. Once the children's interest has been raised, divide the picture into 4 or 5 parts and place it in the middle of a large piece of paper. Arrange the children into groups. Each group starts off with one of the prepared pieces of paper. The papers are then moved in a carousel, with each group doing the new activity with a new part of the picture, building on the work of the last group. With their first part of the picture groups write any questions they have about what they can see in their part. The paper moves to the next group. With the next part of the picture children are asked to add any further questions and answer any questions posed by the first group. The paper moves to the next group.

The children then have a series of questions, raised by the class, to enquire into. Time is given for each group to research in books or on the internet to clarify what is happening in their part of the picture and then as a group write a paragraph which could be displayed next to the picture part to explain. Work goes on to look into more about the concept, theme or religious material that is being studied, but learning can be led by the questions raised by the pupils. This style of enquiry ensures that, whilst the children raise the questions, appropriate content and concepts are studied. A good example of this can be found in the unit 'Why Do Christians' (Moss 2012). There is also a film in the 'Good Learning in RE' series on the National Association of Teachers of RE website (www.natre.org.uk) that shows this enquiry in action.

RE teachers peruse the media, contemporary culture and the local area to find examples of religion in practice to share with their pupils. Belief, with the comfort, joy and challenges it offers, needs to be portrayed as relevant now, not something that was relevant in the time of the children's parents or grandparents. Enquiring into religion in the contemporary world shows the relevance of the subject of RE and supports children to become 'skilled cultural navigators'. At the 2012 Olympics in London, 25% of the athletes were Muslim; it was Ramadan and the height of summer. For some of the athletes this caused a dilemma: would they fast and risk a dip in their performance at this key time? Using a mystery strategy, well explained in *Thinking through Religious Education* (Baumfield 2002), pupils were able to consider the imagined dilemma of the Muslim athlete Imran whilst encountering ideas from Muslim athletes such as Mo Farah, Mo Sbihi and Darren Cheesmen, advice from religious leaders and quotes from the Qur'an and Hadith. After studying the material pupils were asked to offer advice to Imran. Should he fast? Why? Why not? This type of creative thinking engages pupils in an RE-relevant dilemma requiring them to speculate, analyse, make links, interpret, evaluate, hypothesise and explain. An example of this mystery and a series of related teaching and learning ideas, which can be adapted for other sporting events, can be found at www.reonline.org.uk/wordpress/wp-content/uploads/2013/02/Muslim-Athletes.pdf.

## CREATIVE MODELS OF CURRICULUM ORGANISATION

Ten years ago if you went into most primary schools, RE would have appeared on the timetable once a week for about an hour and would have been taught in a series of work units exploring different themes relating to religion and belief. The pattern has changed and RE is organised in a variety of ways. Each organisational approach has its advantages and disadvantages, but many RE subject leaders and advisers have found that some of these models can support sustained learning and sustained pupil engagement. Two popular models are described and exemplified next.

### Blocked time

Some schools use a themed curriculum approach to RE. A series of lessons in the humanities or other subjects is themed with a relevant focus for RE, for a fixed period of time determined by the outcomes to be delivered (see chapter 1 in this volume for a discussion of webbed integration). Blocked learning can last for two weeks or for longer – for example for half a term – and pupils spend five hours a week or more learning RE and relating study to history or geography. In the next half term, the focus may be more on one of the other subjects. The main advantages of this are that pupils get a deeper and more continuous experience of RE. Working in depth allows children the time they need to consolidate their learning. A disadvantage is that some schools use arbitrary themes or fail to plan RE into the programme at sufficient depth. Specialist teachers' involvement in planning is crucial.

Excellent examples of this work are shown when RE is the lead subject in some learning, for example a Leicestershire school where students who were learning about people who have made a difference in a unit that linked RE, history and English studied Rosa Parks and Malala Yousafzi. After studying the Montgomery bus boycott, pupils engaged in a Conscience Alley activity and then suggested what Rosa should say to the bus driver.

> Rosa should say, "I am fed up of being treated as not as good as white people – us black people are people too. We have feelings. I don't want to be treated like this. I am going to get off this bus and walk rather than be disrespected in this way."
>
> Amardeep, 10

> I would say this to the driver. "It says in the bible that you should love your neighbour. I don't think it is a very loving thing to treat one person better than another. I am not going to move."
>
> Gurjit, 11

In a year 1 class the focus of work was on castles, not naturally rich pickings for RE work. Inventive teacher Heather Lee from Cambridgeshire asked her class of 6-year-old children to come up with questions to ask a soldier visiting from a local army barracks. I'm not sure he expected question such as Do you think war is good? What is peace? Are all people who fight baddies? or Why would God ever make bad people to fight? The children then chose their best question as a focus – Why do wars start and why do people fight? Children discussed the statements about why wars started and considered whether these were good or bad reasons to start a war. They went on to learn about what Sikhs, Hindus and Christians think about war. Just war theory was encountered and investigated by 6-year-olds!

## Focussed RE day or week

Some schools use an 'RE Week' or an 'RE Day' to focus learning, then follow up the 'big experience' with linked lessons over several weeks. Such 'big events' planning is demanding of teachers but can for example help the whole school to focus and develop the subject. A day is about 5 hours, so it is not, of course, a substitute for a term's work. Effective work on a week about respect for all religions, an Easter or a 'Creation Week', or a week on spring celebrations in different faiths is possible, as are many other themes. The key to success is clarity about the RE learning that is planned. RE Today produces an e-publication supporting teachers planning RE days or weeks, *Big RE* (Blaylock *et al.* 2013).

One example of this is work by Jo Chrich from Cambridgeshire, who planned an excellent RE Day for 7- to 11-year-olds on the concept of temptation, linking the work to Lent and the experience of Jesus in the desert. The pupils learnt about Jesus in the desert, the practices that different Christians undertake at Lent and what the key concept of temptation might mean to them. Creative strategies such as philosophy for children were used as strategies for learning during the day (see Figure 5.4). One teacher commented after the temptation-themed day, '[I am a] Big fan of the day as it allowed teachers and children to really get stuck in and explore a particular theme.'

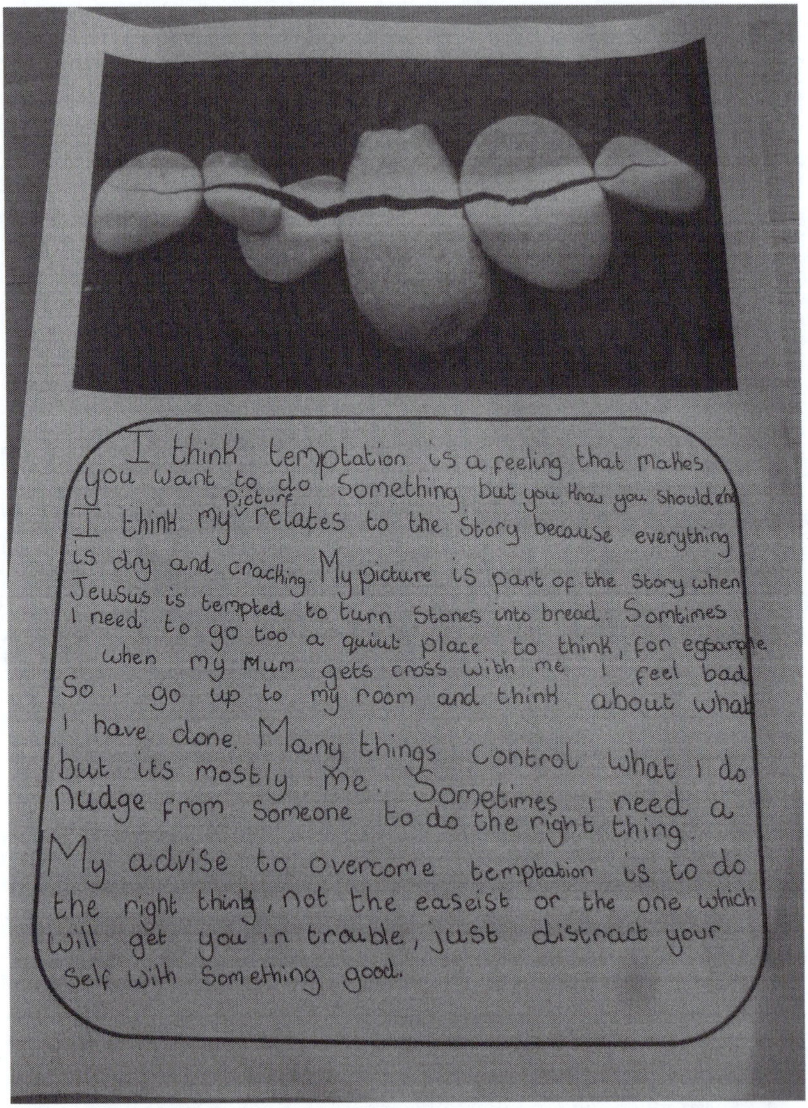

■ **Figure 5.4** Temptation: writing based on a study of the story of Jesus in the desert

An enthusiastic teacher will inspire her pupils and transmit the relevance of the subject. The ideas and techniques in this chapter are designed to support and enthuse primary teachers and their pupils. The enquiry methods practically described show pupils the relevance of RE and deepen their understanding of religious material.

> The most effective RE teaching integrated opportunities for reflection and creativity effectively within the process of enquiry which arose directly from pupils' engagement with religious material.
>
> Section 63, *Religious Education: Realising the Potential* (OfSTED 2013)

The thinking skills approaches described are attractive to both teachers and pupils as whilst they engage learners, they allow opportunities to practise and develop key learning skills in RE.

A teacher who plans for engaging creative teaching and learning will have pupils who become engaged advocates of the subject, like these children from a Leicester Primary School:

> I like RE because it makes you think.
> I like RE because it helps me use my head.

# REFERENCES

Baumfield, V. (2002) *Thinking through Religious Education*. Cambridge: Chris Kington Publications.

Bedford Borough, Central Bedfordshire and Luton SACRE (2012) *Identities, Meanings and Values: The RE Agreed Syllabus for Bedford Borough, Central Bedfordshire and Luton*.

Berryman, J. (2006) *Godly Play: Volume 1 – How to Lead Godly Play Lessons*. Denver, CO: Living the Good Life News.

Blaylock, L. (ed.) (2004) *Representing Religions*. Birmingham: RE Today Services.

Blaylock, L., *et al.* (2013) *Big RE*. Birmingham: RE Today Services.

Blaylock, L., and Moss, F. (2011) 'The Lost Sheep: Teaching Christian Story to 6–7s.' *RE Today* vol. 28, no. 2 (Spring): p. 12.

Butterworth, Nick, and Inkpen, Mick (2008) *The Lost Sheep: Stories Jesus Told*. West Sussex: Candle Books.

Grimmitt, M. (2000) *Pedagogies of Religious Education: Case Studies in the Research and Development of Good Pedagogic Practice in RE*. Great Wakering: McCrimmons.

Moss, F. (Ed.) (2012) *Opening up Christianity*. Birmingham: RE Today Services.

Moss, F. (Ed.) (2013) *RE Ideas: God*. Birmingham: RE Today Services.

OfSTED (2010) *Transforming Religious Education*. Manchester: OfSTED; www.ofsted.gov.uk/resources/transforming-religious-education

OfSTED (2013) *Religious Education: Realising the Potential*. Manchester: OfSTED; www.ofsted.gov.uk/resources/130068

Pett, S. (2013) 'Asking and answering puzzling questions' in Moss, F. (ed.), *Opening up Creativity*, pp. 7–12. Birmingham: RE Today Services.

# SPIRITUAL DEVELOPMENT THROUGH CREATIVE RE

## *Sally Elton-Chalcraft, Penny Hollander and Georgia Prescott*

Creative RE provides many opportunities for children's spiritual development because it involves children in exploring their own inner ideas, beliefs and feelings in response to learning about religious beliefs and concepts. Creative RE allows for individual reflection and expression through art, music, drama, poetry and other forms of creative writing. Opportunities for awe and wonder are provided through visits to places of worship or through individual responses to religious art or music (see chapter 7 in this volume). As teachers we need to be aware of children's spirituality and give avenues for them to explore and express this.

This chapter will explore the following:

- Spirituality and spiritual development (Hay and Nye 2006; Adams, Hyde & Woolley 2008); the four dimensions of spirituality (Elton-Chalcraft 2002); windows, mirrors and doors (Mills 2002).
- Awe and wonder through encounters with religion.
- 'Ows' – spiritual development through encounters with the difficult aspects of life.
- RE and the arts – spiritual development through personal expression.

## DEFINITIONS AND AIMS OF SPIRITUALITY

Before considering *how* to support children's spiritual development, first we must have some understanding of *what* spirituality is and *why* we should be supporting children's spiritual development.

One of the authors of this chapter has explored perceptions of spirituality (Elton-Chalcraft 2002), asking student teachers and in-service teachers for their definitions of spirituality. The authors have continued to ask groups for their definitions and, probably similar to the lists you have compiled in response to Table 6.1, diverse and innumerable forms of spirituality (along the lines of the items in Table 6.2) are often suggested.

While each group's list is always unique and seemingly different to another group's definition, nevertheless four main themes can always be found (see Table 6.3): the inner, the social and moral, the environmental and the transcendental (Elton-Chalcraft 2002). Myriad and diverse definitions, or forms of spirituality, can usually be categorised into

---

■ **Table 6.1** What is your definition of spirituality and why should we be supporting children's spiritual development?

---

*Before reading any further (resist peeking ahead!)*

1. Write *your* definition of spirituality
2. Why should we support children's spiritual development?
3. Discuss with a peer/group of peers (perhaps write words/phrases on a big piece of paper)

---

■ **Table 6.2** Examples of student teachers' definitions of spirituality

---

Inner peace, metaphysical, something more than the physical, beautiful scenery, relationships, morals, faith, God, destiny, personal, innate, mysterious, other worldly, search for meaning

---

■ **Table 6.3** The four dimensions of spirituality (adapted from Elton-Chalcraft 2002; Hay and Nye 2006; Prescott 2014)

---

**Inner dimension – *Looking Inwards* to your self**
Self: Our feelings/experiences/what is important to us. An inner quest for meaning, creativity/inspiration, feelings of elation

**Social and moral dimension – *Looking Outwards* to others**
Others: The way we interact with others and our important relationships. Choices about how to live life, ethics and values

**Environmental dimension – *Looking Downwards* to the Earth**
The world: Responses to the physical world/appreciating what is amazing about the world and nature and how that fits into our worldview

**Transcendental dimension – *Looking Upwards* towards God/the transcendent**
One's place in the universe: Response to the 'Ultimate'/the Divine, a sense of 'the other'; destiny, religion/faith/belief system

---

these four dimensions of spirituality, which have been recognised by other authors such as Fisher (1999) (cited in Elton-Chalcraft 2002), Nye (1998) (cited in Elton-Chalcraft 2002) and Brigstocke (2012).

Elton-Chalcraft (2002) found that teachers struggled to find appropriate activities to develop children's spirituality because they struggled to agree on a consensus definition for spirituality. Elton-Chalcraft suggests a metaphor which likens spirituality to a hologram (Elton-Chalcraft 2002, 313). A hologram has dimensions of height, breadth, depth and hue but is not tangible and can come in various forms – a piece of jewellery, a woman's face, a part of machinery. Similarly, spirituality is also intangible but has four dimensions – inner, social and moral, environmental and transcendental – but may have totally different forms. Like a hologram, spirituality can take many forms: your own spirituality may be very different to the writers of the chapters of this book, and certainly our individual spirituality will be different to those of a different culture, religion, age, gender, country, political stance etc. Table 6.4 attempts to capture these myriad forms of spirituality which, nevertheless, could be categorised into the four dimensions.

So if there are myriad forms of spirituality 'out there', even if they can be categorised into the four dimensions, which forms of spirituality (if any?) should we be nurturing in our children? (See Table 6.5.) And should we be engaged in this in any case? Isn't this a job for parents/the child's faith community/someone else or left to the child to undertake without intervention?

We would argue that all humans are spiritual. In fact spirituality could be defined as what it is to be 'truly human'. We agree with Heelas (2008, 2) that 'human flourishing' is under threat from a wide range of restrictions and regulations and that, to be truly human, to be truly spiritual, is to be liberated from the 'iron cages' of 'mainstream society and culture, with their measurable and narrow criteria of what it is to be a "successful" human' (Heelas 2008, 3). Especially within the English education system, where OfSTED grades and SATs results are often cited as measurements of success, we should remember that certain governmental documents can be found which encourage developments of children's creativity and spirituality (NACCCE 1999; OfSTED 2013a).

We would agree with Wright (2000) that education is often viewed in the West as 'nurturing', hence the call for teachers to 'support children's spiritual development' (OfSTED 2013a). However, we would also agree with Wright's (2000) insistence to supplement the nurturing with a critical stance, recognising that 'spirituality is a vital yet fundamentally controversial issue' (139).

So before we proceed to suggest creative activities for developing children's spirituality in each of these four dimensions, it is necessary to advocate aims for spiritual development which should underpin any activities.

---

■ **Table 6.4** Different forms of spirituality categorised into the four dimensions

**Examples of different forms of spirituality**
- Anuj, a nine-year-old Indian boy, offering flowers at the Ganesh shrine in his wealthy Bangalore home (transcendental dimension) in the hope that he will do well in his school test and make his parents proud.
- Sarah, a ten-year-old white Cumbrian girl, in the crowd at Wembley watching Blackpool win 2-0 in the playoffs in 2012 may experience the (inner dimension) feeling of elation as she screams in unison 'YEH' with her equally excited divorced dad in mutual (social and moral dimension) happiness.
- Martha, a four-year-old Afro-Caribbean girl from Derby, gathering different-sized stones and leaves to make an Andy Goldsworthy (*Art in a Natural Environment* 2014) artwork in the local park, observing intently (environmental dimension) the impact of the gentle rain on her sculpture.

---

■ **Table 6.5** Why should we develop children's spirituality? Which form of spirituality?

**What are your responses to these questions?**
Do all humans have the capacity to be spiritual?
Should teachers be responsible for developing children's spirituality?
If not, why not?
If so, then what form of spirituality should we be 'nurturing' or 'developing' in children?
And how?

---

Wright (2000) argues that teachers must balance nurture with critical thinking. We have translated these two almost conflicting pedagogies of spiritual learning into aims:

1) *Nurturing* a child's preferred spirituality (according to their preferred web of belief/ belief system – see chapter 1) in terms of the inner, social and moral, environmental and transcendental dimensions.
2) Inviting children to *critically challenge* their own and others' definitions of spirituality and grapple with pluralism, difference and the human desire for truth, conflicting views of ethical behaviour and lifestyle.

But are these two aims achievable? We would argue yes, and we offer some practical activities which should ensure each child in your class is aware of their own spirituality and develops critically and mindfully as a successful human being. It is also important that we give children the opportunities to have their spiritual voices heard and not dismissed or silenced by adults (Adams, Hyde & Woolley 2008).

For teachers looking to include a spiritual dimension into their lesson planning, it might be useful to consider the visual image of a doughnut. Liz Mills (2002) developed the concept of the Spiritual Ring Doughnut to represent the whole child. The outer ring is the tangible (mind and body) with the hole representing the intangible (spirit). If there was no hole there would not be a doughnut. The exploration and development of that 'hole' is what makes us whole as human beings.

## EXPLORING SPIRITUALITY WITH CHILDREN – WINDOWS, MIRRORS AND DOORS

Liz Mills' work also built on that of David Smith (1999) in developing the concept of 'spiritual windows' through 'windows, mirrors, doors' (Figures 6.1, 6.2 and 6.3). These three openings for spiritual development can be included in different curriculum areas.

> What is this life, if full of care
> We have no time to stand and stare
>> From 'Leisure' by William Henry Davies (1911)

Discussing with children the wonders of the created world is relevant to both RE lessons and other curriculum areas, particularly science; these provide the 'wows'. Conversely, the things that are difficult about life – suffering, war and poverty – are also part of the world in which we live. They are the 'ows'. It is important to consider how we provide children with the space, tools and frameworks to deal with these 'ows'. The window provides an encounter for learning about the world in which we live. Mills (2002) says that in experiencing such opportunities, children are learning about life in all its fullness thus answering Ofsted's (2013b) challenge.

■ **Figure 6.1** Windows: provide opportunities to look out on the world, to gaze and wonder at what is there.

■ **Figure 6.2** Mirrors: provide opportunities for children to reflect on their own experiences, to look inwards and meditate on life's big questions, exploring their own insights and those of others. They are learning from life.

Taking the children's own experience into consideration, a group of primary school teachers created a reflective display for their classrooms to help children express their own 'ows' in life and to move from this 'ow' to a 'wow' (see Table 6.6).

The concept and practice of using displays as a focus for spiritual development is further discussed in Prescott (2012).

## A unique spiritual identity

Every human being is unique, and as teachers we have a responsibility to aid children's spiritual development by giving opportunities for them to pursue a quest for meaning, values by which to live and to develop a sense of truth and mystery.

■ **Figure 6.3** Doors: give children opportunities to respond, to do something and go through the door – creatively expressing, applying and developing further their thoughts and convictions. In doing this they are learning to live by putting into action what they believe and value. The following display was used to encourage children to think about the ways in which they could approach the need to forgive others and also to ask for forgiveness.

---

■ **Table 6.6** Ows and wows in RE – display ideas from primary teachers

We developed the notion of ows and wows, aiming to help children know that life contains both and that a journey can be made between a place of ow and a place of wow. The central signpost clearly shows a journey. The cross at the bottom is to ensure that the message is one of forgiveness, redemption and the centrality of Christ.

Each activity offers children a space and time to own their feelings and act on them both personally and on behalf of their friends:
- Write down your ows and leave them in the ow box.
- Write down your wows and put them in the wow box.
- Take a notelet and write a message for a friend.
- Write a word of encouragement for a friend.
- Use the rays of hope as a prompt to help you move from ow to wow. Say something kind, take time to think, give someone a smile, do something for someone else.

---

Rickett *et al.* (2012) have used the 'windows, mirrors, doors' principles to map out a series of grids to give children a progression of *experiences* to aid spiritual development across the different age ranges. They give practical examples within four areas of spiritual learning: self, others, the world and beauty, beyond (church schools may wish to make this more specifically linked to God or the Divine, but the process is the same).

In each section there are suggestions to provide for learning about life: encounter (*window*); learning from life: reflection (*mirror*); and learning to live life: transformation (*door*). Another way to express this is to encourage children to look *inwards*, *outwards*, *downwards* and *upwards* (see Table 6.3).

### Things to discuss

Some examples from Rickett *et al.* (2012) include the following:

### Self

What makes me happy?
Who am I?
What do I deserve in life?
Where does my identity come from?

### Others

What makes a good friend?
How do I treat others?
Why should I care for those who may be in need but I have never met?
Why should I accept different values and beliefs from my own?

### World and beauty

What makes a special place?
Respond to a stimulus and verbally express reaction to something wonderful.
Diversity within world environments.
What is a perfect world?

### Beyond

Puzzling questions – what does God look like?
Where is God?
What is the purpose of the earth?
Is there life after death?

Lat Blaylock from RE Today has produced many practical activities to aid children's spiritual development (Blaylock 2012). On the NATRE website (www.natre.org.uk) in the Spirited Arts section there are examples from the Art in Heaven section and Spirited Poetry in the Galleries section. A few of these are illustrated here and show children's engagement with questions relating to themselves, others, the world and God.

My art in heaven work is about Hope for the world. Because I want peace to come to the world. I want everyone to stop arguing and to make the world a better place. My picture is called My Hope for the World. My name means hope in Albanian. And the words on the picture mean hope in other languages.

'My Hope for the World' – Shepresa, age 10

*How we should live*

### My Beatitudes

Blessed are those who starve and thirst
For they understand God's feeling.
Blessed are those who appreciate others' respect and love
For they will respect and love back.
Blessed are those who tolerate the world
For they listen to each other.
Blessed are those who are responsible for their actions
For they are responsible for God.
Blessed are those who care for their neighbours
For they care for God's love.
Blessed are those who trust their neighbours
For they trust God and the world.
Blessed are those who feel friendship in others
For they will be friends with the world and God.
Blessed are those who show happiness to the world
For they show happiness to God.

Aiden Tompkins, age 8
(www.natre.org.uk/spiritedarts/index.php)

*How we should treat our friends*

### Keep a Promise

If you keep a promise
You will keep a friend
You will keep your friend
From beginning to end
Do not break a promise
This you should not forget
Please don't break a promise
Or your friend might get upset
We should always try to keep
The promise that we make
Like the one I made at rainbows
Which I really don't want to break
Promises are special
To you and to your friends
Friendships keep you together
This is what God recommends

Anna Beresford, age 5
(www.natre.org.uk/spiritedarts/index.php)

*What is life like?*

**Celebrating Life, Celebrating Love!**

> **Life and Love are dangerously exciting.**
> My picture is of lots of lightning striking across the sky. The lightning is like life and love. It can be exciting and beautiful but it can also be really scary and dangerous.
>
> Kieran, age 8
>
> (www.natre.org.uk/spiritedarts/index.php)

## STILLING AND GUIDED VISUALISATION

Mary Stone's book *Don't Just Do Something, Sit There* (1995) and Stone and Brennan (2009) have helped teachers design opportunities for spiritual development. Stilling means 'being still' both physically and mentally, beginning with exercises of self-control and moving on to guide the mind into visualisations about a particular theme (e.g. wonder at the natural world, focusing on a leaf, a stone etc.) or a particular event or story from religious tradition (e.g. Jesus' parable of the tax collector, the Buddha's first visit outside his palace, Moses' experience at the burning bush etc.).

Stone and Brennan (2009) describe guided visualisation as using the imagination to recall an event, an object or a situation, which for the purpose of creative RE helps develop deeper reflection. The child is led through a story sequence, for example in the role of a bystander, and the teacher narrates using 'you' to ensure the child is actively involved (Stone and Brennan 2009:5). Guided visualisation is inclusive because it does not involve reading or writing and most children find it enjoyable. The teacher's narrative, in the guided visualisation, introduces children to historical contexts through engaging children's awareness of the sights, sounds, smells and textures of the situation. So when the teacher tells the story of Buddha leaving his luxurious lifestyle in the palace, the child takes on the role of the charioteer who takes Buddha outside the palace gates. The child, through guided visualisation, observes Buddha's reaction to the world outside the royal enclosure when he saw an old man, a sick man and a corpse. Through guided visualisation the child can reflect on Buddha's feelings and gain insight into the impact this experience might have had on the Buddha. (The story can be found at www.buddhanet.net/e-learning/buddhism/pbs2_unit01.htm, and the teacher can retell it in the guided visualisation style.)

The following visualisation takes the child through a journey as a leaf by appreciating and entering into the natural world; see Tables 6.7 and 6.8 (Stone 1995,18–20).

## THE POWER OF COLLECTIVE EXPERIENCES

When head teachers are asked how their school provides opportunities for spiritual development, one of the things they often talk about is their residential trips and visits outside of the classroom. The power of these collective experiences is not to be underestimated in terms of how they can help children to develop spiritually. They usually include the first two dimensions – inner, social and moral – and often can also include environmental and transcendental dimensions, depending on the context and nature of the trip.

---

**Table 6.7** How to begin and end a stilling/guided visualisation session – adapted from Stone
(1995)

---

Before you begin ensure the room is quiet and the children have been suitably briefed about
spending some time in silence, ideally with their eyes closed (this does take some practice
and perseverance but after a few weeks most children begin to enjoy stilling). Ensure your
voice tone is gentle and relaxing – children should pick up on the cue that there is a different
atmosphere. Make sure you pause frequently to enable the children to think deeply.

  i. I wonder if you can sit in an 'alert' and 'relaxed' position. . . . Is your back straight . . .
     your feet on the floor . . . your hands in your lap in a cupped position? Can you shrug
     your shoulders to relieve tension?
 ii. While you are sitting in an alert and relaxed position can you let your eyelids very gently
     close.
iii. Now breathe in and out slowly and gently, perhaps counting in your head 1, 2, 3 as you
     breathe in and 1, 2, 3 as you breathe out and feel any tenseness in your body release.
 iv. We are going to go on an imaginary journey.

*Take children through the guided visualisation.* An example of guided visualisation of a leaf is
given in Table 6.8

  v. Now we are going to leave our imaginary journey . . . and slowly return to the
     classroom.
 vi. Feel the hardness of your chair and the sounds inside and outside the room.
vii. When you are ready slowly open your eyes and have a good stretch.
viii. Would you like to make a comment about the visualisation?
 ix. What did you find out today?

*Discuss the visualisation. Possibly (but not always) the children could be asked to paint,
sculpt, discuss, write a poem, design a group poster etc. to express their responses to the
guided visualisation.*

---

> The bonding that takes place during a residential or on a day trip out of school is both
> strong and subtle. Children learn different things about each other that they may not
> have learnt in the classroom. Hidden strengths and talents as well as sometimes hum-
> bling challenges alter set preconceptions of what someone is like.
>
> (Prescott 2014)

Children begin to see each other in new and different ways. A confident child may not
be as brave or strong outside of the classroom and may be unwilling to try new activities and
in need of support from their peers to succeed. Conversely, a quiet child can be very confident and surprise their classmates with their inner strength, bravery or abilities. The previous
perceptions of them are expanded and developed. A child who can be very challenging in
the classroom is sometimes utterly engaged on school trips and contributes with enthusiasm.
The class experiences things together and bonds together more strongly as a group because
of it. At leavers' assemblies at the end of Year 6, day and residential trips are often relayed
as amongst their most memorable experiences from their time at primary school.

Trips give children new encounters and opportunities, and they can grow through
these. The sense of achievement at trying something new like canoeing or sailing or con-
quering their fears going for a night walk is huge. Many of the outdoor education trips and
residential visits will involve the environmental dimension of spirituality, as they include

---

**Table 6.8** Journey of a leaf stilling/guided visualisation session – adapted from Stone (1995,18)

---

1.  I am going to give one of you a leaf. . . . Examine and 'get to know' your leaf, look at the patterns, the veins, the colours, the texture . . .
2.  This leaf given to you by a tree is unique. There never has been one exactly the same and there never will be. If I were to ask you to put it on a pile with everyone else's leaf would you be able to pick out your leaf? . . . Good. . . . But now just place in in front of you.
3.  (Follow steps i–iv from Table 6.7.)
4.  Now you are going to imagine you are that leaf . . . feel what it is like to be that shape . . . that weight . . . those colours.
5.  Imagine you are on top of a tall tree . . . attached to a twig. Feel the gentle wind on both sides of you . . . listen to the splash of the raindrops on you . . . feel the rain.
6.  Now go back in time to when you were a bud. Feel what it was like to be tightly closed up . . . feel the warmth of the spring sunshine . . . feel the life force from the tree surging through your veins . . . feel yourself uncurling . . . facing the sun.
7.  All through summer you feel yourself growing . . . you have a marvellous view . . . what can you see?
8.  Autumn approaches and you feel a difference . . . the strength of the sap surging through your veins ceases . . . your colour begins to fade . . . a gust of wind blows you from the twig on which you have spent the whole of your life.
9.  You finally settle on the ground . . . what happens to you now?
10. (Follow steps v–ix from Table 6.7.)

Depending on age group, children could discuss what it felt like to 'be' a leaf.
Does this have an impact on how they now view leaves and the natural world?
Can they explore how different religious groups view the environment?
For example

■ Many Christians view humans as 'stewards' looking after the world and using resources wisely, so God created the natural world for humans to care for but also enjoy.
■ Many Hindus do not see the divine as separate from nature. The natural world (living and non-living things) are part of the Divine and so many Hindu rituals are designed to harmonise humans with the natural world.

---

children being in the outdoors and experiencing it in new and different ways. The 'wow' moment at reaching the top of a mountain and seeing the world from a different angle can be very powerful, as can the amazement at seeing the minute and intricate details of nature in a flower or a spider's web. Likewise, for a child from a rural area, the first experience of a city environment can provoke a sense of awe and wonder.

Within the transcendental dimension, RE has a significant part to play through helping children to experience a range of places of worship, both in their own locality and farther afield. You do not have to be a Muslim or a Christian to feel awe and wonder at the beauty of a mosque or the grandeur of a cathedral. We should allow children the chance to be still and absorb the atmosphere of a place of worship in a multi-sensory way (Ewens and Stone 2001).

Pauline Lovelock (2011), who spoke movingly about showing children around the Julian Shrine in Norwich and giving them experiences of stilling there, recorded one child as saying, 'I lit a candle and I felt all shaky – but I'm not a Christian. That never happens in football.'

If we provide children with these kind of inner and, at times, transcendental experiences, and a way to express their responses afterwards, we are going some way towards 'allowing their spiritual voices to be heard' (Adams, Hyde & Woolley 2008, and Euade 2008).

## Igniting a spark

A head teacher we know had a saying on the wall in her office which read, 'Every child has a spark; it is our job to ignite it.' This is a powerful statement which encapsulates what being a teacher is about and also what spiritual development consists of. If we get to know our children and encourage them to develop by supporting them through challenges and giving them a wide range of experiences and opportunities, we are helping to nurture their inner being at the deepest level. A good school is one where children seem to be 'alight' with their enthusiasm for life and learning. We can almost feel the sparks in the air (Prescott 2014). Creative RE has a real role to play in ensuring this happens.

# REFERENCES

Adams, K., Hyde, B. and Woolley, R. (2008) *The Spiritual Dimension of Childhood* (London: Jessica Kingsley Publishers).

*Art in a Natural Environment* (2014) BBC presentation of artwork of Andy Goldsworthy. Available at www.bbc.co.uk/learningzone/clips/andy-goldsworthy-art-in-a-natural-environment/8230.html (accessed 20 April 2014).

Blaylock, L. (2012) *Reflection, Inspiration, Engagement: Spiritual Development through RE 31 Practical Activities*. Cumbria SACRE Conference, RE Today.

Brigstocke, M. (2012) Are you there God it's me Marcus. *RE Today* 30.1: 4–7.

Davies, W. H. (1911) 'Leisure – a poem' in *Songs of Joy and Others* (London: A. C. Field).

Eaude, Tony (2008, 2nd ed.) *Children's Spiritual, Moral, Social and Cultural Development: Primary and Early Years* (Exeter: Learning Matters).

Elton-Chalcraft, S. (2002) Empty wells: How well are we doing at spiritual well-being? *International Journal of Children's Spirituality* 7.3: 309–28.

Ewens, A. and Stone, M. (2001) *Teaching about God, worship and spirituality: Practical approaches for 7–11 year olds*. Norwich: Religious and Moral Education Press.

Hay, D. and Nye, R. (2006, rev. ed.) *Spirit of the Child* (London: Fontana).

Heelas, P. (2008) *Spiritualities of Life: New Age Romanticism and Consumptive Capitalism* (Oxford: Blackwell).

Lovelock, P. (2011): *Can You Feel the Silence?* Presentation at the Westhill Trust Seminar Leeds 2011: 'Spirituality and RE: Imagination, Spiritual Development and the RE Curriculum'.

Mills, E. (2002) *Spiritual Development: The Doughnut and the Hole*. Available at www.crackingre.co.uk/htdocs/crackingre/secure/teach?Supp/donut.html (accessed 4 February 2014).

NACCCE (National Advisory Committee on Creative and Cultural Education) (1999) *All Our Futures: Creativity, Culture and Education* (Birmingham: RE Today). Available at http://sirkenrobinson.com/pdf/allourfutures.pdf (accessed 20 February 2014).

OfSTED (2013a) *Religious Education: Realising the Potential*. Available at www.ofsted.gov.uk/resources/religious-education-realising-potential (accessed 20 January 2014).

OfSTED (2013b) *Not Yet Good Enough*. Available at www.ofsted.gov.uk/resources/not-yet-good-enough-personal-social-health-and-economic-education-schools (accessed 4 February 2014).

Prescott, G. (2012) Spirituality in the classroom: Interactivity and imagination. *RE Today* 29.1: 46–8.

Prescott, G. (2014) *From Unconscious Incompetence . . . ? A Personal Journey to Understanding Spiritual Development* (Birmingham: RE Today).

Rickett, A., Rickett, S. and Holloway, D. (2012) *Progression in Spirituality*. Salisbury Diocesan Board of Education.

Smith, D. (1999) *Making Sense of Spiritual Development* (Nottingham: Stapleford Centre).

Stone, M. (1995) *Don't Just Do Something, Sit There* (Norwich: Religious and Moral Education Press).

Stone, M. and Bennan, J. (2009) "See" RE Stories from Christianity: Guided visualisation for children aged 7–11 Norwich: Religious and Moral Education Press.

Wright, A. (2000) *Spirituality and Education: Master Classes in Education Series* (London: Routledge).

# ENRICHING RE THROUGH MUSIC AND ART

### Carrie Mercier and Siobhán Dowling Long

Religious education (RE) is not in the National Curriculum. It holds a unique position as a part of the basic curriculum that is required in all schools. Some might argue that this allows for greater flexibility in terms of how the subject is taught and organised. Teachers responsible for RE will find that many local agreed syllabuses for the subject encourage an approach in RE that works creatively with other areas of the curriculum. In this chapter we will explore ideas for enriching RE through music, art and creativity and through engaging pupils in the aesthetic dimension of religion. However, music and art are not just to be considered as an add-on or enrichment. In this chapter, we argue that we cannot make sense of religion without engaging with music and the visual arts.

## MUSIC IN RE

The sound of music features in the liturgies and prayer services of many world religions, in the recitation of chants and mantras, and in the singing of hymns, songs and prayers. Music is used to communicate teachings and beliefs, as well as to promote reflection and to aid meditation. It plays an integral role in the religious practices of individuals, and it is heard at services of daily worship, on holy days and feast days, and at celebrations of various rites of passage, including religious festivals. Most notably, it is the medium through which many sacred scriptures are recited or intoned. Participation in music making during communal and private worship fosters religious identity and a sense of belonging. Music invokes a variety of moods in those who listen, and features as the only art form with an innate capacity to transcend the boundaries of temporal existence.

The inclusion of music in RE, thus, complements any study of world religions as well as supporting the values, aims, and attainment targets of the National Curriculum as outlined in the *Non-Statutory National Framework for Religious Education* (QCA 2004) and in various agreed syllabuses throughout England and Wales. Its use in RE also promotes 'positive attitudes, including self-awareness, respect for all, open-mindedness and appreciation and wonder' (QCA 2004:13). Similarly, the report *Making More of Music: An Evaluation of Music in Schools* notes the positive impact of music on the personal development of pupils in approximately three-quarters of all primary schools inspected (OfSTED 2009:12). Effective teaching and learning were also observed in teachers who engaged the musical intelligences of pupils by playing music as the pupils entered the room; empha-sized listening to enable pupils to hear their own music and make connections to the music of others, including the music of established performers and composers; demonstrated and modelled music making; enabled pupils to play and explore sounds; and allowed them to use their musical imaginations (OfSTED 2009:40). Good and outstanding practices such as outlined in this report on music can also be applied to the use of music in RE.

The inclusion of music in RE enables every child, including gifted pupils and pupils with special educational needs (SEN), to participate in class discussions about lyrics under-pinning songs and mantras and to become involved in the composition and performance of short musical works in small and larger class groups. This view concurs with the vision outlined in *The Importance of Music: A National Plan for Music Education* (DfE and DCMS 2011:7), which aims to 'enable children from all backgrounds and every part of England to have an opportunity to learn a musical instrument; to make music with oth-ers; to learn to sing; and to have the opportunity to progress to the next level of excel-lence' (DfE and DCMS 2011:9). This aim also features as the second aim of the National Curriculum for *Music Programmes of Study for Key Stages 1 and 2* (DfE 2013b:1). The importance of singing includes multiple benefits for children including 'improvements in learning, confidence, health and social development' (DfE and DCMS 2011:11). In par-ticular, the National Plan notes that 'singing can change lives and build communities' (DfE and DCMS 2011:11). Singing religious songs, hymns, and carols as a class choir in RE thus promotes many of the benefits outlined in the National Plan, including a sense of social cohesion within the class group and in the school community as a whole. Out of respect for the sacred traditions, however, it is recommended that pupils refrain from the recitation of sacred texts and that they would sing only those sacred chants and mantras (prayers) drawn from their own religious traditions. This is an area of sensitivity, which teachers ought to consider. However, it does not rule out the possibility of performing spirituals or other sacred music as part of a class or school choir. Pupils can still learn about (attainment target 1) and engage with the sacred music of other religious traditions through listening and composing their own personal chants and mantras (see Table 7.1).

'Sing Up', which is also mentioned in the National Plan (DfE and DCMS 2011:11), hosts a website for interested teachers and schools to provide subscription access to a song bank featuring backing tracks, scores, and tracks of melody lines and individual parts of songs for part-singing. This website features songs for a number of subjects in the curriculum, including over seventy-six religious songs for use in RE (www.singup.org/songbank/song-bank/tags/164-religious-education). Songs from a variety of genres are

---

■ **Table 7.1** Using music with Year 5 to support spiritual development

---

Play a recording of the well-known Tibetan Buddhist mantra 'Om mani padme hum' ('Om, Jewel of the Lotus'), which is recited by Tibetan Buddhists for purification and as a means of acquiring spiritual merit. Point out that the recitation of this mantra is often accompanied by the spinning of a prayer wheel (Mani Wheel) and by bells and wood blocks. Invite the pupils to critically reflect on the meaning of the words and to comment on the powerful meditative effect of the music. Then ask them to compose, in small groups, their own mantras with words and music that will have a positive effect on all who listen and sing. The mantras can be performed with tuned and non-tuned percussion instruments. This activity could also be extended to include the composition of a class mantra.

---

included, e.g. the spiritual 'Dem Dry Bones' (based on Ezek. 37:1–14) and the children's song 'The Wise and the Foolish Man' (based on Matt. 7:24–7), along with signed videos, Braille scores and recommendations for pupils with moderate learning difficulties, specific learning difficulties and profound and multiple learning disabilities to enable the participation of all. Similarly, the National Association of Teachers of Religious Education (NATRE) has included on their website a database of songs divided into different themes to support the National Curriculum for teachers interested in 'Developing Religious Education through Music' (www.natre.org.uk/music). Music Today Services also provides information about publications that develop RE through the arts, along with articles in its newsletter, *RE Today* (www.retoday.org.uk; see especially the spring 2010 issue). Penny Hollander and Ruth Houston's book *RE and Music Education: Singing from the Same Song Sheet?* (Hollander and Houston 2009) provides teachers with a wealth of imaginative and creative ideas for using music in RE. Practical suggestions for preparing assemblies are included on the website www.assemblies.org.uk, including relevant songs and a list of resources: e.g. Ronnie Lamont's *Primary School Assemblies for Religious Festivals* (Lamont 2012) and Gordon Lamont's *Primary Assemblies for a Just World* (Lamont 2008).

## Music and spirituality

The importance of exposing children and young people to a wide variety of music genres for the purpose of spiritual development is explored in the *Religious Education CPD Handbook*. Here Lat Blaylock (2011) argues that if RE is to engage the spiritual, then the widest range of spiritually inspiring music across the world's religions needs to be explored. Ruth Wills (2007) also points out that music is a medium through which spirituality is often encountered with children, and with this purpose in mind she has compiled a list of suitable music for developing children's spirituality (this can be found at www.schoolswork.co.uk/thinking/childrens-spirituality-and-music/P1). Much of the music listed and more can be sourced on YouTube and can be easily accessed by specialist and generalist teachers who may want to use examples of religious music to promote pupils' spiritual development, as well as to illustrate the use of religious music in real-life contexts. It is advisable however to download music prior to lessons since this facility is often blocked in schools, and where it is available, valuable time can be wasted waiting for videos to buffer. Free video downloading software is available on the internet to enable YouTube video downloads onto a computer or memory stick.

## Non-specialist teachers of music

For non-specialist teachers of music, taking a risk to include music in RE will result in more creative and imaginative approaches in teaching and learning, as well as fulfilling the general requirements of the National Framework to promote key skills through RE (QCA 2004:15) and making cross-curricular links with the National Curriculum for *Music Programmes of Study for Key Stages 1 and 2* (DfE 2013b:1–2). But taking a risk requires confidence on the part of the non-specialist teacher who may want to include music in RE. The new government agency the National College for Teaching and Leadership (NCTL) has provided a new online resource, ITT Primary Music Guidance and Resources, to support the training of initial primary teachers who are teaching music as part of the National

Curriculum. Over twenty-one different Initial Teacher Training (ITT) providers designed and delivered training modules during 2012, which were funded by the then Training and Development Agency for Schools (TDA) in response to the National Plan for Music. The online resources, which are freely available, provide helpful suggestions for initial teachers as well as for more experienced generalist teachers who may need guidance on and resources for teaching music in primary school. These resources can also be used to aid in the inclusion of music in RE.

The success in using creative approaches in teaching and learning cannot be underestimated and has been noted in various OfSTED reports, including *Transforming Religious Education* (OfSTED 2010), which is based on the findings of an earlier report, *Making Sense of Religion: A Report of Religious Education in Schools and the Impact of Locally Agreed Syllabuses* (OfSTED 2007). The occurrence of good and outstanding teaching and learning was noted when teachers used 'imaginative and evocative resources to stimulate the pupils' imaginations and to explore their personal responses' (OfSTED 2010:17). It was also noted that sustained learning happened when RE was linked to other areas of the curriculum, most notably English, art, drama and music (OfSTED 2010:17).

## Music and the Bible

There is a vast quantity of classical and popular music composed on every book of the Bible. For this reason, teachers might consider using classical or contemporary musical retellings of biblical stories. In this way, they would employ a more creative approach in RE and also make valuable cross-curricular links with the music curriculum through 'listening to, reviewing, and evaluating music across a range of historical periods, styles and traditions, including the works of the great composers and musicians' (DfE 2013a:1). Throughout the history of music, the Psalms have been a popular choice for composers' settings in choral and instrumental works. Teachers who may want to use a musical setting of Psalm 150, for example, could play either a recording or preferably a clip on YouTube of a performance of Benjamin Britten's 'Psalm 150' for children's chorus and instruments, Op. 67. The latter would enable the pupils to see and hear some of the instruments being played, some of which are mentioned in the psalm, and would also give them an opportunity to see and hear other children singing this great hymn of praise. Following this exercise, pupils could discuss how the composer, Benjamin Britten, expressed the joyous sentiments of Psalm 150 in music. After this discussion, they could compose their own hymn of praise to God using tuned and untuned percussion or on instruments made by the pupils themselves (cf. DfE 2013b:1). As an alternative, the words of Psalm 150 could be set to other well-known tunes and performed with percussion instruments.

## Religious founders and music making

Some founders of religion were also composers and musicians, and they used the medium of hymns to spread their teachings. For example, in the Lutheran and Methodist denominations of Christianity, Martin Luther (1483–1546) and Charles Wesley (1707–88) composed hymns in the vernacular for the purpose of spreading the Christian message among the ordinary people. In Sikhism, Guru Nanak (1469–1539), who was a composer and a musician, also communicated his teachings through this genre – such as *Shabad Kirtan*

('Singing the Praises of God'), found in the *Guru Granth Sahib*. Guru Nanak placed great importance on the singing of divine music and believed singing hymns shaped an individual's character as well as enhanced physical and spiritual well-being. To make a cross-curricular link with history, teachers could play a recording or even play on an instrument or sing Martin Luther's paraphrase of Psalm 46, *Ein' feste Burg ist unser Gott* ('A Mighty Fortress Is Our God'). Following a discussion of the lyrics and music, the pupils could do a project on the story behind this hymn, which is also known as the 'Battle Hymn of the Reformation'. Similarly, to promote pupils' literacy, the children could make a booklet containing the stories behind their favourite Christmas hymns and carols or a booklet which explores the variety of hymns among world religions.

Although there is no founder associated with Hinduism, music has been closely associated with the Hindu gods and goddesses, who are depicted playing or holding musical instruments. The three gods of the Hindu trinity – Brahma, Vishnu and Shiva, who play the hand cymbals, conch and damaru (drum) respectively – symbolize 'the Nada-Brahman, the sacred sound represented by the symbol Om, which generates the universe' (Beck 2006:114). Teachers could show visuals of the gods with their musical instruments, including Vishnu's avatar, Krishna, who is depicted playing the flute, and invite pupils to critically reflect upon the meaning and significance of different objects and instruments held in the hands of the gods (see Figure 7.1). Pupils could reflect on the story of Krishna and his flute, found in the Bhagavata Purana, through storytelling, art and drama (see Table 7.2).

■ **Figure 7.1** Children at Janmashtami Festival (Krishna's Birthday) at Bhaktivedanta Manor ISKCON (Hare Krishna) Temple

Photo credit: © Universal Images Group/Superstock

■ **Table 7.2** Ideas for questions – Krishna playing the flute – Year 3

Questions to stimulate critical reflection:
Why did Krishna choose the flute as his instrument?
What was the effect of Krishna's flute playing on the milkmaids (*gopis*) and the animals?
What does Krishna's flute symbolize? Explain.

## Symbolism of musical instruments

While in some religions the use of instruments is prohibited during religious services of worship, in some others there are exceptions at permitted times, and in some more they play an integral part in the religious worship of the community. Many instruments used in religious services are imbued with symbolism. This point could be highlighted for example in lessons based around Rosh Hashanah and Yom Kippur, around Buddhist sand-painted mandalas, or indeed on a visit to a sacred place such as a gurdwara, temple or church where the pupils might see or hear the instruments being played.

For a lesson on Rosh Hashanah for example, teachers could play a recording of the shofar for the pupils and explain why this sound is significant for Jewish people today. Made from a ram's horn, it makes a mystical sound that calls to mind a number of events in the Hebrew Bible including the Creation of the World (Gen. 1), the Sacrifice of Isaac (Gen. 22), the experience on Mount Sinai (Exod. 29:6–19), and the Destruction of the Walls of

■ **Figure 7.2** Sounding a Yemenite shofar

Photo credit: © Shutterstock/Howard Sandler

Jericho (Jos. 6:1–20) among others. In particular it reminds Jewish people today of God Almighty, Judgment Day, and the future Resurrection of the Dead. The site www.chabad. org provides teachers with many creative ideas and resources, including videos and recipes for Rosh Hashanah and other Jewish festivals (see DfE 2013a:4).

For a lesson on Buddhist sand-painted mandalas, the pupils could watch a video clip on YouTube illustrating its construction and deconstruction by Buddhist monks. This activity is done to the accompaniment of instrumental music also played by monks. Teachers could ask the pupils to critically reflect on the significance of the disconcerting sound of the instruments being played. Blaring trumpets, for example, are understood to either drive away evil deities or call benevolent ones, while the low tones of the *dung chen*, a metal trumpet five to twelve feet long, mimics the sound of the elephant. The *dung kav* sounds either warnings or announcements, and the *kang dung* calls the living and the dead. Percussion instruments such as cymbals (*rom*), drums (*nga bom*), conch shells and bells feature as part of the ensemble (Miller and Shahriari 2012:234–5). To link up with the Design and Technology Curriculum, the pupils could design their own sand mandalas using coloured sand or paints with Buddhist music played in the background (see DfE 2013a:1–3 and Figure 7.3).

Bells, which feature prominently in Buddhist music, feature in other religions too, most notably in some denominations of Christianity: e.g. in the Church of England where they are played before and after religious services of worship, and during the Mass in the Catholic denomination at the epiclesis and the consecration, at the point of elevation of the bread and wine, to focus attention on significant events and moments of great holiness

■ **Figure 7.3** Sand mandala destruction ceremony

Photo credit: © Shutterstock/Artur Bogacki

■ **Figure 7.4** Isolated church bell and crucifix

Photo credit: © Shutterstock/Hanzi-mor

(Figure 7.4). Teachers could ask the children to think about the importance of bells in their own religious tradition(s) and to compare and contrast their use by worshippers in other religious traditions.

## Islam and music

Many sacred scriptures and texts of the principal world religions are chanted or intoned in heightened speech, but in some cases, such as in Islam, the sound produced is not regarded as 'music' as understood in Western art music terms. In Islam, it is a highly controversial subject among Islamic scholars and there is much debate over its legitimacy. For this reason, teachers ought to be mindful of the language used in explanations about Islamic recitation of the Qur'an and the *Adhān* (the call to prayer). Different categories of sound are classified into non-music (*non-mūsīqā*) and music (*mūsīqā*). *Non-mūsīqā*, which is considered legitimate (*hallāl*), includes Qur'anic chant, the call to prayer, pilgrimage chants, eulogy chants, chanted poetry with noble themes, family and celebration songs, occupational tunes and military band music. Controversial *mūsīqā* includes vocal and instrumental improvisations, serious metered songs and music of pre-Islamic or non-Islamic origin. *Mūsīqā* considered illegitimate (*harām*) involves all types of sensuous music (Nasr 1997:222). For classroom use, there are many examples on YouTube of songs in praise of Allah (*qasida*) and songs in praise of the Prophet Muhammad (*naat*), including recordings of the *Adhān* (Figure 7.5).

■ **Figure 7.5** Muslim 'bilal', or the assistant to the imam, calls for prayer, or performs 'azan' (*Adhān*)

Photo credit: © Shutterstock/Bianda Ahmad Hisham

By way of contrast, the attitude of the Sufis to music is different from the attitude of other branches of Islam. Abū Hāmid al-Ghazzālī, who is regarded as one of the greatest Islamic thinkers, argued in favour of music, stating its importance for preparing the heart to intensify the worship of God. The ritual dance of the Sufis, which is part of the *sema* ceremony, is a devotional act called *dhikr* (also called *zikr*) and is based on this understanding. The dancers spin in a circle on one foot at varying speeds to assist the soul's movement towards Allah. As part of this ritual, the music and whirling enables the dancers to enter a trance-like state in which they become ecstatic (Miller and Shahriari 2012:271). The most well-known group associated with this ceremony is the Mevlevi sect, more commonly known in the West as the 'Whirling Dervishes' founded by Jalal al-Din Muhammad Rumi (1207–73 CE). The ritual is performed in traditional dress, in a sleeveless white garment, a long-sleeved jacket, a belt, and a black overcoat, which is removed before the whirling begins (see Figure 7.6). It might be possible for teachers to invite a Sufi group to the school who could perform and explain the ritual to the pupils. Alternatively, clips sourced from YouTube could also aid reflection on the significance of the movements, removal of garments, and music used to accompany the dance. These two contrasting approaches to music in Islam can be explored by the children sensitively (Table 7.3).

The importance of music or sacred recitation in RE cannot be underestimated. Music, as briefly illustrated, plays an integral part in communicating beliefs, teachings, practices of worship, and rituals in all the principal religions. The inclusion of music in RE thus

■ **Figure 7.6** Turkish Sufi dancers perform 'religious dancing', Turkey, 2008

Photo credit: © Armend Nimani/AFD/Getty Images

---

■ **Table 7.3** Attitudes towards music in Islam – Exploring attitudes towards music in two branches of Islam – Year 6

---

Do NOT ask children which approach is right/wrong (e.g. chapter 7 this volume). Rather encourage the children to critically appraise the beliefs and understand why they are so different.
Why do the Sufis think music intensifies their worship?
Why do some Muslims abhor sensuous music?

---

enhances creativity in teaching and learning, fulfils the curriculum requirements for including the creative arts in RE, and above all promotes pupils' spiritual, social, moral and cultural development.

# ART IN RE

The deepest mysteries and most treasured truths at the heart of the world's great religious traditions are often communicated through the visual arts. The icons and symbols of a faith often capture the distinctive core beliefs central to the religion. For example, the tortured on the cross says something very different about the nature of the spiritual path from the message communicated in the image of the Buddha in meditation. These contrasting images remind us that we cannot encourage our pupils to think that all religions are saying basically the same thing. We need to pay attention to the significant differences between faiths as well as seek the common ground. Unless we help our pupils to develop the skills to interpret religious art and to ponder questions about its meaning, a whole dimension of religion will remain closed to them and they will lack the confidence to interpret the many outward forms of religious faith.

In this section of the chapter we will focus on two ways to bring art and RE together in a creative curriculum. First we will look at reasons for engaging pupils in the creative process of interpreting the symbols, icons, images and visual expressions of religion and identify some strategies for doing this. Second, we will look at opportunities for pupils to explore religious themes, concepts, beliefs, stories, ideas and feelings through creating their own artwork, making their own symbols and expressing themselves in a variety of visual forms in RE.

One reason for getting pupils engaged in looking at religious art is to help them understand the nature of religion. Through his phenomenological approach, Ninian Smart (1968) offered a framework for the study of religions identifying six dimensions: ritual, doctrinal, mythological, ethical, social and experiential. Later he introduced a seventh: the material or aesthetic dimension. These dimensions have influenced the way teachers approach the study of religion, but perhaps the aesthetic dimension has too often remained an afterthought and has been left out of the planning for RE. Engaging with the material or aesthetic dimension is essential for ensuring that pupils become 'literate' in terms of understanding religion, or as Gates (1975) calls it in his essay 'religiate'. It could be argued that developing skills in visual literacy in RE is just as important as securing the skills for interpreting religious language, words and texts.

A second reason to get pupils looking at religious art in RE is to develop a wide range of essential skills for the subject such as enquiry, investigation, interpretation, creative thinking and empathy, as well as communication and skills of expression. These skills can be found listed in nearly every local agreed syllabus for RE. They are also identified in the National Non-Statutory Framework (QCA 2004).

A third reason for engaging pupils with the artwork of the great religious traditions is that it can enhance opportunities for their spiritual development. Religious art can raise deep questions about existence and reality. It can inspire a sense of awe and wonder, as this artist remembers when he was confronted with three massive twelfth-century carvings of the Buddha in Sri Lanka:

> I was half the height I am now, so they appeared twice as big. I could see that the rock was the same and therefore they had somehow been formed from the cliff face, but I couldn't imagine what possible agency was involved. The cliff wasn't there but the Buddhas were: something huge was missing and something huge was present. . . . it left a deep impression connected to a raw physical apprehension of presence and absence.
>
> (Deacon 2014)

Of course we cannot take our children to Sri Lanka for an afternoon, but pupils looking up at the form of a great cathedral might well feel a similar sense of awe and wonder. Or, to give a different example, the exquisite detail in a painting such as *The Adoration of the Kings* by Jan Gossaert (1500) can capture the imagination of the child and yield deep questions and insights. This painting is included in the National Gallery's *The Image of Christ: Resource Pack* for schools (National Gallery Education Department 2000); it is also available online (www.nationalgallery.org.uk/paintings/circle-of-jan-gossaert-the-adoration-of-the-kings). If the teacher cannot take pupils to the cathedral or the art gallery, then the internet offers virtual tours of places of worship and other technologies offer ready access to the great works of religious art in the classroom. So why is it that religious art is used so little in RE when it enhances creativity and learning?

One of the reasons why the teacher may be cautious about using art in RE could be anxiety about breaking certain rules or conventions or the fear of giving offence. It is certainly true that the relationship between religion and art is not straightforward. Some groups within religious traditions are very cautious about the use of artwork. One of the reasons for this has been the risk of the image becoming the focus of worship rather than the truth it represents. Early in the history of Buddhism there were no images of the Buddha. The dharma or truth was represented in symbols such as the wheel, the sacred footprint or the empty throne. In the Jewish tradition the commandment to avoid the creation of any graven image runs very deep. The synagogue windows of the Jewish Museum in Manchester tell the story of the Exodus in colour and shape, but there is no picture of Moses and no humans are depicted in the stained glass. In the history of Islam there have been periods when pictures of Muhammad were employed to help tell the story of the Prophet. However, later guidelines did not permit this and to represent Muhammad or any of the prophets in visual image is forbidden in Islam.

It is also true that neither human beings nor other animals should be represented in the decoration of mosques or the illumination of the Qur'an so as to avoid the risk of idolatry. A direct outcome of this ruling has been the extraordinary richness of the calligraphy and the ornate designs for the tiles and walls of mosques based on elaborate plant forms and geometric patterns. All the faiths have their guidelines on how the truth can be represented. There is a summary of the way in which different Christian traditions have either forbidden or exploited the depiction of Christ in Northcote's book for teachers on using art in RE (Northcote 1999). In exploring the different guidelines about how images are used you might want to take in a family photograph that you treasure and that you would not want someone to spoil or misuse. There are significant challenges here for creating art in the RE classroom – but engaging with these challenges makes for good RE.

If we want to encourage pupils to engage with the symbols, icons, images and visual expressions of faith we might ask what teaching and learning strategies are to be recommended. It would not be appropriate to expect the pupil to respond as a believer, to kiss the icon of Christ or meditate on the image of the Buddha. So the question is, how can we engage the pupils in responding to the artwork of religion in a way that is both appropriate and likely to enhance learning and creativity?

In her visit to a church in *Eggshells and Thunderbolts* (BBC and Culham College Institute 2003), Mary Stone invites the pupils to respond directly to what they think and feel as they sit in quietness for a few minutes. Her message is 'don't just do something, sit there' (Stone 1995). The pupils reflect and come up with their own thoughts, feelings, insights and questions. They can then go on to explore and find out more about the things they see in the church.

The teacher will need to judge the situation and the likely response of their own pupils; there may be occasions when what they see is going to appear very strange, and there is a danger of a flippant response or a lack of respect that may cause offence. The teacher will need to provide a platform for learning so that pupils can feel engaged rather than uncomfortable. Table 9.3 shows a strategy that we can use to encourage thinking skills and creative engagement with the visual arts in RE. It is taken from the three Rs of the Visual Literacy Toolkit (Woods 2008; see Table 7.4).

---

**■ Table 7.4** Response, Research, Reflection

Response

This is an invitation for the pupils to make an initial, personal response to the image or piece of artwork. The pupils are invited to talk about their observations, their immediate thoughts and feelings. It is an opportunity to think about what the colours, shapes and symbols might mean or to imagine why they were chosen.

Research

In this second stage pupils find out more about the artwork through their own enquiry and research. They can investigate who made it or find out how it was made or what it is made of. The pupils might also try to find out what the image is about and explore the content of the picture or the icon. This is an opportunity to unpack and interpret the symbols or the story behind it. Another line of enquiry that they might pursue is to ask about the audience – who was this piece of artwork intended for and how is it used in worship or religious practice? In this way the pupils can unpack the context of the work of art.

Reflection

In the last stage of the strategy and in the light of their findings, pupils reflect on how they view the artwork from their new and more informed standpoint. They may see things differently from how they first viewed it. They might want to change their minds about its meaning or they might want to think about how a piece of artwork can have different meanings. A further stage in the act of reflection might be to involve the pupils in painting their own icons, designing their own mandalas or illuminating their own favourite texts.

---

**■ Table 7.5** Reflecting on Hindu and Christian images

- Reflecting on the Hindu image of Siva dancing can help pupils explore ideas about creation and questions about the nature of God, about cycles of life, about destruction and re-creation. Investigating a faith through the different cultural traditions is important in terms of ensuring an inclusive curriculum.
- The variety of images of Jesus from across the world and through the centuries challenges us to see the Christian experience of faith from a range of different perspectives. The way artists have represented Jesus can generate fresh ideas about familiar material (Blaylock 2004) and throw light on the universality of the Christ figure (see chapter 10).

---

Art helps us to see things differently and from engaging with it we get a new perspective on life or see the world around us in a new light. Things can become more vivid or more extraordinary as a result of our encounter with the work of an artist. Using art in RE encourages a range of important skills such as interpretation, creative thinking, seeing things from another perspective and perceiving different levels of meaning. See Table 7.5.

Some forms of religious art are designed to tell stories of courage and faith or to communicate moral teachings and guidance. In most gurdwaras there will be images of the Sikh gurus on the walls of the langar or in the entrance hall. They are rarely found in the main prayer hall so as to avoid the risk of the image becoming an object of worship. The gurus are there as role models and inspiration for good works and *sewa*, or selfless action. Through research and discussion pupils can begin to identify the teachings and unpack the details of the stories. One of these images and its story could be the stimulus for a lesson using the community of enquiry or P4C approach (see chapter 3). Using the resource in this way would provide a valuable opportunity for developing questioning skills and creative thinking.

Some religious art is intended to help believers fathom the mystery of the transcendent or a reality beyond the one we see in the everyday world. For Orthodox Christians, icons are intended as windows into another reality or invisible world (Cook 2005:13). They expand the concept of the Christian community to include those who have lived, believed and trodden the path of faith in previous ages. Pupils can find out about the way icons are made and learn about the layers of spiritual meaning that are expressed in the many layers of paint. They can go on to create their own examples of icons, perhaps of people that they believe have shown the way in terms of faith, courage or compassion.

In RE pupils will encounter a range of religious concepts such as incarnation, covenant, ummah, remembrance, reconciliation, promised land, heaven, karma and nirvana. We can try to explain these terms using texts, stories and discussion. But these concepts are bigger than the words and phrases we employ to explain them. Pupils can bring together their thoughts, responses and ideas and express them in colour, shape, texture, form and visual designs. They can create a poster advertising 'The Promised Land' or design a display for a wall of 'Reconciliation' in the classroom. Religious art is often the work of a community and usually belongs within the context of the family of believers. Classroom displays can express shared values and vision and capture something of the nature of the religious art enterprise (see chapter 6).

If we provide opportunities for pupils to express themselves in RE through the use of colour, shape, texture, image and symbol, they can begin to see how knowledge is not only to be found through the scientific process of enquiry but that there are other kinds of knowing and other kinds of wisdom to be explored through art and creativity. Creative work in RE allows pupils with visual and kinaesthetic learning styles to express themselves and explore meaning without using words. For example, having visited the Salvation Army church or having discussed its motto they can design a flag to represent the meaning of 'Blood and Fire'. Or to give another example, pupils might watch a video of a Muslim child talking about how they pray at home and discuss what they have seen and heard. They can then think carefully about their own design for a carpet that would be appropriate for prayer or quiet time (see Figures 7.7 through 7.12).

What does the teacher need for a creative classroom where pupils are doing art or making music in RE? Paul Key (2009) believes that three things are essential. First, the teacher needs flexibility to allow space for imagination. Second, teachers must be ambitious in terms of the high expectations for the quality of the learning. There must be a desire to raise the challenge. Third, there must be a relationship of trust between teacher and child to allow space for the creativity and imagination. There must be a readiness to trust in their ability to respond and 'to allow creativity to unfold' (Lowenfeld and Brittain 1982).

This closely mirrors the view of Lealman, whose chapter in *Religion and the Arts in Education* (Lealman 1993:60) reminds us that 'teacher and student must connect. They are partners in exploring. . . . This requires a real mutuality of participation and exposure; a willingness on behalf of the teacher to share her/his processes of thinking and responding; willingness to make space for the innerness of the students. There must be a desire to acknowledge its mystery; to respond to one enigma – story, parable, metaphor, whatever – with another enigma, rather than with analysis or explanation.'

■ **Figure 7.7** Photographs of examples of pupils' work reproduced from display at the York RE Centre 1994

 Figure 7.8

■ Figure 7.9

 Figure 7.10

■ Figure 7.11

 **Figure 7.12**

## Acknowledgements

We would like to thank the School of Education, University College Cork for funding the procurement of the images used in this chapter.

We would like to acknowledge the use of photographs of pupils' work formerly exhibited at the National Society RE Centre at what was once the College of Ripon and York St John.

# REFERENCES

BBC and Culham College Institute (2003) *Eggshells and Thunderbolts*. London: BBC Education (originally published 1993).

Beck, G. L. (2006) 'Hinduism and Music' in G. L. Beck (Ed.) *Sacred Sound: Experiencing Music in World Religions*. Waterloo, Ontario: Wilfrid Laurier University Press, pp. 113–139.

Blaylock, L. (2004) *Picturing Jesus: Fresh Ideas*. Birmingham: RE Today Christian Education Movement.

Blaylock, L. (2011) 'Spiritual Music: A Source of Spiritual Life and an Energising Power in All Human Life' in *The Religious Education CPD Handbook*. http://re-handbook. org.uk/section/curriculum/religious-education-across-the-curriculum/creativity-and-religious-education#tab-2

Cook, K. (Trans.) (2005) *A History of Icon Painting*. Moscow: Grand Holding Publishers.

Deacon, R. (2014) 'How I learned to see' in *Tate etc.* London: Tate Gallery.

DfE (2013a) *Design and Technology Curriculum for Key Stages 1 and 2*. London: DfE.

DfE (2013b) *Music Programmes of Study for Key Stages 1 and 2*. London: DfE.

DfE and DCMS (2011) *The Importance of Music: A National Plan for Music Education*. London: DfE and DCMS.

Gates, B. G. (1975) in N. Smart and D. Horder (Eds) *New Movements in Religious Education*. London: Temple Smith.

Hollander, P. and Houston, R. (2009) *RE and Music Education: Singing from the Same Song Sheet?* Nottingham: The Stapleford Centre.

Key, P. (2009) 'Creative and imaginative primary art and design' pp. 117–133. in A. Wilson (Ed.) *Creativity in Primary Education*. Exeter: Learning Matters.

Lamont, G. (2008) *Primary Assemblies for a Just World*. London: SPCK.

Lamont, R. (2012) *Primary School Assemblies for Religious Festivals*. London: SPCK.

Lealman, B. (1993) in D. Starkings (Ed.) *Religion and the Arts in Education: Dimensions of Spirituality*. pp. 55–56. Sevenoaks: Hodder & Stoughton.

Lowenfeld, V. and Brittain, W. L. (1982) *Creative and Mental Growth*. New York: Macmillan.

Miller, T. E. and Shahriari, A. (2012) *World Music: A Global Journey*. New York & London: Routledge.

Nasr, S. H. (1997) 'Islam and music: the legal and the spiritual dimensions' in Lawrence E. Sullivan (Ed.) *Enchanting Powers: Music in the World's Religions*. Cambridge, MA: Harvard University Press, pp. 219–236.

National Gallery Education Department (2000) *The Image of Christ: Resource Pack*. London: National Gallery.

Northcote, V. (1999) *Using Art in RE, Using RE in Art*. London: National Society Church House Publishing.

OfSTED (2007) *Making Sense of Religion: A Report of Religious Education in Schools and the Impact of Locally Agreed Syllabuses*. London: OfSTED.

OfSTED (2009) *Making More of Music: An Evaluation of Music in Schools*. London: OfSTED.

QCA (2004) *Religious Education: The Non-Statutory National Framework*. London: QCA.

Smart, N. (1968) *Secular Education and the Logic of Religious Education*. London: Faber.

Stone, M. (1995) *Don't Just Do Something, Sit There: Developing Children's Spiritual Awareness*. Lancaster: St Martin's College.

Wills, R. (2007) 'Children's Spirituality and Music'. http://schoolswork.co.uk/thinking/childrens-spirituality-and-music/P1

Woods, R. (2008) *Visual Literacy in RE Teaching and Learning: Rethinking 18*. Nottingham: The Stapleford Centre.

<table>
<tr><td>CHAPTER<br>8</td><td># DEVELOPING EXPERIENTIAL RE CREATIVELY<br>*John Hammond*</td></tr>
</table>

## INTRODUCTION

The methods of experiential RE are designed to encourage pupils' reflection on their own interior life as a means to understanding better the nature of religion. The publication of the teachers' handbook *New Methods in Religious Education: An Experiential Approach* (Hammond *et al.* 1990), advocating an experiential approach, had a considerable effect nationally on teaching and learning in the subject. The rationale and strategies of the handbook are examined here, and the success of the approach in engaging and motivating pupils is related to its methods and the use of symbol, story and structured silence. Further practical examples of classroom implementation are suggested. Exercises using symbol, story and silence are then related to religious celebration and ritual, and a case for the educational use of ritual is explored together with examples for classroom use.

The publication of *New Methods in Religious Education* in 1990 was met with enthusiasm in classrooms and the acknowledgement by pupils that RE was about them: their hopes and fears, puzzles and struggles. The teachers' handbook, for it saw itself as a book to do, introduced a novel approach and a wealth of teaching strategies and examples; it had a huge impact nationally, renewing the practice of many serving teachers and inspiring numerous trainees.

The authors conveyed the distinctiveness of the experiential approach by using the story of an explorer. An explorer discovers a new land of stunning beauty populated by remarkable animals and exotic plant life. On her return she enthusiastically goes on to all who will listen about the splendour of the place and her awesome experience. Her hearers catch her enthusiasm and beg for a map to enable them better to grasp the detail. She hesitates. What she really wants is for them to take the trip and to go and experience the land for themselves. She fears they might just settle for the map. But they persist, and she relents and draws the map. Grateful, the friends eagerly study the map and make it a subject of seminars. They illuminate and frame it and hang it in galleries, and produce electronic versions with commentaries to send to their friends. But as she feared, all this activity and accumulation of detail becomes a substitute for setting off. They settle for the second-hand. They don't go to experience the place for themselves. She wished she had never made the map.

In the late 1980s, when *New Methods in Religious Education* was devised, the map stood for information on the religions – the details spelled out in the SCAA Model

Syllabuses of the time: the people, histories, beliefs and practices that characterised the particular faiths. Accurately portrayed, this was vital to know. However, you could know all this and still miss the point: the experience of the believer and the power of the faith to move mountains, heal the sick or stir up a holy war. How could one avoid getting lost in the detail and instead get to the essence and lived experience of the religion? What would be the equivalent in the classroom of going to experience for oneself the breath-taking land discovered by the explorer? Not conversion to a particular faith – although that might happen. Was there another alternative, something between an objective description of the elements of a faith and the life of the fully committed believer? For the authors of *New Methods in Religious Education* there was, and it was reached by getting in touch with your own inner or spiritual life. By making this 'interior' journey the learner could come to that place in human experience that the religions addressed and from which he or she could better understand what the faiths were about. The exercises in the book were designed to this end: to bring pupils to a deeper awareness of their own inner life and so enable them to come to a real understanding of the nature of the religions.

The initiative was also a response to what was perceived as an ongoing problem at the heart of the subject: how, in an increasingly secular society, can pupils be brought to a valid understanding of the religious dimension of human experience? The question had preoccupied *Schools' Council Working Paper 36* which in 1970 had spoken of the need for bridge building across the cultural gap between the religions and many pupils' experience of the world. David Hay, the principal author of *New Methods in Religious Education*, had shown through extensive research into religious experience (Hay 1987; Hay and Nye 1998) that a dominant secular culture was continuing to marginalise personal religious experience and a religious view of the world. Though he was able to show that some 40% of people were claiming intense spiritual or religious experience, the vast majority of this group had never before felt able to speak of it. Why? Because they would be thought odd or weird. There seemed to exist a widespread conspiracy which compelled nearly half the population to remain silent about a personal and highly significant dimension of their lives. The exercises in *New Methods in Religious Education* were designed to reinstate this marginalised dimension by providing a means for pupils whereby the validity of these experiences could be acknowledged and their relatedness to the lives of religious people explored.

*New Methods in Religious Education* worked for teachers and their pupils because the experiential exercises it offered motivated and engaged learners. They provided a space where pupils felt safe to reflect on who they are, their hopes and their fears, and thus the possibility of a personal openness and the 'first-person' encounter with the faiths: a real opportunity to 'learn from religion'. The descriptive and analytical skills appropriate to an objective or 'third-person' perspective and the acquisition of Attainment Target 1, learning about religion, were seen as insufficient for 'learning from religion', Attainment Target 2. For this an experiential or first-person approach is necessary.

The approach was not without its critics. It was seen to have a 'subjectivist view of religious truth' (Cooling 1991: 123), to be too preoccupied with 'inner experience' and so promoting 'privatised religion' (Thatcher 1991: 23, 25). It was also described as 'New Age' education (Heelas 1996) and thought, as RE, to be light on religion.

In so far as a number of the – highly popular – exercises were drawn from the writing and practice of humanistic psychology, the criticisms were not without some weight. But the rationale and many of the exercises were explicitly related to religion, and subsequent writing on experiential RE has tied it closer to the practice of the faiths without compromising the considerable gains made by the handbook in bridging the cultural gulf between pupils' experience and the world of religion.

In part, the success of the project was down to the team of experienced teachers and teacher trainers who developed the methods and tested them in a group of pilot schools. But it was also about the nature of the methods used. The exercises selected in the handbook could be grouped under three headings. They involved:

- working with *symbols*;
- using *stories*;
- practising structured *silence*.

Is there something essentially motivating or engaging for learners about exercises involving symbol, story and silence? There appears to be. All three are characterised by an invitation and a required response. They all require of the learner an engagement, an openness, a certain personal commitment to the activity. So in choosing or creating a personal symbol I need to draw on my understanding of who I am and what I value. To engage successfully with the activity and to create a symbol which feels authentic requires a response which is a truthful expression of my identity and history. Symbols cannot be validly created or interpreted without this personal engagement. The meaning in the symbol is, in the first instance, its meaning for me.

Similarly with stories. Good stories are irresistible. As J.R.R. Tolkien knew, they draw us into their world to better understand our own. The experience of the people and places in the story can help me see more about my life in the world beyond the page. On finishing the story I might be a wiser person. The world of the story beckons, but to benefit I must respond, be open to it and bring my own understanding to engage with the events, to challenge and be challenged by them.

Again with silence. Through the process of a stilling exercise I can begin to set aside distractions, the clamour of all the deeds done and the demands of others, and just be still, aware of and present to myself. All I have to do is do nothing. Let go of the business of hiding or justifying; just be still and wait. In this state of quiet openness and apparent passivity I can come to an awareness of myself and gain insights available only within the silence.

All three – symbols, stories and silence – give meaning and extend understanding but only through an act of interpretation, and interpretation is always personal. Exercises that incorporate any of the three have the potential to both fascinate and reveal. Involvement with symbols, stories and silence can provide new insights, a way of going beyond or transcending present knowledge, which is why they are embedded in the religions. Over the millennia, symbols, stories and silence have been at the centre of religious discourse and practice. The success of *New Methods in Religious Education* was that it used some very old methods. But it used them to engage and motivate in an educational rather than a religious setting. The aim was to deepen personal awareness and acquire a better understanding of religion, not bring about commitment to a particular faith.

Within the faiths, symbol, story and silence usually sit within the overarching structure of celebration or ritual. But before examining ritual further and asking whether it is advisable or educationally sound to conduct rituals in classrooms, let us consider some teaching strategies drawing on symbol, story and silence.

Symbols, the philosopher Paul Ricoeur reminds us in a nutshell, give rise to thought. They are the source of endless meaning which we supply as we respond. Pupils therefore choosing a symbol for themselves – perhaps an animal, a song or piece of music, or a colour, or a flower or tree, or something they paint or make like a shield or coat of arms – are creating meaning. They invest the chosen symbol with elements of their identity and can, in subsequent discussion of their symbol, begin to read out of it more of who they are. And there are no wrong answers. The artwork may be more or less accomplished, and the discussion more or less sophisticated, but if the exercise is undertaken seriously, they get it right. For in this context the symbol means what they think it means. This can be a particularly good learning experience for those who often don't get it right.

But this is not the case with the great universal symbols. The symbols of light and darkness, of the tree or the journey, are invested with near timeless cultural meanings which are learned rather than chosen. Across the globe light and darkness invoke good and evil, hope and despair, the blessed and the cursed. The tree is a sign of life and growth, renewal, change and heritage. The journey is a symbol of life's pathway, from place of origin to time of end, mapping the decisions, satisfactions and frustrations. Though these symbols can be given a personal spin, their meanings are largely determined by our culture and language, so through meeting them in books or films, in art or ads, pupils learn more of the complexities of human life and, by gaining expertise with the currency, express with more subtlety their own experience.

The rich and complex world of religious art embodies the meanings at the heart of a faith and provides windows into its central beliefs and practices. By exploring the cross or the crescent or reflecting on a seated Buddha or working with the Islamic geometric patterns which decorate mosques or a statue of the dancing Siva, pupils can come to understand more of the insights and motivation of the believers. These symbols which draw on universal symbols give rise to the particular meanings at the heart of the faith.

The following three examples show how this might look for Key Stage 2 (KS2).

## SOME EXAMPLES USING SYMBOLS AND STORY

1.    Using the symbol of the tree.

Start by reflecting with the class on images of great and ancient trees. Trees are the biggest living things on the planet – the sequoias, or giant redwoods, in California can be taller than St Paul's Cathedral, measuring 115 metres high. Trees are also the oldest living things – the bristlecone pines, in the White Mountains of Nevada, live up to 4,000 years. Present-day trees were mature specimens before the pyramids were built.

What huge and ancient trees do the pupils know? What is it like to stand under the branches of a towering tree? How many generations have come and gone during the life of this tree?

Trees have been seen as bridges, through time, across the generations, and through space, between the earth and the heavens. A great tree can span centuries, many generations of human endeavour, its roots drawing nourishment deep from the earth and our past. And every spring it renews itself and our world with the appearance of new growth at the tips of its branches.

Provide, or enable each pupil to make, a number of paper green leaves and some brown twisted roots. Like trees we have roots; these are our past, all the people and things that make us who we are: our families (siblings, parents, grandparents, great-grandparents), the places we have lived, the languages we speak, local communities, all our experiences, health and sickness, struggles and successes. Each pupil writes on or marks several paper roots to show something of their own 'roots' and what has made them who they are.

And like trees we are growing and changing. What are our new shoots? What are the new things we are learning, getting better at? What are the new friendships? How else am I changing? What would I really like to achieve? Taking the paper leaves, pupils write on them or mark them to show some of these changes, the new aspects of themselves which are making them the person they are to become.

Then on a large wall-mounted outline of a tree with branches and roots pupils can attach their own roots and shoots to form a class tree which shows their collective past and future growth. Given time to view the tree, they may be prompted by the roots and shoots of others to want to add extra ones of their own. Can we give a name to our tree? What else can the tree tell us? What does it say about the complex and different roots which make up this one class? On a living tree every root feeds every shoot. So on our tree the pasts of others mix with our experience to shape in some way our own new growth and future. The symbol of the tree can continue giving rise to thought. The exercise can be extended through images of the tree found in religious art: the Christian cross as a living tree, the tree of life on Islamic prayer mats, the tree showing the spread of the Buddhist Dharma.

2.      Working with 'the spider webs' of God.

The intricate, tessellated patterns in mosaic which decorate the great mosques are stunning. The recurring, complex designs follow strict geometrical patterns and colour-coded rules. They enhance the beauty of the architecture but also carry an important theological teaching at the heart of Islam: as the presence of Allah who cannot be seen or imaged gives shape and order to his creation, the universe, so 'the spider webs', the 'invisible' white lines, give shape and order to the coloured mosaics which form the beautiful patterns. The presence of Allah, who must never be represented, is 'evident' in the absence of colour, the white borders that create and order the patterns.

An exercise using symbols in Islamic art to convey Muslim belief might run as follows. Provide photocopied sheets from books of Islamic art (A. Roeder 2010). The patterns repeat infinitely, so provide interlocking copies from any one pattern, one for each pupil in a group of six. Provide copies of different patterns for each of the other groups. Show them pictures of great mosques, point out the patterns and explain the colour coding: same shape of mosaic, same colour and the spaces between ('the spider webs') are left white. Each pupil within the group takes responsibility for their own sheet but the common colour coding needs to be decided jointly before they begin. Let them know that when completed, all six copies will be mounted and joined together to form one continuous pattern.

The colouring-in requires concentration and attention to detail. As one sloppy contribution will ruin the effect of the whole, the groups tend to provide their own quality control. The activity is calming, almost meditative, and the effect of the completed and mounted set impressive: the makers are justly proud of their joint endeavour. The sets could also be used to decorate an outline of a wall-mounted mosque.

Then return to the images of the great mosques, interiors and exteriors, and compare them with images of cathedrals. Pupils can grasp that whereas the divine image is present in and on the Christian cathedrals, in paintings and images of the Trinity and statues and pictures of Jesus, there is nothing of this in or on the mosques. For the mosques the decoration is confined to verses from the Qur'an in Arabic, the geometric patterns, and perhaps arabesques, swirling leaf-like designs. A review of the account of Muhammad's victorious entry into Mecca and subsequent ridding of the images of the gods from the Kaaba will show dramatically the prohibition against representing Allah in early Islam. But a careful consideration of the patterns can show that in the emptiness of the spaces that order the coloured shapes, there is a reminder of the Muslim belief of the sustaining presence of the un-representable Allah.

3.   The symbol of the journey.

The familiar concept that life is a journey is mapped in some detail by the poet W. H. Auden in an essay on J.R.R. Tolkien, 'The Quest Hero' (Auden 1968). Applying the idea to Tolkien's trilogy, *The Lord of the Rings*, itself an epic journey, Auden identifies six characteristics of any journey which is a quest, that is, a journey with a point. These are the heroine or hero who undertakes the journey, the journey itself, the obstacles encountered, the helpers who smooth the passage, the hinderers who add to the difficulties, and finally, a goal or treasure achieved at the journey's end.

Like the quest, our life's journey – from birth to present and into the future – involves dealing with obstacles, receiving help and encouragement from others, coping with people who add to our difficulties and pushing on towards a dream or ideal. The symbol of the journey is a symbol extended over time and space and so a narrative, a story. This symbol exercise can therefore be used also as a means of working creatively with stories.

Starting with a quest story (Beast Quest, The Hobbit, Harry Potter, Dora the Explorer, Jason and the Argonauts, Red Riding Hood . . .), pupils can be asked to identify the six elements. What other stories do they know that are quest stories? Can they find the six characteristics in these?

If they were the hero or heroine of a quest what would their journey be? Their responses can be expressed graphically, in the form of a route they draw or paint that winds across a large sheet of paper. On this route, showing their journey from their birth to the present, can be plotted significant obstacles – depicted as they choose, literally or symbolically – then, again expressed in appropriate images, their helpers and hinderers and finally their goal or treasure and, what is more difficult to imagine and express, the treasure that still lies in the future.

The symbol of the journey can prompt serious reflection on the course of a life, enable the recognition and naming of obstacles and reveal the sources of support and obstruction. It also raises, unselfconsciously, the question of a worthwhile aim – what is life about?

The classic stories of religion and mythology, and the endless subsequent texts they inspire, confront us with the glorious and the tragic and the transcendent and provide models to imitate or reject. Engaging with this literature extends horizons and enriches lives. Auden's categories can also be a means of exploring explicitly religious texts: the wanderings of the ancient Hebrews in their search for a promised land; Islamic calendars date from the Hegira, Muhammad's flight or journey from Mecca to Medina. The enduring significance of the journey in Islam is evident too in the Haaj, the pilgrimage to Mecca and one of the Five Pillars. The Buddha sets off on a quest for enlightenment following his confrontation with sickness, old age, death and a wandering holy man. There is also – in all the faiths – the phenomenon of pilgrimage: the journey of transformation where the pilgrim leaves the comfortable and familiar to face danger and uncertainty on the way to the holy place. From this place of heightened awareness and spiritual intensity the pilgrim will return, changed, to live a better life.

One version of pilgrimage, for those who couldn't quite manage to go, could be imported into a school playground. The labyrinth, set in stone on the floors of medieval cathedrals, gave an alternative trip to Jerusalem for those unable to undertake the rigours of the physical journey. The labyrinth in Chartres cathedral is 13 metres in diameter with its unicursal – single path and so no choices – pathway, winding 60 metres from entrance to the centre, the holy city of Jerusalem. The labyrinth is a microcosm of a pilgrimage and a life journey. Painted on a playground, the ancient pattern excites interest and invites participation. Pupils aware of its origin and purpose can make their own journey, in silence, to the centre and back. As they enter they can be given a version of the question put to generations of pilgrims: 'What do you seek?' The silent walking, governed by the dynamics of the labyrinth, seems to create a calm and reflective attitude in participants, enabling a measured consideration of present experience and a space to consider where life is going (http://labyrinthsociety.org).

Silence isn't easy. Noise and other people don't seem to want to leave us alone. But the benefits claimed for structured silence are considerable:

■ Helping concentration and the ability to learn.
■ Experiencing physical relaxation.
■ Developing imagination.
■ Helping creativity.
■ Finding a peaceful place within the mind that can be restful and that can help us understand and accept ourselves. (Fontana and Slack 1997: 37)

In the particular context of RE we could add that a developed ability to be still and silent can enable pupils to better recognise and understand the significance of the meditative traditions which are central to many of the world's faith.

Exercises appropriate to KS1 and KS2 involving a range of stilling and meditative exercises that attend to posture, breathing and the use of the imagination, plus guidelines for their management, are available from a number of sources (Fontana and Slack 1997; Erricker and Erricker 2001; Hammond *et al.* 1990).

## Ritual and celebration in the classroom

Earlier it was suggested that symbol, story and silence were constituent elements of celebration or ritual. For example, many rituals (Easter, Passover, Divali, Wesak, Eid, Vaisakhi) incorporate readings from the scriptures, the founding narratives or stories of the faith; they will involve symbolic objects, clothing and gestures. Silence, as meditative practice, will have a ritualised setting that takes account of posture and breathing and can draw on music and narrative. Rituals are woven from symbol, story and silence. If, as we have seen, exercises drawing on these elements can be highly effective ways of motivating learners and enabling a better understanding of religion, should we also be using rituals in the classroom? To come to a conclusion we need first to take a closer look at the nature of ritual.

With reference to *The Encyclopaedia of Religion* and the writings of anthropologists (Turner 1969, 1974; Driver 1992; Schechner and Appel 1990), a description of ritual might run as follows: rituals consist of repetitious and stylised bodily actions – sequences of gestures, words and objects, performed in a special place to influence powers or forces beyond the immediate world of the actors. Rituals are bodily – you can't perform them in your head – and made more effective by repetition: they don't wear out with use. They are performed in a place set apart from ordinary everyday activity. They transform those who perform them; in fact their business is to effect transformations that cannot otherwise be brought about.

They consist of three distinct phases:

- **separation** – the participants go out of their everyday world to a separate place, made special by architecture, decoration, lighting, music;
- **'liminality'** – the place of transformation, of crossing a threshold or 'limen' into a new awareness or a new reality;
- **reaggregation** – the return, as a changed person or group, into the everyday world.

So in marriage rituals two people dressed in special clothes go to a place apart – church, mosque, temple, synagogue or registry office – to exchange promises, make statements of intent, receive blessings (or perhaps break glasses or walk round a fire) and then return to the world changed into a couple with a new joint identity. The description fits rituals in places of worship and pilgrimage but is not confined to things religious, or even human. Other primates have rituals of mating and conflict, and numerous social, political and sporting events fall into the ritual pattern: participants separate to the place of the match, rally or concert. In an atmosphere altered by a heaving crowd, decorations, special lighting, chanting, speeches, gestures, food and drink, they undergo a transformation or affirmation of identity which can strengthen bonds and shift perceptions. Then they return, more or less changed, into the routines of everyday life.

As we have seen, exercises incorporating symbols, stories or silence effectively engage and involve learners. Consequently, the cumulative effect of all three as ritual can – as is the case of a religious celebration, a political rally, a concert or a big match – make a powerful impact on participants. Are the effects of ritual appropriate to the classroom?

Earlier we saw how the authors of *New Methods in Religious Education* looked for a 'middle way', a position between an objective description of religious phenomena and commitment to a particular religion. The same question can be applied to ritual in classrooms: is there a 'middle way' between observing and describing ritual, on the one hand (important, but flat) and the participants' committed involvement, on the other (powerful, but inappropriate). It seems there is and it is called theatre. (For more detail on this see Hammond 2002 and the work of Sue Phillips 2011.)

In their structure and origins, ritual and theatre are close relatives. But as well as similarities there are important differences. Whereas both use 'dramatic' elements – dress, decoration, lighting, music – and the dynamics of the group to heighten participation and convey meaning, ritual will have a transcendent focus and requires belief, while theatre's focus is on the here and now of the performance and the audience is left to provide its own meaning. So it is possible to draw on those elements of theatre/ritual which predispose the performer/learner to a reflective and engaged attitude without entailing a commitment to a specific belief. Take the example of a Passover meal, the annual celebration by Jewish communities of the historic exodus from slavery. Pupil participation in the meal through sitting at the decorated table, hearing the readings and tasting the foods and drink produces a dramatic effect, encouraging reflection and involvement. But this is theatre in education, serious and respectful of an important celebration in the life of the Jewish people but not requiring or resulting in belief. The predisposition towards engagement and reflection encouraged by the 'atmospheric' setting and participation in the event can result in important insights into what religious ritual does for those who perform it. This understanding, gained by means of performance, is of a different order than that acquired by reading a description or seeing a film.

Both religious and non-religious rituals can be used. As well as festivals there could be rites of passage – initiations, coming-of-age ceremonies, marriages and funerals. Because enactment tends to hook in the performers' own experience, the last needs particular sensitivity. Forms of celebration could be used to mark important events in the life of the class or school: beginnings and endings and significant changes. They can provide a context for the unselfconscious sharing of joy or sadness and bring fresh insights to problems. In *Thinking Like a Mountain: Towards a Council of All Beings* (Seed, Macy, Fleming and Naess 1988), the task of identifying with elements of the natural world or threatened species, the activity of mask making and gathering in the circle of the 'Council' to speak through one's mask as one's 'being' provide an involving means of thoughtfully exploring environmental issues and a structured opportunity for expressing fears and hopes for endangered species and the life of the planet.

## CONCLUSION

We have argued that RE's second attainment target, learning from religion, requires a particular kind of teaching strategy. The experiential approach as set out in *New Methods in Religious Education* and developed subsequently has been and will continue to be an important element in any scheme which enables pupils to reflect seriously on their own lives and relate their thinking to the teaching and practice of the world's religions. Because the key processes of the approach – symbol, story, silence and celebration or ritual – are shared in common with the faiths, then there is a sense in which success in 'learning about' (AT1) and 'learning from' (AT2) appears to be best served by 'learning with' religion. However, though the elements of language and meaning making are common across a spectrum of human pursuits – education, theatre and religion – the context and intent of the classroom and the aims of education to provide knowledge and understanding remain of a different order from the loyalty and life-long commitment which are the intention of the faith communities.

## ADDITIONAL RESOURCES

Hammond, J. (2005) 'Children Use Their Imagination for Spirituality', *RE Today*, vol. 22, no. 3 (Summer): 6.

Turner, V. (1969) *The Ritual Process*. Ithaca, NY: Cornell University Press.

## REFERENCES

Auden, W. H. (1968) 'The Quest Hero' in *Tolkien and the Critics*, ed. Isaacs, N. D., and Zimbardo, R. A. London: University of Notre Dame Press, 40–62.

Cooling, T. (1991) Book Review, New Methods in Religious Education, *British Journal of Religious Education*, vol. 13, no. 2: 122–4.

Driver, T. (1992) *The Magic of Ritual*. New York: Harper One.

Erricker, C., and Erricker, J. (eds) (2001) *Meditation in Schools: A Practical Guide to Calmer Classrooms*. London: Continuum.

Fontana, D., and Slack, I. (1997) *Teaching Meditation to Children: A Practical Guide to the Use and Benefits of Basic Meditation Techniques*. Shaftesbury: Element.

Hammond, J., Hay, D., Moxon, J., Netto, B., Raban, K., Straugheir, G., and Williams, C. (1990) *New Methods in Religious Education Teaching: An Experiential Approach*. Oliver and Boyd.

Hammond, J. (2002) 'Embodying the Spirit' in *Issues in Religious Education*, ed. Broadbent, L., and Brown, A. London: RoutledgeFalmer, chapter 15.

Hay, D. (1987) *Exploring Inner Space*. Oxford: Mowbray.

Hay, D., and Nye, R. (1998) *The Spirit of the Child*. London: Harper Collins.

Heelas, P. (1996) *The New Age Movement*. Blackwell.

Phillips, S. (2011) theatreoflearning.org

Roeder, A (2010) *Islamic Art Colouring Book*. New York: Prestel.

Schechner, R., and Appel, W. (1990) *By Means of Performance*. Cambridge: Cambridge University Press.

Seed, J., Macy, J., Fleming, P., and Naess, A. (1988) *Thinking Like a Mountain: Towards a Council of All Beings*. London: Heretic Books.

Thatcher, A. (1991) 'A Critique of Inwardness in Religious Education', *British Journal of Religious Education*, vol. 14, no. 1: 22–7.

Turner, V. (1969) *The Ritual Process: Structure and Anti-structure*. Chicago: Aldine Publishing.

Turner, V. (1974) *Drama, Fields and Metaphors: Symbolic Action in Human Society*. Ithaca, New York: Cornell University Press.

# INTERFAITH DIALOGUE IN THE CLASSROOM

*Julia Ipgrave*

## INTRODUCTION: DIALOGUE AND RE

Few primary school teachers in the United Kingdom can be strangers to the concept of dialogic learning. The development of children's linguistic, social and thinking skills through classroom dialogue has been a prominent theme over the last three decades and more in what has been described as 'a gathering momentum' of dialogic pedagogy (Alexander, 2008). In their training and professional development, today's teachers are likely to have encountered the work and thought of Robin Alexander, Neil Mercer and other champions of classroom dialogue (Alexander, 2001, 2008; Mercer, 2000). While Alexander's focus has largely been on teacher–pupil exchanges in class, Mercer and colleagues have developed a pedagogy for group discussion, *Thinking Together*, which was incorporated into the *Primary National Strategy* and has been very influential (Dawes *et al.*, 2004; Littleton *et al.*, 2005; DfES, 2006). Dialogic pedagogies are particularly attractive to primary school teachers as they combine key elements of learning, relational skills of social interaction, linguistic skills of communication and cognitive skills of critical thought. The *Strategy* expects children at the end of their primary education to be able to 'acknowledge other people's views, justifying or modifying their own views in to the light of what others say' and 'share, test and evaluate ideas' in group discussion (DfES, 2006, p36). *Thinking Together* views dialogue as negotiation between different perspectives, a convergence of understandings leading to joint discovery of 'new and better ways of making sense' (Mercer, 2000, p102–3). The dialogue process creates a 'community of inquiry' in the classroom (Littleton *et al.*, 2005, p9).

These generic pedagogies are intended for application across the primary curriculum, though tailored to the requirements of specific subject disciplines. The question for this chapter is where RE and its subject matter sit in relation to this interest in classroom dialogue. The view of the Religious Education Council (REC) is that the relationship between RE and dialogue is very strong. There are several compelling reasons for its view that 'dialogue has to be at the heart of good RE' (REC, n.d., p4) (see Table 9.1).

Reasons for putting dialogue at the heart of RE are both relational and cognitive. If care is not taken, these two purposes can conflict. Various influences have licensed an increasingly robust critical approach to religion in RE. In response to 9/11 and the 2005 terrorist attacks in London, the 2007 OfSTED report on RE recommended that 'we should

---

■ **Table 9.1** Arguments for dialogue in RE

---

■ RE, like other curriculum subjects, has its own language (or languages) that can be acquired and understood through verbal interaction in lessons.

■ The essential condition for dialogue – difference – is especially obvious in the religious plurality in British society.

■ Many classrooms in the country reflect this plurality, containing students of different religious and non-religious identities. Still greater variety can be engineered through dialogue with children in other schools, whether face-to-face or by electronic communication (McKenna et al., 2008).

■ RE was given a particularly prominent role in the educational drive for 'community cohesion'. While the 2001 Cantle Report on some northern towns depicted a community segregated along religious lines (Home Office, 2001), RE could serve community harmony by bringing people together across religious difference and promoting mutual understanding.

■ The subject matter of RE, the diversity of religious perspectives and the interest in different levels of meaning offer particular cognitive challenges to the learner; dialogue around these issues promotes higher level thinking skills, an aspect of RE pedagogy that has been receiving increasing attention in recent years (McCreery et al., 2008, chap. 5).

■ There already exists a long and rich tradition of inter faith dialogue from which RE can learn (as this chapter aims to demonstrate).

---

dispense with the notion that we should encourage pupils to think uncritically of religion as a good thing' (OfSTED, 2007, p40). Secular voices, in particular that of the British Humanist Association, recommend a thinking RE where pupils are engaged in 'analysing, evaluating and criticising beliefs and philosophies', even though, it is acknowledged, 'some students may take criticisms personally' (IPPR, 2004, p8). Educationalist Michael Hand suggests that students should be actively encouraged 'to question the religious beliefs they bring with them into the classroom' so 'they are genuinely free to adopt whatever position on religious matters they judge to be best supported by the evidence' (Hand, 2004, p162).

This emphasis on analysis, evaluation and criticism resonates with the thinking-through-talk approaches promoted by advocates of dialogic pedagogies, but there is potential for tension and hurt when they are applied to the context of religious dialogue. The 2010 OfSTED report on RE acknowledges 'some uncertainties about the relationship between fostering respect for pupils' beliefs and encouraging open critical investigative learning in RE' (OfSTED, 2010, p6). Tensions between dialogue as relation building and dialogue as cognitive challenge are suggested in the following uncomfortable combination of meeting others and criticising their views:

> Developing respect for the commitments of the other while reinforcing the right to question, criticise and evaluate different viewpoints is not just an academic exercise: it involves creating opportunities for children and young people to meet with those with different viewpoints.
>
> (OfSTED, 2007, p41)

The same document recognises that where religion is the theme passions and emotions are involved. While the fact of religious diversity makes RE a particularly appropriate

---

■ **Table 9.2** Four platforms of inter faith dialogue

---

■ Dialogue and personal faith
■ Dialogue and faith community
■ Dialogue and 'the other'
■ Dialogue and God

---

forum for dialogue, the nature of the relationship between the participants of that dialogue and the subjects they are discussing mean that the ordinary rules of classroom dialogue are not sufficient. The stipulation that one should 'distinguish between personal criticism and criticism of ideas' (Littleton *et al.*, 2005, p10) does not cover the case where ideas take on the character of deeply held beliefs.

RE teachers may find support for dealing with these tensions by engaging with long-standing traditions of inter faith dialogue that explore the exciting possibilities while working within the parameters of religious sensibilities. Encounters and intersections between the world's peoples and cultures over the ages mean that meeting between religious differences and having dialogue between religions are part of the story of humankind. In modern times new patterns of migration have resulted in new potential and new need for dialogue. The UK has seen a proliferation of inter faith groups meeting regularly at national, regional or local levels for people of faith to get to know each other and discuss together things that interest and concern them. The Inter Faith Network for the UK recorded details of 260 organisations that prioritise inter faith relations in its 2009 directory (IFN, 2009), and there are numerous small inter faith projects, events and activities not included in this number. Records indicate a sharp rise in inter faith activity after 2001 (IFN, 2005, p11). In a context of religious plurality and potential interreligious tension these organisations seek to develop relationships of friendship across differences, to tackle prejudice and lessen the likelihood of discord. The focus of inter faith dialogue may be interreligious cooperation on a matter of common concern or increased understanding of each other's faith traditions (ibid., p13). The second focus is particularly appropriate for RE.

The national non-statutory guidance for RE specifies that students' learning experience should include reflection on the significance of inter faith dialogue (DfES and QCA, 2004, p12), but more attention could be given to the way the principles of inter faith dialogue might translate into classroom practice and a dialogical RE. In what follows I shall take in turn four platforms of inter faith dialogue (see Table 9.2).

For each platform I shall consider application to the primary school RE class. I include in my considerations the young age of the children concerned and the possible presence in the class of pupils with no experience of religion in their upbringing. Rather than being a 'how to' of inter faith dialogue in RE, this chapter sets out principles to guide classroom practice. Examples of children's dialogue from my own research in the field will be used as illustrations.

## DIALOGUE AND PERSONAL FAITH

One way in which inter faith dialogue often differs from dialogic pedagogies is the attention it gives to the stability of practitioners' religious identity and beliefs. As a 2007 guide for Muslims states,

> Inter faith dialogue means to hold on to one's faith while simultaneously trying to understand another's faith.
>
> (Shafiq and Abu-Nimer, 2007, p2)

This 'holding on' contrasts with the 'letting go' present in Mercer's formula for classroom dialogue where, instead of protecting their own identities and interests, pupils are to move on to 'new and better ways' (Mercer, 2000, p102–3). The emphasis on continuity of faith and identity in inter faith dialogue both offers reassurance to those considering engagement that their integrity will not be compromised and reflects the experience of proponents and practitioners that strength of personal belief makes for more meaningful dialogue with others. This is the position held by Jaco Cilliers based on his experience working for the United Nations in conflict resolution in multi-religious communities:

> Engaging in inter faith dialogue is constructive only when people become firmly grounded in their own religious tradition and through that process gain a willingness to listen to and respect the beliefs of other religions.
>
> (Cilliers, 2002, p48–9)

Concern for the integrity of participants' faith position and conviction that a solid base in one's own faith and belief system is a good platform for dialogue are relevant to the context of primary school RE.

In the introduction I suggested that some modes of classroom dialogue might have an unsettling effect on young people's religion. Before a too-ready application of dialogic pedagogies (evaluation, criticism, meaning construction) in RE, teachers need to consider the risks entailed and the extent of the loss should such activity undermine a child's confidence in their faith. Hand's model does not take this cost into account (Hand, 2004). Choice based on rational assessment of evidence privileges cognitive aspects of religion but neglects experiential and relational aspects. It also privileges one particular form of belief, that of secular humanism, which insists on rational evidence as foundational. Research carried out among primary age children in a multi-cultural school in Leicester showed their religious identity to be closely bound up with ties of loyalty to family, to community and to God and to their own sense of self-worth and well-being (see Table 9.3).

---

■ **Table 9.3** Extracts: identity and loyalty

---

I'm proud who I am because it's really my ancestors that started this and I'm going to carry it on for them. (CS,* Year 4, African Caribbean Christian boy)
I'm happy what [religion] God made me. . . . I'd be proud what he made me. (JS, Year 4, African Caribbean Christian boy)
I'm always happy [to be a Muslim] – even though it's hard, so hard, I like the life I'm living. (HN, Year 5, Gujarati Muslim boy)

---

*initials used to preserve anonymity

■ **Table 9.4** Extract: God as an experienced reality

Like if I've been naughty and my mum and dad are cross with me I go to my room and I feel upset. And I feel God's spirit in me and it makes me feel better. (S, Year 4, white British Christian girl)

For many children God is not just an idea but an experienced reality (see Table 9.4).

It would be harsh to shake the foundations of such faith by requiring children to question their beliefs. Political scientist Melissa Lane has argued that it is beyond the remit of a liberal democratic state, through its schools, to impose religious criticism upon children and challenge their religious identity in this way (Lane, 2010). Young people may well go through periods of religious questioning at some stage in their lives and they may use critical thinking skills to do so, but this process should not be planned into RE. This means in practice that pupils should be asked to share what they know, experience and believe from their own perspective rather than argue about the truth or otherwise of a religious proposition; 'tell us what you know about angels' is a more appropriate dialogue prompt for members of the RE class than 'do angels exist?'.

Respecting pupils' religious integrity does not mean that critical thinking is out of place in RE; religions have their own traditions of intellectual engagement which are different from evidence-based scientism. At the level of the child, the status given to one's own faith position in inter faith dialogue entails a particular kind of critical thinking that builds on rather than throws over personal faith. The act of communicating ideas (the selection of words and precision of language required) presents cognitive challenge and helps develop a child's thinking. The use of symbol and metaphor in religious language and the fact that many elements of the children's religious experience have deeper meanings that invite fuller explanation add to this challenge (see Table 9.5). The teacher can assist the reflection process through well-placed

■ **Table 9.5** Extracts: religious language, symbol and metaphor

A simple candle prompted thoughtful reflection on the fundamentals of her faith from a Christian girl as she attempted to convey its symbolism to the rest of the discussion group:

> This represents the light of God – that he's still here, he's not gone, he's still like everywhere, he's watching down, he's following you. (Year 5, African Christian girl)

An African Caribbean boy brings together two non-negotiable positions of his own faith (God's unity and God's universality) and expands his religious language and thinking in response to the questions and positions of others. When his Muslim friends ask him what colour he thinks God is he replies,

> Most people my colour will say he's black, but I think he's all mixed colours, black, white, Asian – blue, pink. I think he's every colour in the world, I don't just think he's one particular colour because . . . God must be like everyone's colour because to me, I think he's everyone's god, because in my religion I think there's only one god and he's everyone's god so he's got to be everyone's different colour. He can't just be black and then he's everyone's god. (JH, Year 6, African Caribbean, Rastafarian Christian)

questions: 'when you say Jesus is a special baby what makes him special for you?'; 'can you tell us why you are so keen to go on hajj when you are older?' Efforts to convey something of one's religion and one's faith to others lead the dialogue participant to think about his or her own religious faith, to revise and extend his or her own religious language.

Not all primary age children have JH's confidence in discussing religious concepts. A teacher can assist the less confident by helping them identify simple, concrete manifestations of their faith that they can describe to their peers: for a Muslim child, how and when he uses his prayer mat; for a church-going Christian child, what she does on a Sunday morning; for a Hindu child, his favourite character from the religious stories with which he is familiar. Some children may not feel ready to discuss their faith and others may have no religious background to share. With the flexibility of the primary school curriculum and timetable there are plenty of other opportunities for them to talk about aspects of their lives (unrelated to religion) that are important to them. Teachers need not be overly anxious about pupils' uneven participation in RE dialogue; as Alexander argues, giving every child a chance to speak in class discussion may not be the best way to advance dialogue as it allows too little time for the expansion of ideas or the development of models of good practice (Alexander, 2005, p8). In RE the less confident and non-religious will increase their religious understanding by hearing about the religious lives and beliefs of others and learning to ask them pertinent questions. Where there are few resources in the class or school for this kind of learning, teachers may invite visitors to talk about their faith.

## Summary: dialogue and personal faith

Inter faith dialogue in RE involves valuing rather than challenging pupils' personal faith; it gives them the opportunity to learn about the personal faith of others.

# DIALOGUE AND FAITH COMMUNITY

The second platform of inter faith dialogue recognises that the dialogue is not just interpersonal but inter faith; it is not just between individuals but between the faith systems, communities, histories, narratives and traditions to which those individuals belong. This reflects reality when two or more people of different faith backgrounds meet together; it is also in large part what constitutes the significance of inter faith dialogue in our society. Whether at the national leadership level of archbishops, chief rabbis and other faith leaders, at the civic level of local faith community representatives, or at the grass-roots level of ordinary Sikhs, Hindus, Muslims and Christians getting together, inter faith meetings are powerful statements to religious believers and society in general that it is perfectly possible for people of different religions and communities to come together in friendship and cooperation for the wider good. Inter faith dialogue in the classroom can be part of this witness. If children in our schools are to learn about, experience and model inter faith dialogue, the communal dimension of faith needs to be taken seriously.

The Non-Statutory National Framework for RE includes both the personal and the communal dimension in the following statement:

RE encourages pupils to develop their sense of identity and belonging. It enables them to flourish as individuals within their communities.

(DfES and QCA, 2004, p7)

Nevertheless the location of the individual child's personal faith with a religious tradition is contrary to some prominent trends of thought in RE. A distrust of religion fed by 1960s and 1970s liberal Christianity and secularist thinking (Hull, 2000); a postmodern prioritisation of the 'small narrative' of the child over the 'metanarrative' of the faith tradition (Erriker and Erriker, 2000); and recognition of the internal complexity of religions (Jackson, 1995) all lead to a focus on the individual rather than the tradition. In keeping with this school, inter faith dialogue programmes often teach pupils to use 'I' rather than 'we' language in their contributions. To exclude the 'we' altogether, however, is to neglect the communal experience so important to the religious lives of many: the congregational worship and fellowship in a Christian church, the crowds of Muslims who converge on Makkah for hajj, the gathering of community to celebrate Diwali, the Jewish family coming together each Friday at the beginning of Shabbat – all are 'we' experiences. In wider society religion's role in creating and sustaining communities is well known; it is the understanding behind the national and local governments' concern to consult and interact with leaders and representatives of the churches and other faith communities in relation to social policy (DCLG, 2008). Alistair McGrath argues that this communal dimension of faith has become increasingly important since 1965, citing the tendency of immigrant communities to define themselves in religious terms (McGrath, 2004, p264–6). Whatever their degree of commitment, regularity of practice or orthodoxy of belief, the vast majority of the world's people identify with a communal faith tradition; for many it is also their primary social reference.

Acknowledging faith that is both personal and communal has implications for dialogue in RE. Dialogue is valued for its role in the formation of community, whether the language is cognitive ('community of inquiry') or relational ('community cohesion'), but inter faith dialogue not only creates a community, it is an interface between communities. When people of different faiths meet, it is not just a dialogue of person to person but each of those persons is bringing to that forum their own conversation with their faith tradition; this is so for adults and for children with their different degrees of experience and knowledge of their home religion (see Tables 9.6 and 9.7).

While children may speak from their experience in a faith community – and some may already demonstrate profound knowledge of the faith to which they belong – in general their early stage in their religious learning within that community mean that they cannot speak *for* the community. They may be out of line with the mainstream teaching of their tradition, whether they are articulating distinctive personal beliefs (such as the

---

■ **Table 9.6** Extract: language of community

In RE, it is an acknowledgement of reality if both 'I' and 'we' language is employed. This reality is reflected by the shift from 'I' to 'we' language in this email exchange (part of an inter faith dialogue online project) in which a Muslim boy describes his community's Eid celebration:

> I have a festival it is called eid. We wear new clothes. We respect our god by praying salaat, furthermore we get exesize from doing it. The boys pray inside a building named the mosque and the girls pray inside the house. We love our festival a lot. (A, Year 5, Gujarati Muslim boy)
>
> (McKenna *et al.*, 2008, p86)

---

▨ **Table 9.7** Extract: significance of the crucifix

---

When a Christian girl shares her understanding of the significance of the crucifix with her classmates, her words speak of the symbol of a faith community, transmission of religious doctrine within that community, laws that guide life in community and a communal relationship with God. Her own understanding may extend beyond this to encompass the wider human community in the 'us' and 'we':

> It's to help about Jesus died for us, for our sins. It's to like teach the children how it is – to be good like the Ten Commandments, to do that, follow all the laws God told us that we have to obey because Jesus died for us. (D, Year 5, African Christian girl)

---

Christian boy who spoke about his belief in reincarnation) or demonstrating only partial understanding of the faith in which they are growing – the Christian girl who announced that Joseph was God because he was Jesus' father, for example, has misunderstood what she has been told. Teachers need to ensure that classroom dialogue about religion is not just ignorance meeting ignorance by helping children put the knowledge they have and the experiences they describe into context, by questioning and commenting on statements that are misleading ('That's interesting but in the Bible story Joseph isn't God because he isn't Jesus' father – he's a kind man who marries Mary and helps her look after the baby'). Above all there need to be other sources of learning about major faith traditions in addition to what children share within classroom discussions.

Children may not represent or speak for their faith communities, but they can, by their religious identities, serve as bridges to those communities, and they can, by sharing their experiences, act as hosts inviting their peers to pay a visit and get a glimpse of that community's life and its inspirations. This hosting role was enacted quite literally in one Year 4 class where a group of Christian and Muslim children paid a visit to the home of a Hindu classmate to see the family shrine in the front room, learn about its use and importance from this boy and his adult sister and ask them questions. The experience and knowledge they gained was then shared with the rest of the class.

Children who do not have reference to a faith tradition in their own lives can learn much from their peers' experiences of community. There is a danger, nevertheless, that they may feel left out, as though they do not have a belonging. To guard against this the teacher can find ways of connecting them to the traditions being studied without requiring religious belief. This can be done through culture, heritage, language and place; familiar artefacts with a religious origin (Easter eggs, stars on the Christmas tree); the faith history of family such as grandparents and great-grandparents; personal names that have religious origins (Kevin, Becky, Ali, Krishna); and a prominent religious site in the child's neighbourhood, such as the local parish church.

## Summary: dialogue and faith community

Inter faith dialogue in RE values the communal experience of religion, witnesses to the possibility of interreligious cooperation and harmony in society and uses the religious affiliations of pupils in class as bridges to further learning about different religions.

## DIALOGUE AND THE RELIGIOUS 'OTHER'

The third platform for inter faith dialogue is 'the otherness of the other'. It is a principle embedded in the Inter Faith Network's pronouncement that 'dialogue and cooperation can only prosper if they are rooted in respectful relationships which do not blur or undermine the distinctiveness of different religious traditions' (IFN, 2014). Not all proponents of inter faith dialogue see 'the otherness of the other' as a principle of engagement; some understand inter faith dialogue to be founded on sameness rather than difference. For RE, John Hull has advocated a dialogue grounded in recognition of common humanity and supported by a universalising theology. He has called for a bold RE prepared to deconstruct historic religious traditions and find an underlying global faith. The model he developed during the 1980s and 1990s was founded on a deep distrust of distinct religious identities and truth claims as tending towards 'parochialism', 'tribalism' and 'religionism'. For religionists 'there must be no mutuality, no sharing of the ideals and hopes of the other, no dialogue' (Hull, 1998, p115). In its search for convergence of identity and meaning, Hull's method is similar to the negotiation models of dialogic pedagogy with which this chapter began. Where religion is the subject and where inter faith understanding is the aim, however, this principle of convergence poses obstacles to dialogue, limiting the activity to a minority of like-minded idealists who share similar liberal theologies though they may come from different religious traditions. Concerns that this universalising religion is what inter faith dialogue necessarily entails or leads to can deter participation. *Interfaith Dialogue: A Guide for Muslims* cites, as reasons why some Muslims hesitate to participate, a fear that 'the underlying purpose is to create one religion for everyone', a conviction that 'saying "your faith is mine and there is no difference" is forbidden' in Islam and concern that 'inter faith dialogue is committed to creating new, blended and diluted worship services common to all' (Shafiq and Abu-Nimer, 2007, p7).

Andrew Wright's assessment of Hull's idealised vision for dialogue concludes that he failed to recognise the possibility of inter faith dialogue in the context of the religious plurality that is our current reality:

> Alongside his advocacy of dialogue grounded in the recognition of common humanity communicating within a universal theological framework, stands the possibility of dialogue grounded in a mutual acceptance of difference, and a mutual agreement to pursue conversation despite fundamental contradictions between belief systems.
>
> (Wright, 2000, p88)

My research has found that young children in a multi-faith context can also struggle with similar issues of mutuality and difference in dialogue. At times when interpersonal relations are strained, religious distinctiveness and superiority may be emphasised – 'our god's better than yours', 'your god's not real', 'our god's more important than yours'. When the attitude that guides relations is one of friendship, then attempts are made to negotiate joint meanings along the lines of Mercer's *Thinking Together* approach. The challenge for inter faith relations is to find a dialogue that is grounded in difference but can still sustain friendship. The children found this difficult; their instinct was to seek agreement. This was the case in combined Christian and Hindu discussion groups where children constructed different theological models – one God with many features; a hierarchy of gods – as they sought to reconcile the tensions between their beliefs in one god or many (Ipgrave, 2009,

---

■ **Table 9.8** Extracts: challenges of encounter between different religions

---

A Christian boy, after interrogating his Hindu friend about the number of gods he worships, concludes with this question:

> But one day will your – Do you go to a temple? Will your temple stick to one god one day, any day? (JS, Year 4, African Caribbean Christian boy)

In a separate discussion, another Christian boy asks,

> Do you praise every one of [your gods] . . . like we pray to Jesus – do you have to pray to all of them? (JN, Year 5, African Caribbean Christian boy)

---

p64). These attempts at convergence also revealed various sticking points at which 'the otherness of the other' could not readily be merged into a shared religious understanding without losing or distorting elements of the faith the children brought to the encounter. One example is the response of a Year 5 Hindu girl to her Christian friend's suggestion that there is only one God though he may be called different names: 'We can't actually say that because we've got so many gods'. Interrogating the dialogues further, I noted a tendency for the monotheist perspective of the Christian children to dominate – their preoccupation with the oneness of God reflects a Christian perspective, sharpened, perhaps, through discussion with the Muslim children in their school. See Table 9.8.

Behind the boys' insistence is their inability to comprehend their friends' religion of many gods, how they relate to them all and what it means for their religious practice. JS's question implies that he views 'sticking to' one god as the preferable position. In further exchanges between Christian and Hindu children it is evident that translating from one religious language to another is an issue (Tables 9.9 and 9.10).

This problem with language is not just an issue for primary school children but is part of the nature of religious difference exercising those most experienced in theologies of different faiths. In his analysis of inter faith dialogue, David Lochhead illustrated this point

---

■ **Table 9.9** Extract: issues of translation

---

In the following exchange the Hindu boy says it is not possible to translate 'Allah' from Islam into his own religious culture, but his Christian friends override his hesitation and do it for him.

> CS (Year 4, African Caribbean Christian boy): It's just the same thing. Allah's just the same as God in a different language.
> JS (Year 4, African Caribbean Christian boy): Yeah, just like they speak in Gujarati, they're saying like the same thing but in a different language, Like – er – so you can say 'Allah' in Gujarati?
> AK (Year 4, Gujarati Hindu boy): No.
> JS: That means – what's 'God' in Gujarati?
> AK: Bhagavan.
> JS: That means you call Allah 'Bhagavan'.

---

---

■ **Table 9.10** Extract: translations of deity

---

In another Christian–Hindu conversation a Christian boy makes an Islamically unacceptable translation of 'Allah' into Christian terms but admits to problems with translating Hinduism into his own religious language:

> So I don't like say all the things that you're calling Shiva. I know like Allah as Jesus because I believe Jesus is just one god and you call Allah one god. (JN, Year 5, African Caribbean Christian boy)

---

with the impossibility of finding an exact translation of the Buddhist concept of 'enlightenment' in Christianity or of the Christian concept of 'salvation' in Buddhism; although both denote the ultimate experience of human liberation, they have very different connotations, deriving their meaning from different 'language games' (Lochhead, 1988, p69). For Lochhead inter faith dialogue involves a form of bilingualism that retains the distinctiveness and meaning of the different religious languages engaged.

Paul Ricoeur's paradigm of translation and concept of 'linguistic hospitality' have useful relevance to inter faith dialogue (Ricoeur, 2006). He offers insights into the processes by which people, separated by language, culture and religion, come to relate to one another in understanding and hospitality. Those involved in inter faith dialogue are engaged in a task of translation, a necessary process if mutual understanding is to be achieved. The translator's task is not to produce a perfect translation, however, but to offer one that remains faithful and hospitable to both sides across the linguistic divide. The task is challenging; the translator is tempted to give up the attempt in the face of its perceived impossibility (like AK in the exchange in Table 9.9) or to try to force one language into the framing of the other (like JS). Finally the translator will recognise that the foreign language is 'irreducible' (p10) to her own, and although she loses her ideal of a perfect translation, she gains a new partner in the language she has been struggling with as well as a new sense of the singularity of her own language.

The efforts of the Christian boys to translate their Hindu friends' religious language into their own frames of reference are not ill-meaning but made out of friendship; they want to understand and relate better. However, theirs is a domineering friendship and they need to progress to another level of dialogue if real 'linguistic hospitality' is to be achieved. As they explore the language of their own faith, searching for connections with that of their dialogue partners, and listen attentively to the language of their partners' faith in attempts to gain understanding, the children discover much about both. The next stage is for them to recognise that these religious languages are *not* reducible one to the other or to a third common language but are nevertheless capable of speaking to each other, learning from each other's distinctiveness and welcoming each other's company.

The move to this higher level of dialogue is a big step for children of this young age, but teachers can prepare them for it by encouraging them to identify and discuss the differences between faiths, differences so easily blurred by overemphasis on their similarities – this exercise is particularly important when thematic approaches to RE are being used. Children studying Festivals of Light, for example, could be asked, 'Is Hanukkah the same as Christmas?' To answer, children need to delve more deeply into both traditions, find the commonalities (joyful celebration, miraculous event, lighting of candles), but also the differences – one is a Jewish, the other a Christian festival; one has meaning within the history of a chosen people and its relationship with God and the other presents the specifically Christian theology of incarnation. Considering one festival in relation to the other throws into relief what is distinctive about each. Neither is reducible to the other and together they are irreducible to any universalising concept of celebrating light that would be a distortion of both traditions. To realise that Shiva does not correlate exactly with Jesus or Hanukkah with Christmas is to deepen one's knowledge of one's own and other religions and to expand religious language and understanding. The same method can be used to check too-ready correlations between secular and religious experience – the Five Ks do not equate with school uniform; the Qur'an is not a special book in the same way that the Harry Potter series might be special to a child.

## Summary: dialogue and the religious 'other'

Inter faith dialogue in RE is wary of pressures to fit one religion into the framing of another or to reduce religions to a universal religion; it deepens understanding of religions through exploration of difference as well as commonality.

# DIALOGUE AND GOD

The fourth platform for inter faith dialogue is the understanding of many practitioners that their dialogical activity takes place in relation to, and through the strength of, an entity infinitely greater than the human participants involved. This is the creative force in dialogue and the participants are partaking in that creativity. It is through a greater power that the participating individuals are able to talk of faith – when the Shin Buddhist pronounces the name of Amida it is through Other-power not self-power that he or she does so (Sato, 2010, pp70–5). It is through a greater power that individuals come together across religious difference – the Anglican Communion statement on inter faith dialogue, *Generous Love*, speaks of the 'unrestricted and constantly surprising' working of the Holy Spirit that frees and leads Christians to find ways of engaging with people of different faiths in seeking the common good (NIFCON, 2008, p11). It is in conformity with and imitation of the activity of a greater power that individuals come together in dialogue – as the Muslim guide states, 'dialogue is no stranger to Islam for the Qur'an is a Book of Dialogue between Allah (God) and his Creation' (Shafiq and Abu-Nimer, 2007, p5). Similarly the wisdom of Krishna in the *Bhagavad Gita* is revealed through his dialogue with Arjuna. Inter faith meetings often acknowledge a divine presence in their dialogue activity by beginning and ending with prayer or silence. For religious believers inter faith dialogue is particularly meaningful when they recognise that both they and their partners are conducting their dialogue and relationship with each other in confidence that they are simultaneously in dialogue and relationship with this greater power. To quote *Generous Love*,

> For example, believing ourselves to be in a dialogue with God enabled through the words of the Bible, it can be a profoundly humbling and creative experience for us to read the Bible alongside Muslims who likewise believe themselves to be addressed by the one God through the text of the Qur'an.
>
> (NIFCON, 2008, p6)

So how does this dialogue with God or other-power translate into the primary classroom? First it is well to be aware that religious children may feel God is present in their RE discussion and that what they say and hear should respect that presence. Teachers sometimes find children of different religions hesitate to use certain words, to read or view certain texts, pictures or objects in RE classes. Such hesitations should not automatically be interpreted as negativity about people of other faiths but could reflect uncertainty about what is acceptable in God's eyes. Where this is a persistent obstacle to engagement, conversations with the children, their parents and their community, and a religiously aware model of inter faith dialogue in line with the principles in this chapter, may help to reassure them, but the issue cannot be forced.

More often religious children's awareness of an other-power opens up dialogue. Children in the Leicester primary school did not consider God (or their gods) merely as an object for intellectual debate ('is there one god or many gods?', 'is your god the same as my god?') but spoke of his personal connection with themselves ('I know my God's good', 'my God made me', 'I love Jesus') and of him as a person with wishes and feelings ('God wants us to love each other'; 'God might be getting bored'; 'I think God must be quite annoyed'). There was in their expressions both certainty and mystery – they knew God and yet did not know him (see Table 9.11).

This mixture of certainty and mystery is central to religious experience involving confession of faith and recognition of the limitless nature of God – the 'I cannot tell . . . but this I know . . .' of William Fullerton's powerful hymn (*Hymns Old and New*, 1986, hymn no. 212); it is also particularly pertinent to inter faith relations where participants may be convinced of the truth of their own faith, and sure that God requires them to reach out in hospitality to their neighbour, but still find mysterious the purpose of other confessions in God's scheme. Some things are beyond human judgement. As one Christian teenager expressed it, 'It's not for us to judge, "oh, you're going to heaven and you're not"; God in his perfection and justice will be able to say' (from research in Northern Irish schools, Ipgrave, 2012, p271).

This tolerance of ambiguity and this humility in the face of what cannot be known are valuable attitudes for harmonious and equal inter faith engagement. While the quest for greater understanding is part of the excitement of religious learning, dialogue in RE should not require answers for every question.

---

■ **Table 9.11** Extracts: certainty and mystery

JH expresses a sure knowledge of God's positive purpose for humankind:

> [God] never put us on this earth to kill people. He put us on this earth to be friends and love each other like brothers and sisters. (JH, Year 6, African Caribbean, Rastafarian Christian boy)

At the same time God remains a puzzle to him:

> I want to know – how did God ever make? – how did it? – when did he? – because if I ever get to heaven . . . there's a big question I'm going to ask God when I get there: how did he make the earth? (JH)

---

■ **Table 9.12** Extracts: God talk-around story

In a Year 4 lesson I observed, the children considered the puzzle of God's actions (or lack of action) in relation to the people of Nineveh, his failure to carry out the punishment he had threatened them with and Jonah's reactions to this change of mind. In the story God has a major and very distinctive role, and in their discussion the children engaged with concepts of God's justice and mercy, moving from the seeming 'unfairness' of God to the 'unfairness' of Jonah:

> Jonah's in a bad mood because he got into trouble for disobeying God and they didn't. (R, African Christian girl)

> God's forgiven [Jonah] for not obeying him and now he's upset when he forgives the people doing bad things so it's not fair. (O, African Christian boy)

In keeping with the concept of continuing mystery, the teacher ended the lesson by asking her pupils to identify 'one thing that still puzzles me'. She also asked them to record 'the most important thing I learnt' – potentially an opening for an exercise in 'otherness' where children consider the different messages of the story for those (Jews, Christians, Muslims) for whom it is part of their religious tradition and those for whom it is not.

Learning in RE requires familiarity with language about God, but there may well be children in the RE class who are unaccustomed to and feel uncomfortable with this 'God-talk' (using John Macquarrie's (1967) term). These children can learn much about religion and its significance to the religious by listening to the language of their peers, but can they engage in such talk themselves in a way that respects the personal meaning of God to the believer yet does not force them into expressions of belief or disbelief? One strategy for engagement that respects both believing and non-committed positions is to work with a religious text where God (or other religious power) is present as a character in the story. Without having to make judgements on the truth or otherwise of the story, both religious and non-religious children can discuss the significance of God's actions and words within it (Table 9.12).

## Summary: dialogue and God

Inter faith dialogue in RE respects religious pupils' sense of the presence of God or other-power in their activity; it allows for both certainty and mystery in the children's 'God-talk', valuing knowledge and tolerating ambiguity.

## INTER FAITH DIALOGUE IN RE

Interest in dialogue in the primary RE class is part of a broader enthusiasm for dialogic pedagogy. However, the nature of the subject, its religious content and the diverse religious (and non-religious) backgrounds of the children mean that a wholesale translation of generic dialogue principles to the RE class is not adequate; the dialogue needs to be inter-preted and handled differently. Guided by the experience of inter faith dialogue, an appro-priate RE dialogue can be developed that is sensitive to the positions of children nurtured in different religious faiths and in none; that respects children's relationships with their faith communities; that respects faith traditions in their distinctiveness; that recognises the importance to the believer of their personal relationship with God or other-power. Where these platforms are in place a dialogical RE can develop that enables children to gain real insights into the significance and power of religion in the lives of so many, encourages them to reflect on their own faith and be interested in the faiths of others and teaches the important lesson for our diverse society: that it is possible and enjoyable for people of different faiths to converse and cooperate with each other and that we are increased and not diminished by this encounter with difference.

## ADDITIONAL RESOURCES

Mercer, N. and S. Hodgkinson (eds) (2008) *Exploring Talk in School*, London: Sage.
Near Neighbours Press Release (2011) *Eric Pickles Officially Launches £5m Near Neighbours Programme*, 14 November. www.cuf.org.uk/near-neighbours/press-release/14Nov2011, accessed 13.12.12.

## REFERENCES

Alexander, R.J. (2001) *Culture and Pedagogy: International Comparisons in Primary Education*, Oxford: Blackwell.
Alexander, R.J. (2005) *Towards Dialogic Teaching: Rethinking Classroom Talk*. London: Routledge.
Alexander, R.J. (2008) *Essays on Pedagogy*, Abingdon: Routledge.
Cilliers. J. (2002) 'Building Bridges for Inter Faith Dialogue', *Inter Faith Dialogue and Peacebuilding*, D.R. Smock (ed.), Washington, DC: United States Institute of Peace, 47–60.
Dawes, L., N. Mercer and R. Wegerif (2004, 2nd ed.) Thinking Together: A Programme of Activities for Developing Speaking, Listening and Thinking Skills, Birmingham; Imaginative Minds Ltd.
DCLG (2008) *Face to Face and Side by Side: A Framework for Partnership in Our Multi-Faith Society*, London: Communities and Local Government Publications.
DfES (2006) *Primary National Strategy: Primary Framework for Literacy and Mathematics*, London: Department for Education and Skills.
DfES and QCA (2004) *Religious Education: The Non-Statutory National Framework*, London: Qualifications and Curriculum Authority.
Erricker, C., and J. Erricker (2000) 'The Children and Worldviews Project: A Narrative Pedagogy of Religious Education', *Pedagogies of Religious Education: Case Studies in the Research and Development of Good Pedagogic Practice in RE*, M. Grimmitt (ed.), Great Wakering: McCrimmons, 188–206.
Hand, M. (2004) 'Religious Education', *Rethinking the School Curriculum: Values, Aims and Purposes*, J. White (ed.), London: Routledge, 152–64.
Home Office (2001) *Community Cohesion: A Report of the Independent Review Team Chaired by Ted Cantle*, London: Home Office.
Hull, J.M. (1998) *Utopian Whispers: Moral, Religious and Spiritual Values in Schools*, Norwich: Religious and Moral Education Press.
Hull, J.M. (2000) 'Religionism and Religious Education', *Education, Culture and Values: Spiritual and Religious Education*, vol. 5, M. Leicester, C. Mogdil and S. Modgil (eds), London: Falmer Press, 75–85.
*Hymns Old and New* (1986) Bury St Edmunds: Kevin Mayhew Ltd.
Inter Faith Network UK (IFN) (2005) *The Local Inter Faith Guide*, London: Inter Faith Network UK.

Inter Faith Network UK (IFN) (2009) *Inter Faith Organisations in the UK: A Directory*, London: Inter Faith Network UK.

Inter Faith Network UK (IFN) (2014) www.interfaith.org.uk, accessed 18.1.14.

Ipgrave, J. (2009) 'My God and Other People's Gods: Children's Theology in a Context of Plurality', *Hovering over the Face of the Deep: Philosophy, Theology and Children*, G. Y. Iversen, G. Mitchell and G. Pollard (eds), Münster: Waxmann, 53–70.

Ipgrave, J. (2012) 'Relationships between Local Patterns of Religious Practice and Young People's Attitudes to the Religiosity of Their Peers', *Journal of Beliefs and Values* 33, no. 3: 261–274.

IPPR (2004) *What Is Religious Education For? Getting the National Framework Right*, London: Institute for Public Policy Research.

Jackson, R. (1995) 'Religious Education's Representation of 'Religions' and 'Cultures'', *British Journal of Educational Studies* 43, no. 3: 272–89.

Lane, M. (2010) 'What Is Religious Education For?' *The Philosopher's Magazine* 48. www. philosophypress.co.uk/?p=989, accessed 12.1.14.

Littleton, K., N. Mercer, L. Dawes, R. Wegerif, D. Rowe and C. Sams (2005) 'Talking and Thinking Together at Key Stage 1', *Early Years: An International Journal of Research and Development* 25, no. 2: 167–82.

Lochhead, D. (1988) *The Dialogical Imperative: A Christian Reflection on Inter Faith Encounter*, London: SCM Press.

Macquarrie, J. (1967) *God-Talk: An Examination of the Language and Logic of Theology*, London: SCM Press.

McCreery, E., S. Palmer and V. Voiels (2008) *Teaching Religious Education: Primary and Early Years*, Exeter: Leaning Matters.

McGrath, A. (2004) *The Twilight of Atheism: The Rise and Fall of Disbelief in the Modern World*, London: Rider.

McKenna, U., J. Ipgrave and R. Jackson (2008) *Inter Faith Dialogue by Email in Primary Schools*, Münster: Waxmann.

Mercer, N. (2000) Words and Minds: How We Use Language to Think Together, London: Routledge.

Network for Inter Faith Concerns (Anglican Communion) (NIFCON) (2008) *Generous Love: The Truth of the Gospel and the Call to Dialogue*, London: Anglican Consultative Council.

OfSTED (2007) *Making Sense of Religion: A Report on Religious Education in Schools and the Impact of Locally Agreed Syllabuses*, London: HMI.

OfSTED (2010) *Transforming Religious Education: Religious Education in Schools 2006–2009*, London: HMI.

REC. (n.d.) *Religious Education and Community Cohesion* statement of the Religious Education Council of England and Wales. http://www.babcock-education.co.uk/ldp/do_download. asp?did=304365, accessed 12.1.14.

Ricoeur, P. (2006) *On Translation*, New York: Routledge.

Sato, K. T. (2010) *Great Living in the Pure Encounter between Master and Disciple: A Volume of Essays and Commentaries on the Shin Buddhist Text Tannishō in a New Translation*, New York: Buddhist Center Press.

Shafiq, M., and M. Abu-Nimer (2007) *Interfaith Dialogue: A Guide for Muslims*, Herndon, VA: The International Institute of Islamic Thought.

Wright, A. (2000) *Spirituality and Education*, London: RoutledgeFalmer.

# SECTION 3
# COVERING CONTROVERSIAL ISSUES CREATIVELY

# CHAPTER 10

# CREATIVELY WIDENING THE SCOPE OF RE

## WHAT WE TEACH AND WHY

### *Sally Elton-Chalcraft*

Children have little influence on what and how they are taught (Devine 2003). This volume has suggested creative approaches for RE, many of which involve giving the children more ownership of their learning. In this chapter I consider not only *how* to teach RE creatively but also ask the reader to consider *what* they teach and *why*.

For many primary school RE lessons, *what* is taught is usually selected by the RE subject leader (if there is one, even though this is a requirement). The RE content in English schools depends on how the subject leader has interpreted the agreed syllabus. Sometimes ideas from continuing professional development sessions are included in the RE curriculum and sometimes advice from the county or diocesan RE adviser (if there is one) informs subject content; occasionally the views of the staff at their school inform the RE content. So, unlike most other primary school subjects which are compelled to adhere to governmental directives (e.g. Curriculum 2014), RE has a lot more flexibility concerning the choice of what to teach. This is both a blessing and a curse. Of course adherence to the locally agreed syllabus is the statutory requirement in terms of breadth, choice of belief systems studied and so on. Aided schools and academies have their own requirements determined by governors.

This chapter argues that children deserve to understand that a variety of belief systems exist. They do not necessarily need to know about all of these in detail (and neither should the teacher feel obliged to have wide-ranging knowledge). However, I argue that children have a right to be introduced to a variety of belief systems, be offered opportunities to engage in appraisal of these belief systems and understand how adherents view the world. In some countries RE is not part of the curriculum (for example in France and Spain religion is a matter left to a child's family and philosophical study is important in the French curriculum (Weiss 2011). In England, despite various major overhauls of the curriculum, RE has maintained its place in the basic curriculum, as acknowledged in the comprehensive Cambridge Review of Education (Alexander 2010) and by OfSTED and DfE [REC (2013)].

In this chapter I explore the importance of introducing children in the primary phase to puzzling questions through a variety of different belief stances. In the English context each county's agreed syllabus usually suggests children explore belief systems practised in their local community with a choice of studying several of the six major world religions. I aim to challenge the teacher to widen her/his perception of belief systems, in both community and faith schools alike. I argue that the choice of which belief systems to study and which to leave out is itself determining a child's outlook.

This, I argue, will help children to understand that beliefs and values often underpin actions, and consequently actions and the beliefs/values which may underpin them can be subject to scrutiny. The teacher's or school's choice of which belief systems to explore with the children and how these belief systems are presented may have an impact on the child's negative or positive perceptions of that belief system. This is explored in other chapters (Prescott, chapter 3; Ipgrave, chapter 9; Revell, chapter 11; Hammond, chapter 12). In this chapter I give examples of a variety of belief systems which are 'on the margins' and not often explored with primary children, often with legitimate reasons such as teachers' lack of subject knowledge. I hope that this chapter will persuade teachers to take a risk (one of the characteristics of creativity) and include some of these examples in their RE. The chapter offers practical examples of teaching and learning from outside the canon of the six major world religions (Buddhism, Christianity – Church of England and Roman Catholicism, Islam, Judaism and Sikhism), about which plenty has already been written (multiple RE Today publications; McCreery *et al.* 2008; Teece 2001).

As well as being introduced to a wide range of different belief systems, children also need to learn how to 'respectfully disagree' with beliefs that are different from their own (Blaylock 2007:4).

Finally the chapter ends by discussing a teachers' mindset and reappraising the rationale behind the choice of religions/belief systems to be studied. Does a teacher's mindset reinforce or challenge a dominant worldview of 'acceptable' and 'dodgy' religions/belief systems?

## CHOICE OF BELIEF SYSTEMS TO STUDY

Most agreed syllabi require children to learn about two or three of the six major religions – Buddhism, two branches of Christianity, Hinduism, Islam, Judaism and Sikhism. In the QCA (2004) Non-Statutory National Framework which was used as a template for many agreed syllabi, the breadth of study includes 'Christianity, at least one other principal religion, a religious community with a significant local presence, where appropriate, and a secular world view, where appropriate' (2004:25 and 27). But there is no suggestion for which combination of belief systems to cover. I would argue that these belief systems can be categorised into three groups:

- the 'Eastern' religions of India (Buddhism, Hinduism and Sikhism);
- the 'Western' Semitic religions (Christianity, Islam and Judaism);
- the 'other' belief systems ('secular' belief systems such as humanism, atheism; religions with smaller numbers such as Baha'ism, paganism).

The six Eastern and Western religions are the most commonly taught in primary schools – although in practice Islam, Judaism and the Christian tradition of Catholic and Church of England are the most popular. I would argue that it is important for primary children to have some understanding of at least one Western and one Eastern religion plus one 'other' belief system, particularly those which are becoming more prevalent in today's society, such as humanism.

I have argued elsewhere that our curriculum has been, for some time, white, Western, patriarchal (male-dominated) and Christian in outlook (Elton-Chalcraft 2009). Curriculum 2014 does not promise to be any less biased and so it is left to the teacher to ensure children are receiving a more balanced diet, although the REC (Religious Education Council) (2013) has superseded the QCA (2004) non statutory national framework and produced a new recommended RE curriculum which can be used alongside the 2014 national curriculum. Scoffman (2013), in his book *Teaching Geography Creatively* (in the same series as this volume), also asks teachers to encourage a wider perspective. Scoffman (2013:68–9) calls for children to view maps of the world from alternative viewpoints – i.e. Australia at the top – in an attempt to challenge dominant thinking and develop locational awareness. Similarly, in RE, children should have some understanding of the main world religions, the six itemised earlier, but also they should at least be made aware of the existence of other belief systems, even if these are not studied in detail. In the following sections I suggest activities and invite the teacher to make children aware of global Christianity and less familiar Christian denominations. Second, I present approaches for teaching about humanism alongside some of the Eastern world religions.

## GLOBAL CHRISTIANITY

In a topic on 'Jesus' in Christianity the children may be learning about the Jesus of history, the Christ of faith and the Jesus of experience (Teece 2001). I would encourage the teacher to think about this not only from the perspective of the Church of England but also from less mainstream denominations of Christianity such as Unitarians, many of whom do not view Jesus as fully divine (God's son), although this could be quite controversial for many mainstream Christian children and their families who think of Jesus as the son of God. Also the children could investigate images of Jesus from around the world.

I understand that many busy primary teachers may lack confidence in teaching RE in the first place and have little knowledge of the main denominations of Christianity, never mind the less well-known ones (Elton-Chalcraft 2014). After all, Christianity is a global religion with over two billion followers under many different branches of Christianity (Pew Research 2011). However, I am trying to persuade teachers to widen their scope of what to teach – not being content to concentrate exclusively on mainstream beliefs but being willing to 'dip your toe in the water' and introduce the children to a variety of beliefs over the course of their seven years in primary school. This can be achieved by simply thinking about use of language – for example avoiding 'we believe x, y and z' rather than 'many Christians around the world believe x, y and z'. Also a more global perspective can be attained by using pictures from around the world – see links to images below. Margaret Cooling (1998), Faces of Jesus (REjesus 2014) and the RE Today publication *Picturing Jesus* (Blaylock 2004) are useful resources.

## LESS WELL-KNOWN DENOMINATIONS IN CHRISTIANITY

Most teachers would be familiar with the denominations of Christianity called Anglicanism (Church of England) and most teachers would also have knowledge of Catholicism, because many primary schools have a Church of England or Catholic foundation. Yet many teachers have scant knowledge of the history of the Christian church and the variety of denominations and branches of Christianity in existence today. The BBC website has a helpful introduction; see Table 10.1.

---

▧ **Table 10.1** Denominations and branches of Christianity

---

Examples of different denominations and branches of Christian traditions

- ▧ The Amish
- ▧ Baptist churches
- ▧ Christadelphians
- ▧ Church of England (Anglicans)
- ▧ Church of Scotland
- ▧ Coptic Orthodox Church
- ▧ Eastern Orthodox Church
- ▧ Exclusive Brethren
- ▧ Methodist Church
- ▧ Opus Dei
- ▧ Pentecostals
- ▧ Quakers
- ▧ Roman Catholic Church
- ▧ Salvation Army
- ▧ Seventh-Day Adventists
- ▧ United Reformed Church

Listed on the BBC website under subdivisions of Christianity, available at www.bbc.co.uk/religion/religions/christianity.

- ▧ Jehovah's Witnesses

Considered a Christian-based religious movement, available at www.bbc.co.uk/religion/religions/witnesses.

---

Many Christians, including many Catholics and Anglicans (Church of England), believe Jesus is the son of God, whereas some Christians do not, for example Unitarians. Jehovah's Witnesses are not listed by the BBC as a Christian denomination because they are not recognised as part of mainstream Christianity by some denominations; they are listed elsewhere on the site as a branch of Christianity. While there is no expectation for the children, or indeed the teacher, to have detailed knowledge of all the denominations listed in Table 10.1, I would argue that an awareness of the number of different denominations is important. Christianity might be better described as Christian traditions. Believers from these different denominations, while having some ideas in common (for example the existence of Jesus and his character as a positive role model), may disagree in their doctrines (beliefs) and ways of worship. For example Eastern Orthodox Christians place great emphasis on using the senses to enhance worship, with artwork, incense and music playing a central role in services, whereas Quaker meeting houses are plain and play a central part in their services. Teece argues (chapter 2 of this volume) that the purpose of RE is to encourage the child to understand religion from the believer's perspective. In this chapter I argue that there is not one 'perspective' but a myriad of different and in some cases, totally opposite perspectives, as in the case of Christians. This may seem very daunting for the busy primary teacher who has to engage with subject knowledge in a range of primary school subject areas (science, geography, history, mathematics etc.) as well as RE. However, as I outlined at the start, there is an expectation not that the children or teacher should be experts, but rather that they have some knowledge of the diversity within a religion and

---

■ **Table 10.2** Using a 'problem-solving model' to investigate worship in different Christian traditions

---

### Problem solving – lessons 1 and 2

In groups, imagine you are the managers of a satellite station (10 years in the future) and you have one room, with a very large storage cupboard, which can be used for worship on two days of the week. The station has 200 workers made up of Christians from each of the five denominations.

Your team have to plan how the room would be used and furnished for each of the two days.

**Create a five-minute illustrative presentation for the satellite station owners explaining how you will meet the needs of each group of Christians in the satellite crew.**

In groups, collect data about Quaker/ Anglican/ Orthodox/ Adventist/ Catholic denominations

### Investigation and knowledge sharing – lessons 3 and 4

Find out about your denomination/tradition of Christianity and how people worship, e.g. day of worship, what happens at worship, pictures of the spaces used for worship and their significance.

**Create an informative PowerPoint presentation about 'worship in . . .'**

Share your findings with other groups.

What are the similarities and differences?

Which presentation meets the needs of the crew most effectively and why?

---

not focus solely on the most common or dominant aspect. The above lesson ideas offer an example of how to engage children in a community of enquiry to investigate the characteristics of a variety of different denominations within Christianity.

In pairs or threes, Year 5 and 6 children could use the internet to research worship in five contrasting Christian denominations – Quaker Society of Friends, Church of England, Seventh-Day Adventist, Eastern Orthodox and Catholic. They could investigate these different denominations in groups using a problem-solving model (see Table 10.2). For more information about effective group work see Baines *et al.* (2008).

# HUMANISM

Humanism is gaining in popularity as secularism (non-religious belief systems) becomes more prevalent. If teachers are to provide children with a broad understanding of what it means to be human, then atheistic belief systems should be included as part of the curriculum – as I argued at the beginning of this chapter. Sims (2011) explains that some faith representatives disagree with the inclusion of humanism in the school curriculum. Nevertheless, it is becoming increasingly common for children to investigate 'other' belief systems including humanism.

According to the British Humanist Association (2014), humanists:

■ Think for themselves about what is right and wrong, based on **reason and respect for others**.

■ Find **meaning, beauty and joy in the one life we have**, without the need for an afterlife.

■   Look to **science instead of religion** as the best way to discover and understand the world.

■   Believe people can use empathy and compassion to **make the world a better place for everyone**.

Many notable figures are among its followers, including Professor Brian Cox (presenter and writer of TV science programmes), Sir Jim Al-Kalili (presenter, scientist and president of the Humanist Society), Natalie Haynes (comedian and writer), Ariane Sherine (comedian and journalist) and Philip Pullman (writer).

Humanism can be studied in RE during a topic such as 'Journeys', where children look at stages in a person's life. Sometimes referred to as rites of passage, the different stages throughout our lives are often accorded significance by religious ceremonies or secular practices which can be explored by children.

## Journeys – rites of passage

Whereas in the past many families would have drawn on church, synagogue, temple, gurdwara and so on for such ceremonies, many folk in Britain today are now looking elsewhere. The Humanist Society offers a list of officiates who can work with families to custom-design ceremonies.

The approach to studying life stages (see Table 10.4) advocated by the following lesson ideas draws on shared human experience, traditional belief systems and individual patterns of belief from the Westhill project (Rudge 2000:88).

Activity: Children could begin by considering their own life journey, recording this in an imaginative way – either as a cartoon, a timeline with peaks and troughs or a non-linear mind map (Buzan 2014). The way they choose to record their life journey will be an interesting discussion point, as will what they choose to record. In the next lesson the children can explore an aspect from a belief system; the example explores a naming ceremony from a humanist perspective. Throughout the topic children would reflect on the impact of belief on action – how an adherent makes sense of the world. They would also be invited to reflect more deeply on their own attitudes and beliefs and how these impact action. See Table 10.3 for 'Naming Ceremony' lesson ideas for Key Stage 1.

A similar format could be adapted for use with any age group and any rite of passage – e.g. a humanist wedding ceremony can be compared with Hindu traditions in Years 3 and 4.

Again the emphasis is on the child understanding what a couple might be feeling about getting married. In Hinduism the second stage in life, Grihasta or householder, emphasises the earthly roles of earning an honest living and being a good parent and partner. The children could discuss what they want to achieve when they grow up. Children could imagine (imagination being one of the four features of creativity outlined in NACCCE 1999:29) the thoughts of a Hindu couple preparing for their wedding day. The children could investigate why certain rituals are undertaken – the meaning behind the seven steps in the Hindu marriage ceremony (life-power, wealth, happiness, offspring, a long wedded life and life companionship, and the prosperity of the children).

It is important for children to learn about civil partnerships as well as heterosexual marriage. Stonewall has plenty of resources to support teaching (www.stonewall.org.uk); for example their colourful 2014 'Different families same love' poster could be used as a stimulus for discussion.

**Table 10.3** Using the Westhill model (Grimmitt 2000) of shared human experience, individual patterns of belief

### Key questions: *'Shared human experience'*
**Who knows someone who has had a baby recently?**
(Practically every child will have some acquaintance with a classmate who has a new sibling.)

**What 'rituals' happen when a new baby is born? ('ritual' = events/ceremonies/occurrences)**
Class discussions could include what rituals accompany a new baby – e.g. sending greetings cards and presents, visitors congratulating the family etc. The theory behind this is that we have a shared human experience where children 'share' some knowledge and understanding of common practice. Hopefully a variety of practices will be raised by the children which can be discussed respectfully.

### Key questions: *'Traditional belief system'*
**What happens during a humanist ceremony to welcome a new baby?**
Children can use internet sources (e.g. www.humanism.org.uk/ceremonies/find-a-celebrant and www.inspirationalceremonies.co.uk/humanist-naming) to find out about humanist ceremonies and role-play interviews between parents and the humanist celebrant.
Compare the similarities and differences between ceremonies with which they are familiar. Encourage the children to 'get into the role' of being a humanist parent and why they want to have a humanist naming ceremony for their child.

### Key questions: *'Individual patterns of belief'*
**What would you include in a humanist naming ceremony?**
Plan and act out the ceremony, choosing the readings and songs.

**Why did you design your naming ceremony this way?**
Evaluate why they have made those choices. Compare the similarities and differences between ceremonies with which they are familiar. Hopefully a variety of practices will be raised by the children which can be discussed respectfully; avoid comparing in terms of better or worse, like or dislike – rather discuss similarities and differences.

**Table 10.4** Extract from a humanist celebrant's website

Many parents feel that they want to celebrate and share their joy of having a child with family and friends but do not feel that they want a traditional christening or religious ceremony. This may be because they do not hold any religious beliefs themselves or because they want their child to be able to choose their own beliefs when they are older.

Humanist ceremonies are non-religious and therefore have no worship or fixed rituals. They are appropriate for anyone who would like a non-religious ceremony. The only guideline is that they do not include any religious content such as prayers or hymns. However, it is possible to have a moment of quiet reflection during the ceremony to enable people with religious beliefs to have a private prayer.

**Source**: 'Why choose a humanist ceremony' (2013), www.inspirationalceremonies.co.uk/humanist-naming

However, teachers ought to note that rites of passage are themselves a 'construct'. Not all cultures and religious believers have the same framework for marking out specific rituals. There are a variety of different sacraments, rituals and stages in life which are marked in some way by humans all over the world. In some RE resources a thematic approach is suggested. The teacher can use the pictures and text for primary children to compare rituals and customs from a range of belief systems about birth ceremonies, initiation rituals and so on. This can be an exciting and engaging way for children to appreciate the similarities and differences between and within various belief systems. A note a caution is needed because usually the rites of passage are the four mentioned in Table 10.5 – namely birth, initiation, marriage and death. Yet in some belief systems there are many other important stages, also described in Table 10.5.

---

■ **Table 10.5** Different rites of passage in different religions

---

Teaching point:
Take care NOT to use ONE framework and compare all the religions to this one; different religions and denominations within these religions have different rites of passage/sacraments/stages for example.

The rites of passage usually discussed in RE resources revolve around the four Church of England ceremonies:
  I. Birth
  II. Initiation
  III. Marriage
  IV. Death

In Catholicism there are seven sacraments – not all Catholics encounter each:
  I. Baptism
  II. Eucharist
  III. Reconciliation
  IV. Confirmation
  V. Marriage
  VI. Holy orders
  VII. Anointing of the sick (last rites)
       (www.americancatholic.org/features/special/default.aspx?id=29)

In the Hindu tradition there are four main stages to life:
  I. Student, ages 12–24
     Brahmacharya Ashrama
  II. Householder, ages 24–48
      Grihastha Ashrama
  III. Senior adviser, ages 48–72
       Vanaprastha Ashrama
  IV. Religious devotion, age 72 & onward
      Sannyasa Ashrama
      (www.hinduismtoday.com/modules/smartsection/item.php?itemid=5333)

Also in Hinduism there are 16 samskaras, or rituals for the pure and healthy development of a Hindu's mind and body, 5 of which relate to pregnancy and birth. (www.vmission.org.in/hinduism/samskaras.htm).

---

Also when engaging in a thematic study, comparing one belief system with another, it is important to encourage children to look at similarities and differences and to avoid asking which they like best, as I discuss later.

## COMPARING BELIEF SYSTEMS: 'RESPECTFULLY DISAGREEING'

Rather than asking children which is the best/correct/accurate belief, children should be encouraged to justify their opinion about a particular aspect of the belief system in comparison to another belief system, with reference to evidence they have collected. They can then express their opinion in a fair and balanced manner – 'respectfully disagreeing' (Blaylock 2007), if appropriate. It is not expected that primary RE should encourage children to blindly accept a belief system's doctrine and practices in an uncritical way – see chapters 1 and 2 this volume. Rather children can be shown how to draw on evidence about a belief system, look at life through the believer's lens and critically examine but in a respectful manner.

The 2010 Equality Act requires schools to ensure they are places of equality and diversity with no discriminatory practice (Equality Act 2010). Thus it is important for teachers to have a clear understanding of what is and is not allowed to be articulated in the classroom. In the next example the children are asked to engage in a debate about whether they think 'belief in the afterlife makes humans live a better life'. Some children who have strong religious views might agree with this statement, drawing on their own religious convictions. Other children will disagree, possibly drawing on secular worldviews such as the humanist stance. The RE classroom allows a teacher to provide a safe, secure space for children to investigate different viewpoints and offer children an opportunity to debate contrasting views. In the following debate lessons children can first investigate differing views – for example Muslim, Christian and humanist. They can work effectively in groups using ideas from Baines *et al.* (2008), which outlines strategies for successful debates.

Activity: A humanist funeral ceremony and humanist beliefs about death can be explored with Years 5 and 6 including a debate (see Tables 10.6, 10.7 and 10.8). While some teachers might have reservations about holding a debate I would argue that, if conducted respectfully, it will provide children with an opportunity to explore different religious claims in a safe environment – see Table 10.6 of good and bad practices. A debate should *not* be an excuse for children to express preferences – 'I like this belief best', 'I think

■ **Table 10.6** Debates – bad and good practice

| Bad practice:<br>Encourages dangerous inflammatory opinions | Good practice:<br>Acceptable critical debating skills |
| --- | --- |
| Allowing children to express feelings and preferences uncritically e.g.<br>*I like this belief.*<br>*This belief is best.*<br>*I think this belief is rubbish.* | Encouraging children to defend their opinion critically and respectfully with reference to what they have observed, read, heard etc.<br>*I think this belief makes more sense because x, y, z.*<br>*I do not agree with this stance because of a, b, c.* |

■ **Table 10.7** Knowledge underpinning a debate

| Most humanists do not believe in life after death. They believe that: | Most Muslims believe if they have lived a good life they will go to heaven. They believe: | Most Hindus believe if they have lived a good life they will return in another form. They believe: |
|---|---|---|
| "in the absence of an afterlife and any discernible purpose to the universe, human beings can act to give their own lives meaning by seeking happiness in this life and helping others to do the same." (www.humanism.org.uk/humanism) | "in the Day of Judgement when the life of every human being will be assessed to decide whether they go to heaven or hell." (www.bbc.co.uk/religion/religions/islam/beliefs/beliefs.shtml) | "that the soul passes through a cycle of successive lives (samsara) and its next incarnation is always dependent on how the previous life was lived (karma)." (www.bbc.co.uk/religion/religions/hinduism/beliefs/moksha.shtml) |

■ **Table 10.8** Example of a debate for upper Key Stage 2

| Does belief in an afterlife make humans live a better life? | |
|---|---|
| YES: Belief in an afterlife makes humans live a better life. | NO: Belief in an afterlife does not necessarily make humans live a better life. |

that belief is rubbish', even though many television programmes and chat shows delight in such activity. Rather the teacher needs to *educate* the children to voice their opinions in a critical way. It is acceptable to challenge a viewpoint if the challenge is expressed in a measured, defensible and respectful manner.

For more information on debating skills see www.ehow.co.uk/how_8694557_teach-debate-children.html.

As well as the teacher's pedagogic knowledge of how to facilitate a successful debate, the children will need to enhance their subject knowledge for it to work effectively. Boden (2001) argues that subject knowledge is crucial to enhancing creativity. So before the debate ensure all the children have some knowledge of several stances – for example from each of the three belief systems mentioned at the beginning of this chapter, Western, Eastern and 'Other' (see Table 10.7). Groups of children can present information about their belief system in a five-minute presentation (possibly using PowerPoint) and then panellists can engage in debate.

Once children have a secure knowledge – having listened to the presentations – the debate can begin. See Table 10.8 for an example question.

## Anti-racism

Throughout this chapter I have attempted to convince the readers to widen their perspective and introduce children to a range of belief systems, the underpinning rationale being to promote equality and diversity. In this section I invite the readers to assess their mindset to ensure that whichever belief system is investigated and whichever pedagogical approach is adopted, the teaching and learning will be fair, will be balanced and will subscribe to the 2010 Equality Act. There are numerous resources to support the teacher (a few are listed in the 'Additional resources' section of this chapter).

However, Warner and Elton-Chalcraft (2014) argue that some schools may be tempted to abide by the letter of the law but not the spirit of the law. Thus some schools, albeit unwittingly, would be exhibiting 'dysconcious' racism (King 2004) that is affirming the high status of the majority culture (in RE this could be thought of as white, male-dominated Anglicanism and Catholicism) and lowering the status of minority cultures (in RE this could be denominations such as Seventh-Day Adventism, which has a large proportion of black adherents, Unitarianism, Quakers etc.). In this chapter I have attempted to redress this balance by encouraging the teacher to engage in study of minority religions and atheist belief systems.

My argument so far has attempted to convince the primary teacher to branch out and include references to a broad range of religions and belief systems, but I realise that it is impracticable to investigate more than a few in detail with the children and finding resources may be problematic. At every opportunity I would encourage teachers to provide an opportunity for children to investigate alternative perspectives to the white, Western, patriarchal (male-dominated) Christian view which, I would argue, dominates our current curriculum. In Table 10.9, the reader could begin to plot attitudes they or teachers at their school might

■ **Table 10.9** Types of multiculturalism (adapted from Warner and Elton-Chalcraft 2014:254; Elton-Chalcraft 2009:82; original idea from Kincheloe and Steinberg 1997)

| 1 | Conservative multiculturalists (mono-culturalism) | are 'tokenist'. They attempt to address multicultural issues but, deep down, they believe in the superiority of Western (white) patriarchal (male-dominated) culture. They may prefer to use BC and AD as a dating system. *This is a starting place for many teachers, but this stance is superficial – there needs to be genuine celebration of diversity.* |
|---|---|---|
| 2 | Liberal multiculturalists | are dedicated to working towards 'one race'. They attempt to gloss over differences in an attempt to make everyone equal and the 'same' ('they' are the 'same' as 'us' – they just happen to be a different colour). *Some teachers think this is 'equality in action' but actually they are adopting a 'colour-blind' stance, denying diversity exists.* |
| 3 | Pluralist multiculturalists | believe pluralism is a virtue, where diversity is pursued and exoticised. There is cultural 'tourism' where 'they' (as opposed to 'us') live in an exotic parallel world. For example, Hanukkah is the 'Jewish Christmas'. *These teachers attempt to celebrate diversity but they use their 'own' cultural language to describe the 'other' (inferior) culture. There is not genuine equality.* |
| 4 | Left essentialist multiculturalists | are extreme in promoting the minority culture, to the extent that the dominant culture is seen as 'bad' and the marginalised as 'good'. *This stance is the opposite of pluralist – here the teacher elevates the 'other' culture and demotes the dominant culture. Again there is not genuine equality.* |
| 5 | Critical multiculturalists | believe in the promotion of an individual's consciousness as a social being. They promote an awareness (self-reflection) of how and why his/her opinions and roles are shaped by dominant perspectives. They prefer to use BCE and CE as a dating system. *This teacher appreciates that there are differences within, as well as between, cultures and there is open discussion of the dominance of one culture over another, while celebrating diversity and equality.* |

hold concerning multicultural/anti-racist practice. Warner and Elton-Chalcraft (2014) encourage teachers to be critical multiculturalists, which means, for RE, choosing a variety of different religions and belief systems to be explored. For example this teacher would use BCE (before the Common Era) and CE (Common Era) in their lessons to avoid the Christian-centred BC (before Christ) and AD (Anno Domini – in the year of our Lord).

A creative strategy for challenging racism is using persona dolls (Brown 2008; Elton-Chalcraft 2005; and also chapter 12 in this volume). A persona doll with children aged 3–8 years, for example Jeetinder, a Sikh doll, can be used by the class teacher to explore issues of prejudice and discrimination (Elton-Chalcraft 2005).

In the following chapters in this final section of the book, Lynn Revell (chapter 11) discusses looking at teaching Islam in a fresh and anti-racist way. In chapter 12 John Hammond discusses the 'in group'/'out group' mentality that causes scapegoating and how this can be challenged in RE.

So in these three chapters I challenge the teacher to be creative about the what, why and how in RE teaching and learning. As chapter 1 of this volume explained, RE can be boring and easy – as with filling in missing words and drawing a picture, an activity chosen by a teacher unwilling to get involved in the risky business of conflicting belief systems. Or RE can be taught creatively as a transformative subject – encouraging children to challenge their own perspectives, which might at times be uncomfortable, but it can also liberate children to discover new ideas and perspectives and enrich their present and future lives.

## ADDITIONAL RESOURCES

Pictures of Black Jesus, African and Chinese heritage Jesus are available at http://photobucket.com/images/black%20jesus?page=1, accessed 12 March 2014; and at http://media.photobucket.com/user/yujiade/media/Sacred%20Paintings/Chinese%20Traditional%20Style/05023.jpg.html?filters[term]=chinese, accessed 12 March 2014.

Resources about civil partnerships available at www.stonewall.org.uk/at_school/education_resources/default.asp, accessed 12 March 2014.

*Show racism the red card*, http://theredcard.org/uploaded/SRtRC%20Education%20Pack%20 2012.pdf

## REFERENCES

Alexander, R. (2010) *Children their world their education: final report and recommendations of the Cambridge Primary Review*, London: Routledge.

Baines, E., Blatchford, P., and Kutnick, P. (2008) *Promoting effective groupwork in the primary classroom: a handbook for teachers and practitioners*, London: Routledge.

Blaylock, L. (2004) *Picturing Jesus: worldwide contemporary artists*, Birmingham: RE Today Publications.

Blaylock , L. (2007) *Inclusive RE*, Birmingham : RE Today Services.

Boden, M. (2001) 'Creativity and knowledge', in Craft, A., Jeffrey, B., and Leibling, M., eds, *Creativity in education*, 95–102, London: Continuum.

British Humanist Association (2014) 'Home page', available at www.humanism.org.uk, accessed 28 January 2014.

Brown, B. (2008) *Equality in action*, Stoke-on-Trent: Trentham Books.

Buzan, T. (2014) 'Mind mapping', available at www.tonybuzan.com/about/mind-mapping, accessed 18 April 2014.

Cooling, M. (1998) *Jesus through art*, Religious Moral and Educational Press, available at www.rmep.co.uk. accessed 20 February 2014.

Devine, D. (2003) *Children, power and schooling*, Stoke-on-Trent: Trentham Books.

Elton-Chalcraft, S. (2005) 'Anti racism: an attainment target for primary RE', available at http://open.tean.ac.uk/bitstream/handle/123456789/623/Resource_1.pdf, accessed 20 April 2014.

Elton-Chalcraft, S. (2009) *It's not just black and white, miss: children's awareness of race*, Stoke-on-Trent: Trentham Books

Elton-Chalcraft, S. (2014) 'I don't think lecturers are ever going to change a closed mind: student teachers' learning journeys and teaching for diversity'. Paper accepted for ECER (European Centre for Educational Research), Porto, Portugal, September 2014.

Equality Act (2010) www.legislation.gov.uk/ukpga/2010/15/contents. accessed 20 February 2014

Grimmitt, M., ed. (2000) *Pedagogies of RE*, Great Wakering: McCrimmon.

Kincheloe, J. L., and Steinberg, S. R. (1997) *Changing multiculturalism*, Changing Education Series, Buckingham: Open University Press.

King, J. (2004) 'Dysconscious racism: ideology, identity and the miseducation of teachers', in Ladson-Billings, G., and Gillborn, D., eds, *The RoutledgeFalmer reader in multicultural education*, 71–83, Abingdon: RoutledgeFalmer.

McCreery, E., Palmer, S., and Voiels, V. (2008) *Teaching RE: primary and early years, achieving QTS*, Exeter: Learning Matters.

NACCCE (National Advisory Committee on Creative and Cultural Education) (1999) *All our futures: creativity, culture and education*. Available at www.cypni.org.uk/downloads/alloutfutures.pdf, accessed 20 February 2014.

Pew Research (2011). 'Christian traditions', 19 December, available at www.pewforum.org/2011/12/19/global-christianity-traditions, accessed 30 March 2014.

QCA (2004) *Religious education: the non-statutory national framework*, London: QCA & DfES.

REjesus (2014) 'Faces of Jesus', available at www.rejesus.co.uk/site/module/faces_of_jesus, accessed 18 April 2014.

Rudge, J. (2000) 'The Westhill project: religious education as maturing pupils' patterns of belief and behaviour', in Grimmitt, M., ed., *Pedagogies of RE*, 88–112, Great Wakering: McCrimmon.

Scoffman, S. (2013) *Teaching geography creatively*, London: Routledge.

Sims, P. (2011) *Blackburn schools to teach humanism in RE*, available at http://blog.newhumanist.org.uk/2011/03/teaching-humanism-in-re.html, accessed 12 January 2014.

Teece, G. (2001) *A primary teacher's handbook to RE and collective worship*, Oxford: Nash Pollock.

Warner, D., and Elton-Chalcraft, S. (2014) 'Race, culture and ethnicity: teachers and their pupils', in Cooper, H., ed., *Professional Studies in Primary Education*, 2nd ed., chap. 10, London: Sage.

Weiss, O. (2011) 'Reflections on the REDCO project', *British Journal of Religious Education* vol. 33 no. 2 (March): 111–26.

# CHAPTER 11

# ISLAMOPHOBIA, RELIGIOUS EDUCATION AND CREATIVITY

*Lynn Revell*

The focus of this chapter is an examination of the ways teachers can approach Islamophobia so that pupils can understand its controversial and complex nature. RE teachers are not strangers to difficult and sensitive topics, and the argument underpinning this chapter is that to engage with Islamophobia teachers must be proactive and interventionist in their teaching. It proposes a model of teaching that is shaped by Vygotsky's ideas about the role of creativity in developing the way young people engage with the world. This chapter will look at current ideas about Islamophobia and it will suggest strategies for developing skills and attitudes that challenge how we think about our relationship with groups we perceive as outsiders. The discussion of approaches to teaching is based on an understanding of Islamophobia as an ideology and a set of practices that vilify and exclude Muslims through legal and informal processes of 'Othering'.

## WHAT IS ISLAMOPHOBIA?

The events of 9/11 and subsequent terrorist and other violent attacks in the UK and across Europe have led to increasingly bigoted and hysterical reactions to Islam and many Muslims. Several projects, like *REsilience* (http://religiouseducationcouncil.org.uk/educators/projects/resilience), have been developed to support schools as they combat the growth of extremism, misinformation and caricatures of Islam. Schools with a commitment to equality, tolerance and pluralism have sought to oppose racism and prejudice (often through RE) but this hostility remains a difficult area for many teachers. A key part of this difficulty is confusion about what Islamophobia means.

There is an extensive debate over the exact definition of Islamophobia. It can involve physical and verbal abuse, exclusion, vilification and discrimination. The Runnymede Trust (1997) defines it as fear, hatred or hostility towards Islam, Islamic culture and Muslims. Barry van Driel, editor of the journal *Intercultural Education*, says Islamophobia is 'an irrational distrust, fear or rejection of the Muslim religion and those that are perceived as Muslims (Van Driel: 2004, x). These definitions all touch on essential characteristics of Islamophobia, some of them violent and physically abusive, some which exclude and others which are more subtle and ambiguous. Teachers should know what the many forms of Islamophobia 'look like' and the factors and circumstances that cause it.

Many teachers, aware of Islamophobia in their schools or communities, respond by presenting a positive and non-threatening model of Islam to pupils. A great deal is made of the beauty of Islamic artefacts and architecture and of the linguistic, cultural, intellectual and social contribution of Islam to the West, and textbooks often attempt to 'defuse' controversial issues surrounding Islam, like jihad or arranged marriages, by representing them in a way that is balanced or positive. However, these strategies on their own fail to address the cause of Islamophobia.

## Does Islamophobia mean that pupils can't criticise Islam?

It is essential that teachers understand the nature of Islamophobia, especially in the context of RE. Teaching about Islamophobia is not the same as teaching about Islam. Some teachers worry that any criticism of Islam, Muslim cultures or beliefs and practices associated with Islam is Islamophobic, and the fear of accusations of being 'anti-Muslim' is real for many teachers. In the context of a lesson on Islam, pupils may be encouraged to reflect on many different aspects of Islam, not just what Muslims do and believe but the values and cultures associated with Muslim lives. In many RE lessons pupils are encouraged to question, challenge and consider these ideas from their own perspectives. Teachers often encourage pupils to interrogate ideas and beliefs; if pupils were unable to express their lack of sympathy for any religion or their criticisms of certain practices, then RE would become a form of indoctrination rather than a subject dedicated to supporting their personal growth (OfSTED: 2010) or a subject designed to help them live in a plural society. However, being critical of Islam and Islamophobia are not the same thing. It is possible to be very critical of Islam and not be Islamophobic, and one of the challenges for teachers is how to share this distinction with pupils.

If a critical attitude towards Islam is not the defining feature of Islamophobia, what is? Chris Allen argues that if the term is to have any real use we need to be certain exactly what it is about Islam that causes a 'phobic' response. He claims that although it is an enormously problematic and complex term, it has three parts (see Table 11.1):

■ An ideology perpetuates meanings about Muslims and Islam and presents it in myriad ways as the Other. That is, values and practices associated with Islam are understood as alien and essentially different from the values and norms of 'our' society and culture.
■ This ideology is sustained and perpetuated through narratives, legislation, political language and the creation of identities that define themselves against Islam.
■ Exclusionary practices disadvantage, prejudice or discriminate against Muslims and Islam. (Allen: 2011)

This definition of Islamophobia rests on a view of Islam as fundamentally at odds with Western values and culture. Islam is not merely different or exotic in the way that customs associated with Buddhism or Hinduism are sometimes thought of but is considered threatening and aggressive. The hostility towards Islam is rooted in the fact that it has become a symbolic enemy, the polar opposite of the positive values and customs we associate with 'our' own culture. We will return to the model of Islamophobia proposed by Allen in a later section.

■ **Table 11.1** The three parts of Islamophobia

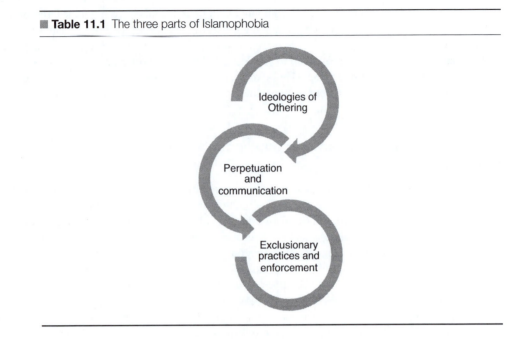

## ISLAMOPHOBIA AND CREATIVITY

Since 9/11 there has been growth in the resources available to schools to oppose Islamophobia. Some of these many excellent resources are recommended at the end of this chapter. However, this chapter argues that a thorough critique of Islamophobia demands more than excellent resources; it also demands teaching that is creative from teachers who can critically engage with the ideas that underpin 'Othering' and Islamophobia.

Most strategies to combat Islamophobia locate its causes either in ignorance or in the fact that people are influenced by sensationalist coverage in the media and the over-representation of Islam as a religion of extremism or fundamentalism. These interpretations imply that the origins of Islamophobia lay in a particular representation of Islam or even in the 'extremist' aspects of Islam itself. Robin Richardson from Insted, an organisation providing commentary and resources on race and diversity in education, argues that the causes of Islamophobia are to be found not in Islam but in the way we define our communities and identities by excluding, marginalising and subjugating others:

> The task of challenging Islamophobia through education ... does not primarily require teaching about Islam. Rather, it primarily requires teaching about Islamophobia. And, more generally, about colour and cultural racism, and about the causes of these. The causes do not lie in the characteristics of the Other, and certainly not in the characteristics of the Other's religion. Rather, they lie in the culture, history and practices of ourselves.
>
> (Richardson: 2012)

Challenging Islamophobia then would entail strategies that asked children to consider how we think about ourselves as groups – nations, neighbourhoods, regions – religiously, ethnically, socially and culturally. The definitions of Islamophobia suggested by Allen and Richardson indicate that teachers should focus on encouraging children to challenge and confront the ways they see themselves in contrast to others and the ways communities and groups communicate messages about these others.

## WHAT DOES A CREATIVE APPROACH TO ISLAMOPHOBIA MEAN?

The work of Russian educational psychologist Lev Vygotsky identifies an understanding of creativity that combines an awareness of how children think and learn and the role of teachers in the classroom. Most teachers accept that creativity is an essential part of the development of the child and that teaching creatively demands that they use strategies and pedagogies designed to encourage children to think in new ways. For Vygotsky creativity is not a discrete area of cognitive activity but the bedrock of imagination. Imagination is the key component of art, science and technology but also of consciousness; the product of the way we speak, our language and our interactions with the world around us. This means that every development of the child is rooted in their cultural and social existence. According to Vygotsky, "Every function in the child's cultural development appears twice: first on a social level, and later on the individual level" (Vygotsky: 1978, 66).

He stressed the importance of previous experiences and emotional states for all learning and the recognition that every aspect of cognitive development is rooted in, informed by and shaped by the social world. He viewed the role of the teacher as instrumental in the way children learn. The teacher does not facilitate or support; she creates the structures and environment in which learning takes place. In doing so a teacher can choose to provide a setting which disrupts previous narratives or which fosters a particular environment of criticality and engagement. The school and the individual classrooms within it can become organisms with their own social norms and expectations.

Vygotsky's belief in the significance of consciousness, the instrumental role of the teacher and the importance of the sociocultural environments of the child means that teachers can expect to play a very particular role in education about Islamophobia. Children encounter Islamophobia not as something peculiar in their lives but as something integral and woven into the language and perceptions of the everyday. We know that even the youngest children give voice to racist and bigoted ideas (Elton-Chalcraft: 2009). Research by Bhola (2009) suggests that when the very young white working class children in her research saw pictures of Muslim women in hijab or the veil, they easily associate them with violence and qualities that mark them as outsiders. Teaching creatively means consciously intervening to disrupt and fragment these narratives, even when they are prevalent in the wider social world. In his work on how Islamophobia should be challenged by teachers, Douglas warns that teachers must be prepared to recognise and acknowledge in their teaching that questions raised in their classrooms may be at odds with views in society or the views of pupils' families (Douglas and Dunn: 2002).

The model of teaching suggested by Vygotsky poses challenges for the teacher who wishes to remain neutral and especially for the RE teacher who may be used to refusing to express a view in class discussions. The neutral teacher is a contradiction in terms for

Vygotsky because the teacher consciously and deliberately chooses the resources, direction and focus of the lesson. If we accept that Islamophobia is rooted in the lived experiences of pupils and in all our communities and that it is morally objectionable, then it is difficult to see how a teacher can maintain the 'procedural neutrality' advocated by Stenhouse (1983). In her discussion of teachers confronting Islamophobia, Wood notes that 'there is no such thing as neutral' because all information on Islam is distorted in some way (Wood: 2007). The implication of Vygotsky's belief that our ideas are shaped and informed by our experiences, communities and social lives is that challenging Islamophobia means engaging in those lives, not as a disinterested observer or facilitator but as adults who are committed to questioning the views on which it is based.

## STRATEGIES FOR ENGAGING WITH ISLAMOPHOBIA

The definition of Islamophobia proposed by Allen has three elements, on which the following suggestions for engaging with Islamophobia in primary schools are based: ideology (the ideas associated with Islam), the mechanism by which those ideas are communicated (representations in the media or textbooks, stereotypes etc.) and the practices used to enforce the values and ideas in the first part (laws, codes and customs).

The next sections briefly elaborate on aspects of Islamophobia and then suggest ways of introducing them to pupils using a single example.

### An ideology of the Other

There is a question in any discussion of Islamophobia that informs a teacher's engagement with it: what is it about Islam or Muslims that incites fear, distaste and revulsion? The most commonly cited reasons for hating or rejecting Islam are:

▨ Islam subjugates women through dress codes (wearing the veil, niqab etc.), marriage (the Qur'an allows men to marry four wives), arranged marriages and confining women to private spaces.
▨ Islam is an innately intolerant religion and one that is prone to religious fundamentalism.
▨ Islam is an innately violent religion and prone to extremism.

(Fekete: 2009)

The beliefs about Islam listed here are part of a wider system of ideas that together make up a narrative about Islam and Muslims that presents them as the mirror image of values and customs associated with the West. Islam then is hated and feared because it is 'our' opposite; it is our 'Other'. These ideas are important for our society not because of what they say about Islam but because of what they say about 'us'. In 1978 Edward Said coined the phrase 'Orientalism' to describe the way in which Western thinkers demonise or caricature the East. In RE we can see Orientalist images and prejudices in textbooks (Revell: 2012) and even in many of the agreed syllabi (Panjwani: 2005).

Islamophobia then, begins as an ideology that legitimises the notion that Islam and Muslims are different from us in some eternal irreconcilable way. Teaching about ideologies is a challenge for teachers of all pupils, let alone those in the primary phases. Yet there are concrete aspects of the 'Other' which creative teaching can address in a manner that is accessible and meaningful to young children.

The legitimacy of the idea of the 'Other' relies to a large extent on isolation of groups and communities from one another. We can only see others as alien and attribute abhorrent qualities to them when we never question ourselves or our own communities and when our views of the 'Other' are never challenged (Wood: 2007). Creating spaces for dialogue between groups is a recognised mechanism for building relationships between them, but when it is used creatively it can also encourage individuals to consider their identity.

One creative approach to dialogue was developed as part of a project to bring together people from different cultural and religious backgrounds. Ipgrave analysed the email exchanges of primary-aged pupils from an inner-city, multicultural school in Leicester and from the more homogeneously white schools in Leicester as part of the Building E-Bridges model. The project did not ask children to form friendships but instructed them to 'provide insights for their partners into the religious and cultural groups to which they belonged" (Ipgrave: 2009, 218). The focus on specific areas of their lives meant that children were expected to think about their identities so that they could explain it to others. Ipgrave found that when some children looked at what set them apart from others, the tone of their communications became respectful and more tentative. More information about the E-Bridges model is at the end of the chapter.

Projects including communication between groups of children can be embedded as part of a whole-school approach to dialogue. Teachers must move beyond inviting guest speakers to schools or taking children on trips to mosques if pupils are to form relationships that can support thoughtful communication. The REDCo project ('Religion in education: A dialogue or a factor of conflict in transforming societies of European countries') found that even though children express tolerance towards others in abstract discussions, they are less likely to do so at a practical level (Weisse: 2011). This finding suggests that the single most creative thing teachers can do to disrupt the ideology underpinning Islamophobia is to seek out communities and groups where pupils can communicate and to support that process. All of the following can be productively used by young people to start or pursue dialogue and with very few resources:

- email
- FaceTime
- text messages
- Facebook
- Skype
- Snapchat
- Instagram
- Twitter
- Myspace

Teachers could create a Facebook page or create times and spaces in the day when FaceTime or Skype conversations could take place. Alternatively children from different groups could work together to create the boundaries and content of a project to find out about each other's lives. They would then be communicating and learning the rhythm and nuances of each other's lives and routines before the project even began.

# PERPETUATION AND COMMUNICATION OF ISLAMOPHOBIA

As an ideology Islamophobia must be communicated throughout society if it is to become a part of the everyday language of that society. Representations of Islam and Muslims that identify them as 'alien' or 'un-British' in the popular media, the news, textbooks and stereotypes are all central to this process.

## Stereotypes

Many of the resources designed for teaching against racism, discrimination and Islamophobia identify stereotypes as a key part of the way ideologies are perpetuated and sustained. Stereotyping is widely recognised as central to communicating ideas and values about groups, so enabling pupils to recognise and challenge stereotypes associated with religious groups is an integral part of RE. An implicit aim in many agreed syllabi is to equip pupils with the skills they need to recognise stereotypes.

Resources such as 'Show Racism the Red Card' adopt a popular approach to stereotypes. It offers pupils a range of images of different 'sorts' of people all wearing head coverings: a nun's habit, a bridal veil, a sporting cap, a hoodie, a crash helmet, a turban, a hijab etc. Children are asked questions about why people wear head coverings. The aim of the activity is to show pupils that the common image (or stereotype of Muslims) wearing veils is inaccurate; the questions are designed to disrupt their possible assumptions about wearing a veil. It points out that nuns also wear a hijab in much the same way as many Muslim women and asks readers to consider how they think society would react if somebody attacked her and ripped off her head covering.

Activities like the one just described are useful because they can prompt pupils to reconsider how they view the world and to question 'facts' that they held to be true, e.g. that only Muslim women cover their heads for religious reasons or that in 'our' society it is weird or strange for people to wear head coverings. It also adopts a tactic familiar to many teachers of RE: asking pupils to put themselves in the shoes of others, to imagine how someone would feel or react in a situation that might not be their own.

Teaching about stereotypes can be developed further if teachers ask what stereotypes of Muslims or Islam are meant to communicate. The core of Islamophobia is the idea that we compare ourselves to a vilification of Muslim values and practices. So one reason there is often a near hysterical reaction to women wearing veils is that they challenge 'our' own ideas of what it is to be a modern women, feminine or capable of gender equality. The 'Other' represents what we are not and is therefore always foreign, alien and apart from us in some way. The significance of the stereotype of the veiled Muslim women lies not in the veil itself but in what we assume it says about her (and therefore all Muslims) and by extension what it says about us.

Older primary pupils can be asked to consider how stereotypes suggest meanings and counter-meanings. The possible meanings and counter-meanings of the stereotype of the veiled Muslim woman are suggested in Table 11.2.

This table can be given to pupils to prompt discussion, or teachers can use partially completed tables and ask pupils to fill in the gaps. The boxes completed by pupils can be used as the basis for further discussion. Similar tables can be drawn in relation to various

■ **Table 11.2** The veiled Muslim woman

| What we assume about her | What she implies about us |
|---|---|
| She is forced to wear the veil against her will | We are free to choose how we dress |
| She is regarded as second class even within her own culture and community | Western women are regarded as equals |
| Her dress is the product of an old-fashioned culture informed by ideas that are no longer accepted in modern democracies | Western dress is modern and embodies the freedom and equality of Western women |
| Her veil marks her out as someone who chooses not to 'fit in', as someone set apart from the mainstream | That we permit her to wear her veil signifies our tolerance of others different from ourselves |

other stereotypes of Islam and Muslims – e.g. the Muslim as bomber and terrorist or the Muslim as fundamentalist and extremist – and the exercise can be adapted in various ways:

■ Stereotypes normally rely on strong visual signifiers; this means that teachers can use images instead of phrases.
■ Pupils can be asked to match the opposing pairs of images.
■ The tables can be developed partially by teachers and then completed by pupils, who can work in groups or individually.
■ The 'truth' of the tables can also be discussed and challenged by pupils. Are the pairings fair? Are they really stereotypes at all?
■ Is there any truth in the stereotypes, and if so does this mean it is not a stereotype?

This is a complex idea to engage in with young children. However, teachers can make this aspect of stereotyping accessible for pupils by helping them consider stereotypes associated with Western society. By considering stereotypes not associated with Islam or Muslims but Western society, pupils will have to question how even 'innocent' activities and behaviours are complex and informed by different beliefs.

An example that yields different discussions is the miniskirt. Pupils can interrogate the miniskirt using the same questions they might ask about why a veil is worn.

■ Does anyone make girls wear them?
■ Is the miniskirt comfortable?
■ When is it not appropriate to wear a miniskirt (and why)?
■ Do old people wear miniskirts?
■ Why do girls want to show off their legs?
■ Is there a stereotype of girls that wear miniskirts?

The aim of the activity is to question the familiar and to understand that all behaviours are symbolic. Pupils can be asked to compare the different meanings and discuss if they agree with them (see Table 11.3).

■ **Table 11.3** Comparing items of clothing

| The miniskirt | The veil |
| --- | --- |
| Fashionable | Secretive |
| PE/sportswear | Foreign |
| Grown up | Spooky |
| Trendy | Makes them look like a tent |
| Sexy | Threatening |

## Islamophobia in school – exclusionary practices

Islamophobia is not just an 'irrational fear of Muslims', a collection of stereotypical views or ignorant assumptions about Islam. Its ultimate power lies in the fact that Islamophobia relies on mechanisms and practices that exclude and discriminate. It is not just an ideology; Islamophobia is enacted through aggressive behaviours, rules, legislation and formal and informal codes of practice.

Teachers may find teaching about this aspect of Islamophobia challenging. Of all these behaviours, 'name calling', insulting remarks and violence should be the easiest for pupils to identify and for teachers to respond to. Child Line reported that in 2013, 1,400 children called to report incidents of racist bullying and that Islamophobia was a significant problem (Independent: 2014). Unfortunately there is anecdotal evidence that teachers are sometimes unwilling to respond to incidents against Muslim children (Richardson: 2004). We also know that teachers can underestimate the extent of racist and prejudiced behaviours in their classrooms and that programmes to educate student teachers rarely provide opportunities for a rigorous and critical engagement with any form of discrimination.

## Fitting in and exclusion

Teaching about Islamophobia creatively can mean that teachers confront and challenge practices that appear to be neutral or 'common sense'. Some practices that exclude Muslims may not appear discriminatory to some because they apply to everyone; however, the reality is that they only really affect Muslims. When the MP Jack Straw asked Muslim women who visited him in his surgery to remove their veils so he could see their faces, for many people this seemed 'like a common-sense' request. It was not considered an act of discrimination because it applied to all members of his constituency. Similarly when schools insist that all pupils wear a uniform, this not only appears to be a part of a British tradition of uniforms in schools but it is justified on the grounds of treating all pupils equally.

Yet these codes affect Muslims disproportionally because they forbid or criminalise behaviour that is mostly associated with Muslims. Rules that exclude Muslims also appear neutral because the practices and customs associated with Western behaviour are seen as the accepted norm and therefore without bias. This means any behaviour that deviates is not normal, is automatically suspicious.

Confronting Islamophobia in education means equipping pupils with skills so they can recognise, challenge and engage with processes of exclusion (Ramarajan and Runell: 2007). Creative teaching and building the ability of pupils to think creatively will aid the development of these skills. A first step to enabling children to engage with the neutral appearance of some of these practices is providing them with skills of critical reflection.

Teachers can select processes, codes, guidelines or incidents that act as exclusionary processes to encourage pupils to engage and understand how exclusion works. Pupils often discuss uniforms and dress codes in religious, PSHE (personal, social, health and economic) and citizenship education. They may be familiar with the symbolic nature of uniforms and the role they play in creating a shared identity.

Teachers who use actual events that can be examined in the media or on the internet bring immediacy and a sense of the seriousness of issues to their lessons. Excerpts from newspapers and reports help ground classroom discussions in situations and conflicts that are real and have real consequences. There are numerous examples of exclusionary practices that have the effect of singling out Muslims.

In 2013 two 14-year-old Muslim boys were placed in isolation in their Lancashire school for a month because they refused to shave off their beards. The head teacher, Mr Xavier Bowers, said the school 'had standards to maintain' and that wearing beards was not a religious activity in Islam. The purpose of introducing this incident to pupils is not to generate a discussion about whether the school has the right to ban Muslim boys who wear beards or whether beards are a part of Muslim practice. The aim of these lessons would be to encourage pupils to interrogate the way codes of practice can sometimes exclude different groups.

Pupils can be asked to compare the uniform code in their own school and a school where the code was very different:

■ Rudolf Steiner School
■ A Muslim school
■ An all-boys' public school (Eton, Harrow etc.)
■ Most American community schools where there are dress codes but no actual uniform

Pupils can discuss the questions in Table 11.4 in relation to each uniform and evaluate the different approaches taken by schools.

Another approach teachers can use to teach about this aspect of Islamophobia is to ask pupils to directly examine particular examples. In relation to the incident where boys were forbidden from wearing beards, they could discuss the following questions:

A.  The head teacher said that the school needed to maintain standards. What standards could he have been talking about?
B.  In what ways could the wearing of beards lower standards?
C.  Think about the rules and values in their school. Are any of the things in boxes in Figure 11.1 forbidden?
D.  What is the purpose of a uniform/dress code in a school? (Should it try and be as inclusive as possible?)
E.  If you wanted to write a uniform code that was inclusive, what reasons would you have for banning things? Look at the list in Figure 11.1; would you ban any of them?

■ **Table 11.4** Uniforms

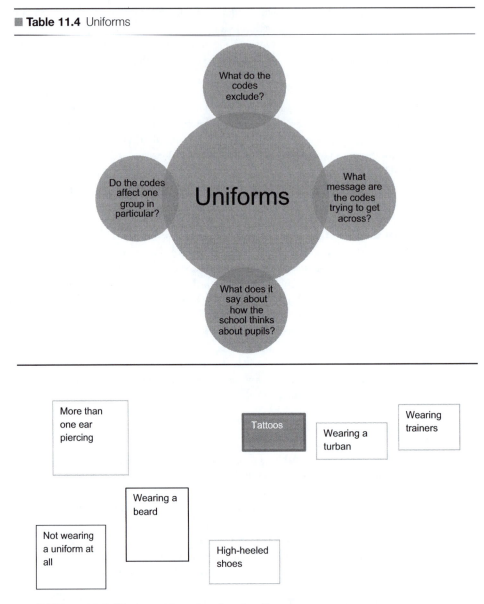

■ **Figure 11.1** What would you ban in school?

## CONCLUSION

One of the most terrible things about Islamophobia is that in many ways it is an 'acceptable racism' (Fekete: 2009). Islam is perceived to be so illiberal, such a threat to democratic or Western values, that some people feel that hostility towards Islam and Muslims is understandable and in some cases even justified (Morey and Yaqin: 2011). It is true that teaching Islam is not the same as teaching about Islamophobia, but RE teachers and specialists in schools have a particular responsibility to confront the ideology behind Islamophobia and expose many of the myths, stereotypes and misrepresentations about Islam in the media and in textbooks. We may share a commitment to equality and fairness with other teachers, but as specialists in the teaching of religion we are best placed to inform the teaching of those values with a deep and rigorous understanding of the significance of Islam and Muslims in today's world.

## ADDITIONAL RESOURCES

Many of the resources discussed in this chapter are free and available online.
www.cps.gov.uk/assets/rara_ppts/classroom_activities_and_pupils_worksheets.pdf
http://insted.co.uk
http://media.education.gov.uk/assets/files/pdf/i/dept%20advice%20template_smscadvice nov13.pdf
www.re-sillience.org.uk/indexphp/en/materials
www.srtrc.org
www.unesco.org/new/en/education/resources/in-focus-articles/fighting-islamophobia-in-schools
http://unesdoc.unesco.org/images/0021/002152/215299e.pdf

## REFERENCES

Allen, C. (2011) *Islamophobia*. Farnham: Ashgate.
Bhola, L. (2009) *What Are Children's Perceptions of Muslim People?* (unpublished research paper).
Douglass, S and Dunn, R. ( 2002) Interpreting Islam in American Schools. 76–98. In Hastings Donnan, ed. *Interpreting Islam*. London: Sage.
Elton-Chalcraft, S. (2009) *'It's Not Just About Black and White, Miss': Children's Awareness of Race*. Stoke-on-Trent: Trentham.
Fekete, L. (2009) *A Suitable Enemy*. London: Pluto Press.
Independent (2014) 'Racist Bullying: Far Right Agenda on Immigration Being Taken into Classrooms'. www.independent.co.uk
Ipgrave, J. (2009) The Language of Friendship and Identity: Children's Communication Choices in an Interfaith Exchange. *British Journal of Religious Education*. Vol. 31. No. 3, pp. 213–25.
Morey, P., and Yaqin, A. (2011) *Framing Muslims*. London: Harvard University Press.
OfSTED (2010) *Transforming Religious Education*. www.ofsted.gov.uk
Panjwani, F. (2005) Agreed Syllabuses and Unagreed Values: Religious Education and Missed Opportunities for Fostering Social Cohesion. *British Journal of Educational Studies*. Vol. 53. No. 3, pp. 375–93.
Ramarajan, D., and Runell, M. (2007) Confronting Islamophobia in Education. *Intercultural Education*. Vol. 18. No. 2, pp. 87–97.
Revell, L. (2012) *Islam and Education*. Stoke-on-Trent: Trentham.
Runnymede Trust (1997) *Islamophobia a Challenge for Us All*. London: Runnymede Trust.
Stenhouse, L. (1983) *Authority, Education and Emancipation*. London: Heinemann.
Van Driel, B. (2004) *Confronting Islamophobia in Educational Practice*. Stoke-on-Trent: Trentham.
Vygotsky, L. (1978) *Mind in Society*. Harvard: Harvard University Press.
Weisse, W. (2011) Reflections on the REDCo Project. *British Journal of Religious Education*. Vol. 33. No. 2. pp. 111–125.
Wood, A. (2007) *What do we tell the children?: Confusion, Conflict and Complexity*. Stoke on Trent: Trentahm.

## CHAPTER 12

# A CREATIVE APPROACH TO RE AND COMMUNITY COHESION

*John Hammond*

## INTRODUCTION

The contribution of religious education to establishing good social or community cohesion is theoretically significant but historically limited. Attempts to address this deficit appear necessarily long term. A parallel but more immediate strategy, offered here, is to address the concept at the heart of any catastrophic collapse of community cohesion, the scapegoat. Drawing on the extensive literature on scapegoating associated with the mimetic theory of Rene Girard, this chapter explores the working and extent of the scapegoat mechanism and provides suggestions for handling the topic in a way that enables Key Stage (KS) 1 and 2 pupils to identify, and identify with, the victims of scapegoating. With this insight they are likely to contribute considerably to a more cohesive society.

Like many Britons I have migratory forebears. Mine, from Eastern Europe (Jews) and the west of Ireland (Catholics), settled in mid-nineteenth-century London. Refugees from violent anti-Semitism and famine, they would have had a less-than-warm welcome in the East End. Respect and empathy were in short supply for nineteenth-century immigrants. Popular stereotyping saw Jews as weak, mean and cowardly, and the Irish as alcoholic, ape-like and racially inferior. Their cultural and religious identities set them up for malicious jokes, abuse and economic marginalisation. Some 150 years later, OfSTED sees RE as potentially playing 'a key role in promoting social cohesion and the virtues of respect and empathy' (OfSTED 2013). Had my migrant forebears had more respect for their cultural and religious identities, and more empathy for their experiences of persecution and privation, London's East End would have been a more welcoming, more socially cohesive and less dangerous place.

Today, global economic inequality, wars and climate change are driving mass migration and promising higher levels of cultural and religious diversity. Politicians across Europe, anxious about civil unrest, talk up 'community cohesion' and see schools as important agents in the promotion of more tolerant societies. The significant role to be played in this by religious education, particularly the model developed in the UK, is spelled out in detail in two European reports. The *Toledo Guiding Principles* (OSCE 2007) sees that knowledge of religions and beliefs can reinforce respect for everyone's right to freedom of religion and belief, foster democratic citizenship, promote social diversity and enhance cohesion. The *Network of European Foundations* (Pepin 2007) claims that the renewed prominence of religion inherent in Europe's increased cultural diversity, and the requirement of the European Convention on Human Rights to respect the rights of parents, challenges schools to take account of religious diversity.

But in OfSTED's reviews of religious education in 2007, 2010, and the most recent report, *Realising the Potential* (OfSTED 2013), RE in the classroom is still falling well short of these aspirations. RE could and should play a major role in bringing about more tolerant and harmonious societies. But it doesn't. What then should teachers do differently?

Looking for strategies in Michael Grimmitt's *Religious Education and Social and Community Cohesion* (Grimmitt 2010) might be disappointing. The book overall is stronger on identifying constraints than offering strategies. There are encouraging pointers about the development of 'dialogic' processes in teaching and learning (see chapter 7 of this volume) and the need for a new philosophy of the subject, but these are inevitably long term. Which is not surprising. With respect to social cohesion, RE (along with other curriculum areas) is engaged in a colossal task – reshaping the values and attitudes of a generation. The task is a positive one: encouraging OfSTED's virtues of respect and empathy and so the promotion of 'inter-religious communication and inter-cultural understanding' (Grimmitt 2010:184). This shaping of an environment in which young people can develop this positive regard is essential, long term and professionally challenging.

There is, however, an additional, more immediate strategy that could be undertaken while working on these long-term aims. Instead of promoting the positive it would address a negative: the practice of scapegoating, a major element of any broken and dysfunctional society. Scapegoating is mentioned in Michael Grimmitt's introduction (Grimmitt 2010:13) but not developed. Here I would like to move it to centre stage. This ancient and seemingly universal mechanism of blaming and violence is key to any catastrophic collapse of social cohesion. It is the process by which communities under stress seek victims, individuals or minorities, to blame for their present malaise. Mounting levels of fear and resentment become focussed on a victim, the scapegoat, whose violent expulsion or lynching provides a temporary respite from the community's distress.

This ancient mechanism still confronts us with countless contemporary examples, both local and global. Related to myth and religious ritual, the concept of the scapegoat falls within religious studies and thus is the subject matter of RE. By enabling pupils to recognise and understand the scapegoating phenomenon, RE will lessen its violent and fragmenting effects and so importantly contribute to maintaining more tolerant and cohesive communities.

The workings of scapegoating have been brought to light in the writings of Rene Girard, the French, formerly US-based literary critic, anthropologist and philosopher. According to his commentators (Girard, Rocha and Antonello 2008:1), Girard knows two big things: the scapegoat and 'mimetic desire'. Through the interplay of these two concepts and with evidence drawn from literature stretching from ancient myths and Greek tragedy through the Christian scriptures to Shakespeare's plays and modern novels, he provides fresh insights into the nature of human desire and the destructive effects of scapegoating. Briefly, the argument goes like this:

■    Human violence is not in the first instance about aggression in individuals or scarcity of objects they want to acquire. Rather, competition and violence arise from the 'mimetic' or imitated nature of human desire. Because we learn what to desire by imitating others, and so come to desire what they desire, we are destined to compete with them, and this competition can lead to violence.

■ Inspired by the work of anthropologists, Girard envisages how this violence arising from the nature of human desire would escalate in early human communities to threaten the very existence of the group. The key to the group's survival is that the rising violence, which (like desire) is imitated by others, is checked by an act of spontaneous collective violence directed against an individual, a scapegoat. This lynching of a single victim is accomplished in an outpouring of energy and emotion which redirects the resentment and violence within the group onto the scapegoat, bringing in its place a sense of calm, unity and restored order, what Girard calls the scapegoat effect.

■ Though the choice of the innocent victim is in some sense arbitrary, Girard sees that the individual who is the target of the mob's violence will be the bearer of what he calls 'victimary signs', certain physical, mental or cultural markers which set him or her apart from the others: ethnicity, culture, language, religion, mental or physical disability. In some way they are not 'one of us'.

The evidence for the phenomenon of scapegoating, Girard suggests, is evident both in the present and in the pages of history. The examples are ugly but not hard to find. A report in the *Daily Mirror* (Aspinall 2013) describes how a disabled Iranian was beaten and burned to death on an English housing estate by people who suspected him of being a paedophile: 'Police took him away for questioning while an angry mob chanted "paedo" "paedo"'. He was returned home by the police without charge but was later attacked and set on fire by his neighbours. All the elements of scapegoating are there: a troubled community plagued by poverty and unemployment, the 'victimary signs' of cultural and religious difference and physical disablement, the accusation of child abuse, the mob violence.

A week earlier (Eccles and Martin 2013) there was a report of Roma families suspected of trafficking children. A blonde 7-year-old was removed by the authorities from a Roma family in Ireland amid fears she was abducted – just days after a Roma couple in Greece were accused of snatching another blonde girl, Maria, the 'blonde angel', found in a Gypsy settlement. These cases also fit the scapegoat mechanism: the Roma, an ethnically and culturally distinct minority, have a long history of suffering persecution. Ireland and Greece, societies still reeling from the global financial meltdown in 2008, are experiencing hardship and, in the case of Greece, serious social unrest. Though the Roma couples were innocent of the accusations – one child was a natural offspring, the other acquired by informal adoption – the children were removed and the Roma communities abused and, in Greece, terrorised by nationalist gangs searching for other blonde children to 'liberate'.

These are not isolated cases. The Minority Rights Group International (2010) report cites numerous examples across the globe where religious minorities are targeted by majorities suffering economic stress and political instability: Christian minorities suffer in Iraq – and now Syria – and Nigeria; Muslims are victimised in Myanmar and earlier in Bosnia; Hindu Tamils are persecuted in Sri Lanka. These are local and global examples of scapegoating in the present but there are also numerous cases in the past:

■ The Nazi Holocaust featured a massacre of six million Jews and targeting of Roma and homosexuals.

- ■  The Turkish army slaughtered Armenians in the First World War.
- ■  The witch-hunts of the seventeenth century claimed some 50,000 victims.
- ■  Jews were persecuted across medieval Europe, particularly in times of plague, for which they were blamed.
- ■  In Rome Christians were victims of an unstable empire.

Wherever and whenever the persecution, the accusations show a remarkable similarity: the victims are accused of crimes which undermine the way of life and most deeply held values of the society. In the past Christians were accused of cannibalism, Jews were said to sacrifice infants and poison wells and witches caused crop failures and killed children. In the present the Roma are said to abuse and traffic children, while immigrants are accused of causing unemployment, taking our women and undermining our culture.

Are there other examples, in the media or in history, of groups under stress making scapegoats? What are the 'victimary signs', and what are the crimes of which they are accused?

Girard finds further evidence for the ancient nature of the scapegoat mechanism in his study of myth and ritual. Whereas the myths, once decoded, recount the process of a rising disorder which culminates in the death or expulsion of a victim, ritual's primary function is to renew by re-enactment the unifying effects gained by the community in the catharsis of the original lynching. Periodically or at times of acute stress, the performance of a ritualised sacrifice would recapture for the group the sense of harmony and restored calm which followed the ancient murder.

Scapegoating shreds community cohesion because there must always be losers, the victims whose rejection makes the rest of us feel better. If, on the other hand, we aspire to living in communities where every group is to be included, scapegoating must be challenged. But that is difficult, because scapegoating is always done by someone else. Whereas 'they' scapegoat innocent victims, 'we' merely point out the facts of the matter, that 'these people' are feckless benefits tourists, preying on our young girls, taking our jobs, undermining our way of life and so on. Scapegoaters are believers. Their energy and violence come from a commitment to preserve their values and punish the deviants who would defile them. But we can only scapegoat if we don't know what we are doing. If the true nature of the process were to be unveiled and we were faced with our part in the lie, we would have to stop.

The evidence of scapegoating, from the earliest human communities down the centuries to the innumerable instances in the contemporary world, argues for the presence of a malign social patterning in which, at times, we are all likely to become involved. Even children? The playground bullying by an excited, edgy group of children of a victim who is in some way different – dress or demeanour, ethnicity or social class, culture or physical or mental capacities – suggests the young are not immune. Children's taunts of 'Paki', 'spaz', 'gay' and 'Chav' are echoes of this same ancient and dishonourable tradition.

But being a pupil is a stressful business. Beginning or changing schools can be times of acute anxiety. Masses of new faces and the need to learn new routines can make children anxious, and an ongoing climate of competition spurs achievement but creates a fear of failure, for the losers must always outnumber the winners. (This can be a problem for the winners too. They are the 'swots', the successes, a visible minority who might be punished

---

▪ **Table 12.1** The elements of scapegoating

---

- ▪ **A community under stress** and experiencing uncertainty – from poverty, unemployment, climate change, crop failure and famine, drought, flood, disease, war – or even the 'ordinary' anxieties of being a child in a school playground.
- ▪ **The blaming of a victim or minority.** The victims are innocent of causing the malaise which afflicts the community. This means that any relief the community feels in punishing the victim will be short-lived.
- ▪ **'Victimary signs'** single out the persecuted – differences of ethnicity, culture, religion, language, social class or physical, emotional or mental attributes. The sign could also be one of celebrity status. Royalty, superstars and the super-rich, once their power begins to wane, can become victims.
- ▪ **The crimes of which the victims are accused** break taboos and undermine the community's deeply held values: fairness, the innocence of children, democracy, accepted sexual mores and 'our way of life'.
- ▪ **The persecution, exclusion or lynching** of the victims.
- ▪ **The community's brief respite** following the 'successful' removal or punishment of the victim is illusory. The real causes of its anger are still there and so the frustration will return. Arguably, now it is even worse, because there is also the resentment of the victims, unjustly accused and punished, looking for retribution.

---

by the majority for their own felt failures.) And then there are the ongoing changes for every child of personal growth: the unstable sense of identity; the need to be popular; the changing relations with peers, family and their own bodies. The price of some respite from the worries and a sense of well-being through solidarity with a group or gang can be the rejection, bullying, sacrifice of an outsider.

A further and immediate contribution RE could make to the building of more socially cohesive communities would be to address, unmask and thus lessen the destructive effects of scapegoating. The elements of scapegoating are outlined in Table 12.1.

Young children are also implicated. They are subject to anxieties and gang up against victims. If the destructive effects of scapegoating are to be exposed and limited, the process needs to begin with children.

Consequently, throughout the years of schooling, the teaching and learning strategies adopted would have to not only describe the scapegoating mechanism and document its historical and contemporary manifestations, but also create an environment in which learners were able to reflect on their own attitudes and actions. Given that countless ordinary people – people just like us – have been involved in the blaming and persecution of all those victims, might we not sometimes be doing the same? Addressing this question requires a safe space for the learner to examine the issue and at the same time be challenged by it. It is not only learning about scapegoating; it is also learning from it, letting the realities of victim and persecutor, innocence and blame impinge on my own attitudes and actions and the way I see others. Addressing scapegoating then will require a combination of the descriptive and analytical teaching and learning strategies appropriate to learning about religion (AT1), but also the experiential approaches relevant to learning from religion (AT2). Table 12.2 shows what this would look like in the classroom.

■ **Table 12.2** Key Stage 1 and 2 – identifying with victims of scapegoating

The aim would be to enable pupils in KS 1 and 2 to identify the victims of scapegoating and to identify with them. And therefore:

- To see that victims are marginalised or bullied because they are different, and to register what these differences are.
- To reflect on times when they have themselves been victims, on how it felt and what it was that made others pick on them.
- To reflect on times when they have been caught up in bullying others, on how and why it happened and in what ways the victim was different.
- To recognise incidents of scapegoating in the media or in their school and to be able identify the 'victimary signs' of the oppressed and the anxieties of the oppressors.
- To have the confidence to speak out about instances of scapegoating and offer support to victims.

Effective classroom strategies for achieving these aims would draw heavily on the use of stories (see chapter 6 of this volume) and Persona Dolls, an effective means of drawing children into a story and enabling them to identify and respond to characters and plot. It is the nature of a narrative to create a world which we or children can enter by willingly suspending disbelief. We know that the world of the story, especially if it begins, 'Once upon a time', is not real. But we also know we can enter this other world and through its places, plots and characters learn more of the realities of our own world. Stories can bring us face to face with scapegoating, with the ugliness of the process, and, when necessary, help us to acknowledge our part in it.

What stories might begin to unpack the scapegoat mechanism for KS 1 and 2? There are many. A few examples are suggested in Table 12.3.

For Babette Brown, using Persona Dolls 'while telling stories makes it easier for children to make connections with their lives . . . and develops the ability to empathise with and relate to others' (Brown 2001:29). The dolls are given specific facial characteristics and dress and sits on the teacher's lap during circle time, while the teacher provides elements of a biography. The doll becomes a 'persona'. The biopic links the doll to the hopes and fears, successes and failures of the listening children and then goes on to describe an incident the doll wants to share. This will be an experience common to the lives of the listening children: perhaps the excitement of holidays or birthdays or the fear of being excluded or bullied. Kay Taus, the originator of Persona Dolls, advocates also using news stories and current events talked about at home (Brown 2001:58).

The medium is effective and powerful. It enables the children present to face difficult issues and to offer support in a context which protects privacy while encouraging participation. It can enhance personal awareness and an understanding of relationships, explore emotions and provide insights into themes of human conflict and trust (Brown 2008:22). Persona Dolls are an ideal context for exploring scapegoating: the concept, what makes a victim, what it is like to be a victim, how to help a victim. See Table 12.4 (as well as Elton-Chalcraft 2005 and chapter 10 in this volume).

Scapegoating is bad for victims and bad for communities. It destroys social and community cohesion because at its heart is the blaming, vilification and persecution of minorities. But given that we are already doing anti-racist and anti-homophobic education, do we

---

▪ **Table 12.3** Stories for use with Key Stage 1 and Key Stage 2

---

KS1:

With *Elmer*, by David McKee (1989), we can see with the multi-coloured elephant how it can be tough and lonely to be different, and we can think about the ways we are different and how sometimes that can set us apart. The story can remind us too that we, like Elmer, might try to disguise what makes us who we are, which would be a mistake, because it is being different that makes him so much fun and, finally, friends with everyone.

In another elephant story, *Tusk, Tusk* by the same author (McKee 2006), we see that the conflict that arises between black elephants and white, causing the demise of both groups, does not end with them. The survivor groups of greys grow ears of different lengths – another source of potential conflict. Why for these elephants and for some people is blackness and whiteness a source of conflict? Where has this happened? Does it still go on? Length of ears looks to be a problem for elephants. What are other differences that people get in groups about against others? Do any of these groups include or exclude me or any of my friends?

KS2:

In *The Feather Wars* by Sally Grindley (2003), a short novel set in World War II, Sam lives in fear of being bullied at school. We see why he is singled out – it's not about him but his dad – and how he gets the strength to confront his persecutors. We see too how mutual suspicion escalates frighteningly to playground mob violence as children evacuated from the bombed cities are confronted by the resentments of their local counterparts. Through the lives of these war-time children who appear as both victims and persecutors, present-day pupils can plot and understand better the workings of scapegoating and explore through the lives of the characters the tensions and threats in their own.

*The Doll's House* is a gem of a short story written by Katherine Mansfield in 1922. It recounts how the present of a doll's house to the daughters of a middle-class family, the Burnells, becomes the occasion of the further persecution of two poor sisters. We are shown how adult class prejudice is unquestioningly taken up by children, who then add their own particular cruelties. But the story adds an alternative. One of the Burnell sisters, Kezia, won't conform and, in the face of adult anger, brings the excluded sisters to share in the wonder of the doll's house. The story presents an opportunity to examine class – then and now – as a marker for exclusion, to raise questions about the experience of victims and persecutors, and to wonder what it is that enables Kezia to see through the corrosive effects of class prejudice.

---

need to get involved in anti-scapegoating? Aren't we doing it already? Do we really need anti-scapegoating as well? I think we do for the following reasons:

▪ As we have seen in our unpacking of the scapegoat mechanism, many kinds of difference can count as a 'victimary sign' and be used to single out a person or group for bullying or persecution. The important work done in anti-racist and anti-homophobic education addresses the plight of two categories of victim, but scapegoating can fasten onto many kinds of difference. By exploring scapegoating, teachers and pupils can come to see that the problem of fragmenting communities lies not only in the negative reactions of some people to other ethnicities or sexual orientations, but also in a deep-seated and continuing pattern where majorities need minorities to blame.

■ **Table 12.4** Using Persona Dolls

An opening sequence spoken by the teacher to the listening group might run as follows:

Doll (given an appropriate name) and her family come from Romania. Doll was pleased to leave because people there shouted nasty things at her. She is happy to be here because people don't yell at her family in the street and she can come to a real school and make friends.

But Doll is worried.

Do you know what 'worried' means?

Have you ever felt worried?

What were you worried about?

What helped you stopped worrying?

Doll is worried because yesterday some children in the playground here laughed at her clothes and called her a Gypsy.

How does that make her feel?

Have you ever felt like that?

What did you do?

What do you think Doll should do?

What can we say to Doll that will help her and make her feel less worried?

**Source:** Adapted from Brown 2001

■ Focussing on this entrenched and underlying social pattern while addressing the situation of particular victim groups might help ensure we don't get stuck on one 'cause', to the neglect of other victims, who may be neither black nor gay. Some early anti-racist work had a blind spot around the significance of religion as a marker inviting persecution.

■ Understanding scapegoating and the role of 'victimary signs' also helps explain the presence and continuing power of Islamophobia (see also chapter 11 of this volume). In Islamophobia (the irrational fear of things Islamic) there is clustering of a number of potent minority characteristics which have become victimary signs. The accumulation of these signs results in the demonising of Islam and the rejection and despising of Muslims. The major signs here are ethnicity (the Middle East, North Africa and Indonesia are the heartlands of Islam); culture (as expressed in dress, language, gender roles and food); religion (not only is Islam a 'foreign' religion, but its evident public practice and insistence on a political voice is unsettling in secular societies where religion is expected to be a private business, seldom seen and rarely heard). Add to this that many Muslims are from immigrant families, the historical animosity between Christendom and Islam, as well as the fear caused by the terrorist actions of certain Islamist fighters, and Islam and its faithful can become a scapegoat for citizens made anxious by forces beyond their control: economic uncertainty and accelerating social and climate change.

▪ An awareness of scapegoating should also be a reminder of our own propensity to blame and that we too are likely to be implicated in the workings of the mechanism: 'If it wasn't for the [English Defence League, Al-Qaida, bankers, unions, the DfE, OfSTED, the head, those pupils . . . ], all would be well in society and the school.'

## CONCLUSION

This chapter has argued for a new dimension in religious education's approach to social and community cohesion. It is one which requires teachers to consider the workings and extent of the scapegoat mechanism and its role in destabilising community life. The basis for this recognition and a deeper understanding of the mechanism is available through Girard's mimetic theory and the secondary literature it has generated. Armed with these insights, teachers can devise strategies using established methods of teaching and learning which will enable pupils to recognise and reject scapegoating, making more attainable those virtues of respect and empathy without which no healthy society can exist.

## ADDITIONAL RESOURCES

Brown, B. (1998) *Unlearning Discrimination in the Early Years*, Stoke-on-Trent: Trentham Books.
Brown, B. (2001) *Combatting Discrimination*, Stoke-on-Trent: Trentham Books.
Fleming, C. (2004) *Rene Girard: Violence and Mimesis*, Cambridge: Polity Press/Blackwell.
Girard, R. (1977) *Violence and the Sacred*, Baltimore: Johns Hopkins University Press.
Girard, R. (1986) *The Scapegoat*, Baltimore: Johns Hopkins University Press.
Girard, R. (1987) *Things Hidden Since the Foundation of the World*, Stanford, CA: Stanford University Press.
Girard, R. (1996) *The Girard Reader*, Ed. J. G. Williams, NY: Crossroad.
Girard, R. (2001) *I See Satan Fall Like Lightning*, Maryknoll, NY: Orbis Books.
Kirwan, M. (2004) *Discovering Girard*, London: Darton, Longman and Todd.
Raven Foundation, a US-based website dedicated to applying the mimetic theory in educational contexts: www.ravenfoundation.org Accessed 20 October 2014.

## REFERENCES

Aspinall, A. (2013) 'Disabled man burned to death by vigilantes who wrongly suspected him of being a paedophile', *Daily Mirror*, 29 October.
Brown, B. (2001) *Persona Dolls in Action*, Stoke-on-Trent: Trentham Books.
Brown, B. (2008) *Equality in Action*, Stoke-on-Trent: Trentham Books.
Eccles, L., and Martin, A. (2013) 'Now blonde girl found at Roma home in Ireland.' *Daily Mail*, 22 October.
Elton-Chalcraft, S. (2005) 'Anti racism: an attainment target for primary RE', available at http://open.tean.ac.uk/bitstream/handle/123456789/623/Resource_1.pdf, accessed 20 April 2014.
Grimmitt, M. (2010) *Religious Education and Social and Community Cohesion*, Great Wakering: McCrimmons.
Grindley, S. (2003) *Feather Wars*, London: Bloomsbury.
Mansfield, K. (1922) *The Doll's House* in *Selected Stories*, Oxford: Oxford World Classics.
McKee, D. (1989) *Elmer*, London: Anderson.
McKee, D. (2006) *Tusk, Tusk*, London: Anderson.

Minority Rights Group International (2010) 'Religious minorities targeted by nationalist and extremist groups in South Asia', 1 July.

OfSTED (2013) *Realising the Potential*, Manchester: OfSTED.

OSCE (2007) *The Toledo Guiding Principles on Teaching about Religions and Beliefs in Public Schools*. Vienna

Pepin, L. (2007) *Teaching about Religions in European School Systems – Policy Issues and Trends*, Brussels, Belgium: Network of European Foundations.

# AFTERWORD

*Lat Blaylock*

## WHAT'S CREATIVE ABOUT RELIGIONS?

In a book such as this, exploring creative work in religious education, it is good to note at the start that a religion is a very creative thing, especially in its most dynamic phases of growth and of renewal. Religions often exalt the divine creativity and see human creativity as exalted. For many believers, in many traditions and communities, God is a maker and humanity shows an imprint of the divine when we make, create, imagine, dream, sing, compose or dance. This takes many forms of course: aesthetic diversity is normal within religions, but word, image, symbol, vision, design and song often energise spiritual life within religions and beyond them all. Plainsong, Zen gardens and Sufi silence are almost the opposite of an Orthodox iconostasis, the complexities of Mosque decoration or the intricate symbolic splendours of Hindu murtis. Still, making space sacred and making time holy are creative activities in all faiths (and atheism can have dynamic creative energy too, of course).

## WHY SHOULD RE BE CREATIVE? FOUR ANSWERS

If religions are creative, then RE should be too. Here are four reasons why. First, RE should be creative because many (all?) pupils have creative abilities and talents. Many pupils do better at RE when using their creative intelligence and skills. Logic and reasoning matter too, but pair well with more imaginative tasks, motivating pupils to love RE.

Second, RE should be creative because the art, architecture, music and texts created by religious communities are among humanity's most splendid and remarkable accomplishments, so RE should enable learning from the creativity of religions.

Third, RE should be creative because teachers enjoy their work more if it is. None of us really believe that RE has been good if all that has happened is that we've transmitted 100 facts from inside our heads to the inside of the pupils' heads. One way or another, creativity is part of good RE.

Finally, RE is a meaning-making subject. I suggest religions and humans need to make meaning, and this is a creative process. If your lifetime is the raw material out of which you make the meaning of life, then RE gives pupils some tools and guidance about how to do this. Philosophy and religion have in common their intention to make meaning out of experience. RE can help any child to do this creatively. The thoughtful chapters of this book – often combining research with practice, always offering thoughtful reflection on the task of the teacher of RE – can make a key contribution to more creative RE for any pupil.

## HOW CAN I ENABLE CREATIVE THINKING AMONG MY PUPILS IN RE?

Perhaps the most important mode of creativity in RE is creative thinking: that's for every learner. Thinking creatively happens where ideas are fresh or are combined in unexpected ways. Juxtapositions of the unusual or new angles on old thoughts make for ideas and approaches that are bold and take risks. A key focus in this book is to offer thoughtful research alongside activities for the classroom that open up creative possibilities.

## CAN CREATIVITY MAKE FOR HIGH STANDARDS IN RE?

The worst kind of RE lacks challenge. Surely no teacher thinks word searches and colour-coding activities promote understanding of religion. Instead, setting up lessons with time enough for imagination to flourish and for thought to grow deeper is essential if RE is to continue to improve. Much in the book will enable teachers to manage the tension between rigour and creativity, between deep thinking and imaginative engagement. Teachers of RE know that creative RE is worthwhile: this book is intended to help you to make it happen.

# INDEX